Praise for *L*

Olivia Hoblitzelle's life story will awaken a deep curiosity about how the mystery of loving awareness weaves through all our lived moments. This is a fascinating, wise, and deeply inspiring spiritual memoir.

— Tara Brach, bestselling author of *Radical Acceptance*

Both a timeless description of contemplative wisdom and an intimate personal account of a fascinating life, *Ley Lines of Love* is a classic spiritual masterpiece: Olivia Hoblitzelle's authenticity, humility, wisdom, and love will awaken your soul. The depth of her experience as a seeker, as well as a mother who faced painful spiritual disillusionment, was expressed with an emotional honesty that brought me to my knees. Then she took me by the hands and raised me up again as her luminous journey of conscious discovery continued, delivering us both to a place of unalloyed wonder. Brava to a generous spirit for taking us with her on an unforgettable journey of the heart.

— Joan Borysenko PhD, bestselling author of *Minding the Body, Mending the Mind*

Olivia Hoblitzelle begins her book with the phrase "Ley lines of love," by which she means "the interconnectedness of everything in the universe from individual lives to the entire cosmos." Olivia's spiritual autobiography is rich and deep, truly embodying these Ley lines, as they manifest outwardly as well as inwardly. In this brave book, she does not lean away from the darkness of disillusionment but rather is willing to learn and grow, bringing so many others along in her own healing and understanding. Writing about interconnectedness is one thing; in this book, Olivia finds a way to embody interconnectedness through her life story and teaches a path of great love. This is indeed a beautiful book and a precious gift to us all.

— Narayan Helen Liebenson, author of *The Magnanimous Heart: Compassion and Love, Loss and Grief, Joy and Liberation*

Olivia Hoblitzelle's extraordinary life has been defined by her deep sensitivity to the mystical and spiritual realm. Answering her calling to bravely probe the meaning of existence through all its darkness and light, she leads us on a journey of continual mystery and wonder. I know no wiser, more loving elder to guide us into seeing our lives and understanding our own hearts.

— Helen Whybrow, author of *A Man Apart: Bill Coperthwaite's Radical Experiment in Living*

Delightfully written, moving and inspiring, Olivia Hoblitzelle's life odyssey pulsates with soul yearnings, cultural undertows and collective waves of becoming. Olivia shares a captivating journey, lighting up multiple facets of the spiritual awakening of our times.

— Monique Pommier PhD, author of *Harmony, The Heartbeat of Creation*

Olivia Hoblitzelle's spiritual memoir *Ley Lines of Love* describes a courageous, insightful journey in search of Truth and the experience of spiritual interconnectedness. In her riveting narrative, she offers example after example of her commitment to spiritual life, describing how outer causes and conditions parallel her inner experiences. I found her discoveries, tools, and insights incredibly inspiring and I will cherish this book as a touchstone for my own journey.

— Lisa Prajna Hallstrom PhD, author of *The Gospel of Shri Anandamayi Ma: Conversations with the Divine Mother*

Moving gracefully between the erudite and the mystical, at once elegant and heartfelt, *Ley Lines of Love* is a beautifully written, courageous illumination of one woman's rich and remarkable journey on the spiritual path.

— Victress Hitchcock, author of the memoir *A Tree With My Name On It* (2024) and director of the documentary film *When the Iron Bird Flies: Tibetan Buddhism Arrives in the West*

Ley Lines of Love is a love story of the soul, filled with the wisdom of numerous spiritual traditions while rooted in life's joys and disappointments. The author's determination to experience the freedom of her spirit leads to the discovery of the liberating power of truth-telling and revelations of divine mystery held in outer realms of consciousness. Readers will be inspired by Olivia's extraordinary courage and devotion, and by the lessons of a life lived deeply, told beautifully with great honesty, reverence, and awe.

— Joan Diver, author of *When Spirit Calls: A Healing Odyssey*

Ley Lines is a compelling life story of a spiritual spelunker who, even as child, felt drawn to what is eternal and life-giving in the religious traditions of both East and West. Olivia opens her heart to the reader, allowing us to share her explorations of the spiritual teachings of Christianity, Buddhism, and Hinduism. In this revelatory book, at once joyful, wrenching and awakening, we accompany a woman whose spiritual journey sometimes takes her through painful, dark periods that test her determination and resilience. The reader rejoices that she always emerges into an open landscape of awareness enlivened by love.

— Dr. Robert A. Jonas, author of *My Dear Far-Nearness: The Holy Trinity as Spiritual Practice*

Olivia Hoblitzelle's compelling memoir describes a life lived in pursuit of the Mystery. She shares the traditions, teachers, and practices that guided and connected her to the invisible sacred. Her stories invite us to cultivate inner awareness, moment by moment, and then "to gather light…to gather light." *Ley Lines of Love* is a spiritual classic.

— Charles Busch, author of *Fields of Peace, Soft as Water*

Ley Lines of Love is a masterpiece in which writer and spiritual teacher Olivia Hoblitzelle deftly weaves the disparate threads of her life into a compelling story that is not only entertaining but deeply inspirational. She takes us with her on her very personal journey, both inner and outer, as she courageously shares her vulnerability as well as her unflinching commitment to honesty. Ley Lines of Love is a most courageous and generous offering to all who read it.

— Barbara McCollough, author of *Digger, A Memoir*

Olivia Hoblitzelle tells the story of her life-long spiritual quest to answer the perennial questions: who are we, and what is the meaning of our human life? Her heart's longing shaped her into an intrepid student and teacher of both Western and Eastern meditation and spiritual practices. Olivia lovingly describes her encounters with many major teachers, giving us a first-person account of how Eastern spiritual traditions were planted in the US. Her vivid and beautifully written stories invite us to open our own lives to what is new and unknown and ancient beyond memory, in our interconnected world. It's an instructive read, full of wisdom and insight. Don't miss it.

— Penny Gill, PhD, author of *The Radiant Heart of the Cosmos: Compassion Teachings for Our Time*

Ley Lines of Love opens her arms to the reader with a gentle ease, an embrace of clarity and focus that carefully weaves the reader into the flow of the narrative. Olivia's story, her spiritual autobiography, is not only her own story. In its full surrender to the power of life to shatter, break open, heal, and awaken us, this book transcends the genre. It does what a true spiritual story must do: it liberates the reader, frees her to hold her own unfolding path with awareness, care, and the love that must inevitably bubble up from our depths. Olivia's easy prose drew me along her journey, through her early inspirations on the spiritual path together with her husband Hob, and their shared passion for insight and awakening; to the flowering ashrams of India, gardens that yet held the seeds of deeper decay and disillusionment; through the reconstruction of her spiritual self as a woman grounded in community with other women, held by the Earth, sustained by the inner weaving of life through ancestral voices, and supported by the awareness practices of the Tibetan Buddhist tradition and its teachers. Olivia shares her profound voyages into the depth of consciousness itself, blasting beyond the ego's territory into the full visionary power of the open heart, a state of unified awareness interspersed with the undulating light of a dolphin's eye. This is a gorgeous book and a must-read for anyone who has ever asked the real questions that animate this life: Who am I? Why am I here? How do I fit into the vastness of this universe? Gone, gone, gone beyond, gone completely beyond. So be it!

— Lama Liz Monson PhD, author of *Tales of a Mad Yogi: The Life and Wild Wisdom of Drukpa Kunley*

Ley Lines of Love

Adventures Along the Spiritual Path

by

Olivia Ames Hoblitzelle

Green Fire Press

Housatonic
Massachusetts

Cover watercolor painting by Amanda Amend — www.amandaamend.com

Cover and page design by Anna Myers Sabatini

Paperback ISBN: 979-8-9899452-0-7
Ebook ISBN: 979-8-9899452-1-4

Library of Congress Control Number: 2024902627

Green Fire Press

Green Fire Press
PO Box 377 Housatonic MA 01236

Publisher's Cataloging-in-Publication data

Names: Hoblitzelle, Olivia Ames, author.
Title: Ley lines of love : adventures along the spiritual path / by Olivia Ames Hoblitzelle.
Description: Includes bibliographical references. | Housatonic, MA: Green Fire Press, 2024.
Identifiers: LCCN: 2024902627 | ISBN: 979-8-9899452-0-7 (paperback) | 979-8-9899452-1-4 (ebook)
Subjects: LCSH Hoblitzelle, Olivia Ames. | Buddhists—United States—Biography. | Spiritual life—Buddhism. | Siddha yoga (Service mark) | Spiritual biography. | BISAC BIOGRAPHY & AUTOBIOGRAPHY / Memoirs | BIOGRAPHY & AUTOBIOGRAPHY / Religious | BIOGRAPHY & AUTOBIOGRAPHY / Women | RELIGION / Buddhism

Classification: LCC BQ962 .O63 2024 | DDC 294.3082—dc23

To my family, friends, and teachers
with profound gratitude for friendship
and the ley lines of love
that connect us across time and space.

CONTENTS

INTRODUCTION

Ever since ancient times when people gathered around campfires under the stars, they have been storytellers. Stories weave connection, inspire, and reassure us. We hunger for stories and for the connection that joins heart with heart.

In your hands you hold the story of a spiritual journey, one that started very early and remained persistent throughout my life. Now in my mid-eighties, I'm sitting around that virtual campfire with you, eager to share an assortment of stories I could never have imagined decades ago. Many are inspiring. Some are heartbreaking. Others are groundbreaking. All brought immeasurable gifts—including the dark ones. That would be an important learning—how to discover the gold that lies hidden in the dark ground of suffering.

The stories have an urgency about them. Why? We live in exceptionally dramatic, challenging, and frightening times. Our hearts break as we watch the destruction of our beloved planet and the cascade of other perils—totalitarian leaders, pervasive racism, climate catastrophes, war, and endless violence.

How do our stories hold the enormity of all these challenges? Besides the social and political actions that we might take, we need to come home to ourselves—to our core of basic goodness, resilience, and compassion. Only that can carry us through the storms that beset us. We need to tend the fires of the heart and find an inner refuge, cultivating qualities that nurture kindness and courage. This is the inner journey, urgently calling in ways that will be unique for each of us.

At the outset, I want to comment on the much-used word *spiritual*, which should be differentiated from the word *religion*, which refers to the doctrinal and institutional forms created by different religious traditions. On the other hand, anything that touches on the mysteries of life, the invisible, or the exploration of consciousness might be referred to as spiritual in nature. Whatever our views, this is an inviting, wide-open subject to contemplate.

My story starts just before World War II and continues now into this second decade of the twenty-first century. I seem to have been born with an undying curiosity to understand the mystery in which we live: where we come from, including our ancestry; and the perennial questions of identity—who am I? Where am I going? And above all, what is the meaning of this life?

The seeds of spiritual curiosity were there in my early childhood, but the first big leap of my journey happened when I was seventeen and met my first spiritual teacher, a charismatic preacher, church founder, author, and mystic named Howard Thurman. I had attended various Christian churches and listened to many ministers, but I'd never experienced anyone remotely like Howard. With his warmth, hearty laugh, and great heart, he seemed enlivened by the stream of spiritual energy that flowed through him, permeating his presence and inspiring his words. Undoubtedly this came from his heritage. As the grandson of a slave, his rise to prominence was remarkable in the mid-1950s.

The next surprising milestone came in my mid-twenties when I was seriously on the prowl for a prospective husband. I was in graduate school at Columbia University. At a small dinner gathering, I met a man who, though very well dressed in a tailored suit, had secured his silk tie with a paper clip instead of with the gold tie clip more appropriate for his handsome attire. His dark, wavy hair was streaked with grey. He was good-looking with an expressive, exceptionally mobile face. His wide forehead had an intricate pattern of lifelines, suggesting that he had been through a lot in his forty-one years. I also noticed that he had beautiful hands with long tapered fingers, perhaps those of a musician or artist. To me, he was an older man, fourteen years my elder in fact, far too old for my taste.

Although our intriguing conversation about philosophical questions piqued my interest, I couldn't imagine anything further happening with this unusual man. Nonetheless, Harrison Hoblitzelle, known informally as "Hob," followed up after that evening.

His idea of a first date was to take me to lunch at the Faculty Club at Columbia University where I was impressed to learn that he was both teaching and Director of Academic Placement. Over lunch, he suggested that I read Alan Watts's book *Nature, Man and Woman.* I'd never even heard of Alan Watts. He handed me a copy and explained that this elegant book could change the way we think, feel, and love. That was a startling statement! Furthermore, Hob continued, the book challenged the assumptions of Western culture and introduced the principles of Chinese Taoism. All this was a totally new world to me. I was both daunted and intrigued.

That was the unlikely beginning of our relationship. Subtly luring me into his world, he sent me off to learn awareness practices with an eccentric German woman; he strongly encouraged me to take voice lessons with his Italian voice teacher; and, most astonishing of all—because he thought I had "a few things to work on"—he sent me off to his shrink. Who was this man who seemed to be subjecting me to some kind of makeover job?

Entangled with all my judgments about how unusual this relationship was, I continued to wobble and question. Hob simply didn't fit my preconceptions about the kind of man I would marry, and I still felt the pull of an earlier love. I found it eccentric that he never explicitly asked me to marry him. Nevertheless, intrigued, challenged, and lured onward, I could hardly believe how fast my life was unfolding. Because of my indecision, Hob instigated a separation. Astonishing me, because I'd never experienced rejection, he announced simply, "If you return, you'll know what it means."

After three weeks of separation, I returned, my decision based on a dream about a wedding. The compelling image was of a champagne glass in which appeared a large, luminous star radiating brilliant light in all directions. That luminous star arose from my soul, and I followed it. This was the unlikely start to our marriage, which was to be an extraordinary, lifelong spiritual partnership.

Olivia and Harrison (Hob) in the early 1990s

Thus began our journey. We were to bring up our two children, Ethan and Laura,[1] through mostly delightful family years, though definitely enlivened by the inevitable squabbles of siblings and parents. Although Hob was intellectually inclined with a PhD in Comparative Literature, he was, at heart, an adventurer of the spirit. That's what had captivated me and what had drawn us together, because those essential questions about life fueled my quest.

1 Laura was to be given the spiritual name "Purnima," which appears whenever the context is the ashram. Otherwise, I use her birth name.

Young family: Hob, Olivia, Ethan (age 7), and Laura (age 4)

Starting in the 1960s, a wide assortment of new movements blossomed—political, psychological, and spiritual—many involving explorations of consciousness in various forms. There was a veritable explosion of experimentation, much of it pushing the boundaries of mainstream culture. Hob and I were right in the middle of all of it. Together in the early '70s, we started by getting initiated in Transcendental Meditation, and then moved on to explore Zen Buddhism. We attended *sesshins*[2] (meditation retreats) at a neighborhood Zen Center where the Zen master, carrying a long, flat-sided stick, would walk slowly around the room of meditators. If you bowed to him as he stood in front of you, he'd whack you on the shoulder to wake you up from your wandering, undisciplined meditations. That practice was definitely bizarre, but I loved the dignity of the place, the formalities of practice, and the profound silence that permeated our days.

2 Given that a number of words may be unfamiliar to my readers, I've included a Glossary at the end of the book.

We then discovered Vipassana, also known as insight meditation, from the Theravada tradition, a form of Buddhist practice primarily from South Asia. That was to become the most adaptable form of meditation for Western culture. As a profound path leading to deep spiritual awakening, one aspect of Vipassana was encapsulated in the word *mindfulness* and led to the stress management movement eventually taught in organizations, schools, churches, government agencies, and even the U.S. military. I was to become a pioneer in this movement, surprising even myself when I ended up teaching Behavioral Medicine, also called Mind/Body Medicine, at a major Boston hospital. This was the crowning phase in my career where my love of both meditation and psychology finally came together.

Like several turning points in my career, this professional leap came by invitation, not because I had sought it out. In a similar way, in my early forties when I started getting involved in the encounter group movement, I decided to train in psychology and group work. Before I'd even received my degree, I was being asked to co-lead groups with leaders in the field, pioneers such as Morrie Schwartz, lionized through the book *Tuesdays with Morrie*; and Philip Slater, expert in group process and author of the underground bestseller *The Pursuit of Loneliness*. Participants in these groups began asking if they could see me for individual therapy. Without having made any career decision, I found myself with a private practice in psychotherapy, seeing individuals and couples, and co-leading groups. It seemed as though I'd fallen backward into my next career.

Parallel with becoming a therapist, when I'd been practicing Vipassana meditation for some years, I was invited to teach meditation in various organizational settings, including schools and churches. Traditionally, one has to be authorized to teach within a meditation tradition by a recognized teacher, something I knew nothing about. But those were the early days of meditation traditions coming to the West, and the field was wide open without any such guidelines.

Olivia in 2007

While I taught basic mindfulness practices, Vipassana, or insight meditation, was to become Hob's lifelong practice. He was eventually ordained a Dharmacharya, or senior teacher, by the much-loved Vietnamese Zen master Thich Nhat Hanh. He became a dedicated teacher with countless students who loved his unique style of teaching, which incorporated his love of comparative literature with his delightful, sometimes irreverent sense of humor.

Hob at Plum Village after ordination

At this point our paths diverged, which sometimes created uncomfortable tensions in our relationship. Given my strong inclination toward devotional practices, I ended up in a tradition from India called Siddha Yoga. I now had a guru, which was a challenge to Hob's Western mind. My deep involvement with this path created challenges, especially when our daughter Laura also became involved, a dramatic archetypal story for spiritual seekers, which I will tell in some detail. Without question, it was one of the most powerful initiations of my life—revelatory, empowering, and spiritually deepening, though later leading to a heart-breaking chapter. I share the whole story with you, dear reader, in hopes that it might shed light on a deeply troubling pattern and its frequency in spiritual groups worldwide.

I will also share an assortment of short vignettes that reveal how the spiritual path can lead us onward in surprising, even startling ways. I now see that a thread of sacred intelligence seems to have been orchestrating my life. I could never have guessed that I would have out-of-body experiences or explore the further edges of consciousness through entheogens (sacred medicines) such as psilocybin and LSD, that I would spend the night in solitary vigil on a remote mountain, or have my life dramatically disrupted by a friend who, in the midst of her spiritual awakening, began channeling my mother's voice, although she had never met my mother and my mother could not speak at the time, her voice having been silenced by Alzheimer's.

Finally, I'll reflect on two parts of my most recent chapter, still unfolding. Following the passion that led me to write my second book, *Aging with Wisdom: Reflections, Stories & Teachings*, I've taught extensively about how to deal with aging in an age-phobic culture. I have also, after forty years, felt called to continue my exploration of consciousness through the sacred medicines, especially psilocybin and LSD. Much is being written these days about the Shift or the Great Turning, the slow but sure movement away from old forms in all areas of life toward a more nuanced, far-reaching view of reality that involves opening to new realms of consciousness. The renaissance of interest in sacred medicines has finally broken through the traditional views of Western medicine, with numerous studies having proven that psilocybin and MDMA, for example, can bring dramatic results with PTSD, depression, and addictions of all kinds, especially alcoholism.

I also want to mention a significant thread that weaves through the various stories in this book. Buddhist, Hindu, and other Asian traditions often use the word *karma* in reference to the basic law of cause and effect, or in biblical parlance, "as ye sow, so shall ye reap." Sometimes people equate karma with the word *destiny*, but karma points to more subtle meanings. It may suggest, for example, the mysterious connections between people, surprising events that contain an inexplicable element, or simply the mystery surrounding some situation. Some of the stories that follow involve the mystery of karma, which shows up for all of us if we examine our lives deeply.

As an example of a karmic connection, no one was more surprised than I when five years after Hob's death I reconnected with Keith, an Englishman I had met in my early twenties. At that time, we had had an instant and powerful connection, but he was married with two children and a third on the way. He'd come to the United States on a Roosevelt Memorial Traveling Scholarship, a four-month visit that began by spending his first weekend with Eleanor Roosevelt at her home at Val-Kill Cottage—a remarkable opportunity! Intense as our relationship was, we respected his marriage. It was an utterly heartbreaking situation; he was the one I still loved when I met Hob. We stayed in touch on and off for more than fifty years, although meanwhile my life had taken me into worlds Keith couldn't even imagine. Still, upon meeting again late in life, we found our strong connection remained intact. Such are the mysteries of karma!

Even though our lives were dramatically different—for we truly lived in worlds apart—after Hob died, Keith uprooted himself from his traditional British life, and we lived together in the United States for fifteen years, bonded by a love very different from the one I had experienced in my marriage. The depth of Keith's connection to both me and my family was remarkable. He ended up writing a book about the Ames family, including the incredible discovery that our ancestors had been serfs on the estate of Lord Wyke in Somerset. Serfs! No wonder I love to get my hands into the soil and plant gardens. Even more extraordinary, Keith found our ancestors' emancipation papers in the archives of Wells Cathedral. Among all the genealogists in our family, it was Keith who uncovered this startling bit of family history.

In contemplative moments, I felt that Hob's and my relationship was more imbued with spirit and the search for inner freedom, for that was our deepest bond. Although I often said that Hob and I were soul mates—for indeed we were—my relationship with Keith was also about our soul connection but was somehow a precious bond of a very different kind. I was blessed with both.

It is human nature to seek patterns, models, or theories to explain the complexities of life. The term *ley lines* is an example of this impulse. The term appeared in the early twentieth century, its origins attributed to early cultures especially in England and Germany who sensed the subtle energies crisscrossing the Earth's surface. As an esoteric perspective, the term *ley lines* describes a central theme in this story—my lifelong curiosity about spiritual traditions, the East/West dialogue, the Mystery, and the search for hidden meanings. The speculations about ley lines also mirror the discoveries of modern physics and theories about the quantum. Though quantum theory is an immensely complex field, one generalization stands out—the interrelatedness of everything in the universe from individual lives to the entire cosmos.

I share these stories with the hope that they might shed light on wherever you are in your own inner journey. We are all given the gift of incarnation, I believe, to experience the great mysteries of life, to find fulfillment, and to help others. Above all, through the adventures of life with all its joys and sorrows, we're called to discover how to give and receive love. My heartfelt hope is that you will discover insight and inspiration as you read these stories from my spiritual journey.

BEGINNINGS

Lost in reverie, I've returned for a day's visit to the world of my childhood. In my mid-forties at the time, I had been drawn back to one of my favorite places from those early days, sitting with my back against the old well that stood in the center of a vast lawn. The well was a leftover from days past when it was an important source of water for that part of the estate. In those years, we were living in a rented cottage on that large estate, a paradise for a young family, with woods and open fields, a pond for skating in winter, the beach in summer, the sheep and farm animals, even a stable with horses.

As a child, I was always intrigued by the well, its round, stone structure now thick with ivy and above, an arching beam where the bucket once hung. As children, we dropped stones down into the deep, dark hole and waited expectantly for the splash as the stone found water. We tried to guess how deep the well might be, which led to my dark fantasies of what might happen if I fell into it. For us as children, the well was surrounded by mystery; it was a dark opening into the ground, an echo chamber for our falling stones, a circular form leading to unknown depths deep in the earth.

Feeling the roughness of the ivy against my back, I had closed my eyes, lost in memories from my childhood. To my surprise, in my mind's eye, I saw a young girl, maybe about five years old. She was climbing over the distant fence that bordered a field filled with sheep, separating it from the great lawn. She continued to walk toward me, and I saw that she was dressed in red shorts and a yellow and white striped T-shirt. Her very blonde braids bounced as she walked, skipping every few steps with a kind of quiet exuberance. She slowed down as she approached me. I had the feeling that she had an important message—a message that would reveal something significant about my life.

She stopped right in front of me and looked down at me. I noticed her vivid blue eyes, her earnest expression, and the sun striking highlights into her blonde hair. I felt a sense of expectancy. She paused, looked directly at me, and then spoke just two words.

"Be free."

Like stones dropping into the well, her words dropped deep into my heart. I felt suddenly overwhelmed by feelings, tears overflowing and running down my cheeks. I sank into the feelings—a longing so deep and intense for something unknown, beckoning, and mysterious. I didn't know what it was, only that it was huge, enveloping me like a cosmic embrace into which I totally let go, continuing to weep.

Then realization suddenly struck me. That little girl was me, a wise child with a message that shone like a beacon throughout a life of spiritual discoveries.

As a child, I sometimes felt as though I lived between two worlds. There was my family and the idyllic place where I had spent my youngest years, and then there was my inner world with all the questions and wonderings.

I'd sit in the window seat tucked under the gabled window in my bedroom and look out into the night sky, vast and star studded, and wonder how it could be so wondrous and overwhelming. Who was I, and where did I fit into this vastness?

The phosphorescence in the night waters of Long Island Sound filled me with delight and amazement, the ever-changing colors surging and receding in response to my swirling hand. How did the water create all that magical color? I was always intrigued by light and light effects. I remember lying in the grass in the sun, remaining very still and squinting until I'd see rainbows in my eyelashes. The angle of light had to be just right for the phenomenon to appear, and I needed to remain very still, mesmerized by the dance of colors. As children, we may instinctively be drawn to these experiences of inner stillness and beauty, doorways to wonder. Or in my bath, I'd stir up soap bubbles and become transfixed by the iridescence in the quivering surface, again suspended in states of absorption. I clearly was drawn to child-like meditative states. How amused I would be many years later when introduced to esoteric meditation practices that dealt with light, much like those that had attracted me as a child.

There were also the recurring questions. Why was I who I was and not somebody else? Why was I in this body while you were in another body? Why couldn't I be free to experience what it was like to be you? Such a young mind couldn't begin to fathom these questions, yet in some simplistic, childlike way, I felt stirrings of curiosity and really wanted to know this: what did your life feel like? Did you wonder about the same things that I did?

Why didn't the grown-ups talk about these things? They did sometimes because my parents were sensitive people who loved books and music and the natural world, but it was never enough for my searching mind. Mysteries and magic were everywhere in my world. I spent hours playing alone in the woods behind our house because my two older brothers mostly ignored me or tried to tickle me to death or occasionally beat up on me. My little sister, Joanie, was too much younger to be a playmate.

As I created little houses and villages with my findings from the natural world, I sensed spirits around me—the spirits of the trees, unseen animals, birds, fairies—a world alive with hidden spirits. I had lots of invisible company. Sometimes I whispered to them. I felt them in the house too. I left food on my bureau to feed them, a practice quietly supported by my mother who helped me choose what to leave, usually a little glass of milk and half a graham cracker. Only a child's imagination, you say? Maybe. Maybe not.

Along with the magical world of our family's place, my maternal grandparents provided another intriguing place in my childhood. Their brown shingled Victorian house on Forest Street in Hartford, Connecticut was spacious, the rooms filled with unusual objects collected on my grandfather's travels. The house was protected by trees on two sides, some of them tall hemlocks that cast shadows into the rooms, creating variations of crepuscular light.

Grandad, as we called him, was our mother's father. I adored Grandad. Bearded and merry, his eyes twinkled with childlike playfulness. He played the clarinet, along with a number of other wind instruments that hung on the wall of his little music room at the top of the carpeted stairs. With delight, he'd recite long poems by heart, such as "The Wreck of the Hesperus," his expressions reflecting the action in the poem. He was a physicist yet hardly felt like the serious academic that he was. He had a mischievous, boyish streak as though the world was his playground. Did his love of science explain the skeleton that hung in the attic, a source of wonder, curiosity and fear in us, his grandchildren? What about one of his books, a collection of essays titled *As It Looks to the Angels?* Everyone knew he was a gifted linguist who spoke nine languages, a combination of his classical education and his marriage to my beloved Danish grandmother, which led to his learning the Nordic languages in addition to French, German, and Italian.

Part of the intrigue about my grandparents revolved around Grandad's brother, my great uncle Edward, who, with his wife Georgie, was a medical missionary in China. There were endless streams of stories about their lives there—the floods, the Japanese invasion that destroyed the hospital they had so laboriously built and would rebuild, how he treated wounded Japanese soldiers as well as the Chinese although they were undying enemies at war. An unfolding of intriguing family stories fed my imagination.

Grandad traveled to China several times to visit his brother. Whether overland or by sea, those journeys introduced him to many countries along the way. Not only had he traveled all through Asia, particularly India and China, but also to much of Europe, thanks to his marriage to a Dane. I used to visit some of the interesting objects around the house—the ceramic Buddha whose arms went up and down as his tongue went in and out, the music box that played the heavenly music of the nightingale, the funny little figures from India that lived in a glass-fronted case—so many curious objects to enrich a child's world.

I loved it most when he invited me to his study. The room looked out over the garden and was lined with windows, the panes leaded in unusual shapes. The sunny side of the room had window seats covered with long, moss-green cushions. Grandad would invite me onto his lap, having chosen one of the big, illustrated books that lay flat at the bottom of his voluminous bookcases. With his arms around me, holding the big books up close in my lap, he'd spin colorful stories about the pictures depicting dramatic mountain scenery reflecting his love of alpine climbing, or bloody scenes of the French Revolution, or images of foreign countries, especially Asia. I particularly loved the books about India—the women in colorful saris carrying copper pots on their heads, the temples with ornate carvings, the exotic sacred cows that wandered the streets, and the elephants beautifully decorated with finery for religious processions.

Did I really remember something about India? Several times I told my mother that I remembered the floods in a faraway place, the vast expanses of churning, muddy water streaming by, all the trees and houses submerged. But she said I'd never lived through any floods. I also described to her the clearing in the forest where I was helped up onto the elephant to ride in a box. She listened kindly but said she didn't think I'd ever ridden on an elephant. Was it my childhood imagination? Scenes from Grandad's books? But I could almost feel these memories in my body. I would persist, because then those impressions were as real to me as anything else in my young life. As a small child, why was I always attracted to anything Indian, especially paisley patterns, artistic designs from India, silks with unusual patterns, Indians on the streets of New York?

All I know is how I loved those grandparents and being in that house filled with its curiosities and intrigue. Besides India, there was my beloved Danish grandmother. My oldest brother had nicknamed her

"Beep." Because I was her first granddaughter, we had a special connection. I felt bathed in her love. As a young woman of only nineteen, she had emigrated from Denmark to pursue her career on the stage—very unusual for that era. Although she was an actress by profession, training actors and actresses into her late years, there was a deep interiority about her. Her hair, now white, was usually braided and pinned up in a crown on her head. Something about her blue eyes as she looked at me with unconditional love conveyed a kind of longing, as though something was missing. She always missed her mother country and would tell me stories about her childhood. She introduced me to the fairy tales of Hans Christian Andersen, a favorite collection which her uncle had published. I didn't understand it as a child, but I still sensed her sadness, maybe finally tinged with acceptance that life had turned out differently from her hopes.

With Beep, my Danish grandmother

Because I was a sensitive child, I picked up these feelings. But as children, we're lost in the world of feelings, unaware of what conditions us. In our family, because my mother had had several nervous breakdowns, my father tried to hold everything together by control. Strong emotions were bridled by discipline, and we were banished to our rooms for any kind of emotional disturbance, especially anger or any other emotional outburst.

I remember being perplexed by the raw, burning feelings of hurt, shame, or abandonment. Did other people feel this way too? Did they ache and hurt and feel as desolate as I sometimes felt? Although I had a mostly happy childhood, I experienced the sufferings of a child with a quiet, inwardly focused acceptance. Besides the inevitable shadows of childhood, there was the dark shadow of war—night coverings for the windows to hide us from the German planes, food and gas rationing, rumors of German submarines near us in Long Island Sound, my mother's work in the airplane spotting tower, and my father's disappearance to Washington, DC, to help with the war effort until we moved there to join him.

How do I make sense of all these pieces of childhood experience? Above all, how do I understand my questions about the mystery of life? Why are we here? What does it all mean? Back then, I couldn't have articulated it that way, but it was all a deep part of my inner world, which would lead to some very unlikely future events.

DISCOVERING OTHER REALITIES

Significant clues about what really matters in our lives may appear in surprising places. Although I harbored questions in my early years, I could never have articulated them in words as I just have. My curiosity was the lived experience of a child, something I felt in my body and innermost being.

The next set of clues appeared while I was only a teenager. The first clue, seemingly insignificant in the larger arc of life, happened when I was sixteen. For the first time in my life, I left home to attend a boarding school just outside of Boston. I was a sophomore, bouncing along through my days like many a teenager, preoccupied with friendships, studies, sports, and the boys who went to school across the street. At first, everything about this new school was a bit overwhelming. I struggled with questions like whether I was smart enough to keep up with the work, who my new friends might be, and where I fit in. But those concerns soon disappeared. I found many friends, relished competitive sports, became a student leader, and overall was very happy at that school.

It was still the first term when I recognized how much I looked forward to the classes with Miss Punderson, our English teacher. We knew her first name was Molly, but we called her Miss Pundy. Though hard to believe, she told me after class the first day that she had also taught my mother, a whole generation earlier. How amazing! That made her very old, at least in my adolescent eyes.

We guessed that Miss Pundy might be in her sixties. Her white hair was pinned up in a bun, usually with a few pieces flying loose around her face. Even though she seemed pretty old to me, she was a lovely looking woman with kindly blue eyes. I noticed how comfortable I felt in her presence compared to my other teachers. I didn't remember any grown-up other than my grandmother Beep looking at me in such an open, curious way with an inviting, thoughtful expression as if she couldn't wait to hear what I might have to say.

Talking about our teachers was part of what we did, and there was something else that intrigued us about Miss Pundy. We had heard that she had a great love who had been killed in World War I. Surely that explained her aura of sadness, creating an air of romance and pathos around her. The deep quiet of her presence and something about her eyes and gentle smile made me feel safe with her.

I had another significant insight about Miss Pundy that I recognized only in retrospect. She saw something about me that I didn't yet know myself. It may have been in the way she asked me questions, the gentle way she guided me, or that my questions in class showed my curiosity that I was looking for something. I knew I wanted to understand things about life that grown-ups didn't seem to talk about. That deep stream of questions about identity and the meaning of life flowed beneath the surface of everything. I have vivid memories of countless discussions with my friends about philosophy and religion, sometimes long into the night after lights out.

In one of those landmark moments in our education, I remember when Miss Pundy asked us to write our first long paper with footnotes. I hadn't known where to begin, what topic to choose, or what books to read. Miss Pundy rescued me when she suggested that it might interest me to write on the subject of symbolism in two of Nathaniel Hawthorne's books. At fifteen, I had no idea how to define the word *symbolism*. But as I read the books, the meaning started to come alive; I saw how symbols were a word or image that stood for something else, allowing us to go beyond what was seen to the unseen and plumb the connection between them. The process was about setting free the hidden meaning.

The concept of symbolism fired my imagination. It seemed to connect to my persistent questions, for symbols point to something hidden, something beyond the ordinary—the unseen, something beyond. The concept seemed to connect to those feelings I'd always had, something about being free. Free from what? Intellectually as a teenager, I hardly knew except that I remembered the feeling of subtle excitement in my body, around my heart. Maybe it was freedom from what's hard in life, like the strangling feelings of anger, loneliness, or sadness. Unlikely as it seems, I look back at this assignment and see how it introduced me to the possibility of experiencing a kind of freedom that I intuited and longed for.

Hawthorne's writing also had a distinctly dark undertone, which mesmerized and sometimes horrified me. I'd led a very sheltered life within a family system that tried to suppress the dark emotions such as anger, fear, sadness, and grief. My father, with his emotionally controlled New England upbringing, wanted to protect my mother and vigorously upheld the ideal of the happy family. My immersion in Hawthorne opened my eyes to the possibility of a darker world.

There was another assignment from Miss Pundy that had a memorable impact on my young mind. It was an excerpt from Plato's *The Republic*, one of the most famous allegories in Western literature. She told us to read it several times and that it would take a lot of reflection to really understand it. Little did I understand then that the allegory related to the two truths in Buddhism—relative and absolute truth—something I would learn about forty years later.

The excerpt described a cave with a dialogue between two people, one of whom was Socrates, Plato's teacher. Plato described how a group of prisoners were living in a cave where they were chained in such a way that they could only see what was in front of them. Behind them were a great fire and a raised wall on which figures were walking by. The prisoners could only see shadows on a wall in front of them. One of the prisoners got free and went out into the world outside and experienced the freedom of the real world. But when he returned to free the other prisoners, he'd been blinded by the light. The prisoners naturally were afraid of that other reality and remained living in the world of shadows and illusion rather than seeking the freedom that lay beyond.

Miss Pundy must have explained that the allegory symbolized the central predicament at the heart of human existence; namely, two views of how we perceive reality—the relative and the absolute. Stated very simply, relative reality is what we experience most of the time—the world as we know it. Absolute reality points to another dimension—ultimate, transcendent, infinite, beyond concepts, ineffable. At that time, I'd never thought about perceptions of reality. All I remember is that I felt pain for the plight of the prisoners and was intrigued by the promise of freedom in that reality beyond the cave. And all that light! I'd been perplexed that the freed prisoner came back blinded, but even that didn't change the allure of freedom for me.

As I look back at these experiences, it astonishes me that they are so deeply etched in my memory. Thanks to an exceptional teacher, I was introduced to new realities I'd never known existed. Both the power of symbolism and the allegory of Plato's cave related directly to that underground stream in my psyche—my curiosity about hidden meanings, how to explain the realities of the world, and the promise of an ultimate freedom. I would forever associate these subtler aspects of our human experience with Miss Pundy and my first ventures into realms that I would subsequently explore in great depth.[3]

3 Miss Pundy's personal story had a surprising and wonderful last chapter. She retired to Stockbridge, Massachusetts where she taught poetry at a local library. One of her students was an elderly gentleman who attended all her classes and one day invited her for dinner. Their friendship deepened. He asked her to marry him, and at seventy-two, she married Norman Rockwell, the famous artist, and off they went to Scotland on a bicycle trip for their honeymoon. This is such a heartwarming story about my memorable teacher!

GIFTS OF THE SPIRIT

There was a flurry of extra excitement in 1976 because my father's seventieth birthday was coming up in mid-June. I was wondering what to give him. He really didn't need anything, but my mother kept talking about what a special birthday it was. Besides my indecision about a present, I couldn't have known ahead of time that this birthday would end up being memorable for me too.

It was a beautiful time of year around our white colonial house. The huge linden tree outside the front door was in full flower with fragrant, little, white blossoms. The whole majestic tree was humming with the sound of bees, a veritable temple of beauty, sound, and fragrance.

Around the side of the house, the garden bed bordering the terrace was filled with a magnificent display of roses, all now in radiant bloom, redolent with heavenly fragrance. I used to think that those roses bloomed especially for my father's birthday. The rose was the symbol on the Ames family crest, and my father always wore a signet ring, gold with a garnet at the center into which was carved the image of a rose. He wore the ring on the little finger of his left hand, so when I sat on his left at my usual place for dinner, I would watch the candlelight play on the deep red garnet—a sweet childhood memory that somehow connected us. As a child, I usually called him Pa. His given name was Amyas, though most everyone called him Ammie.

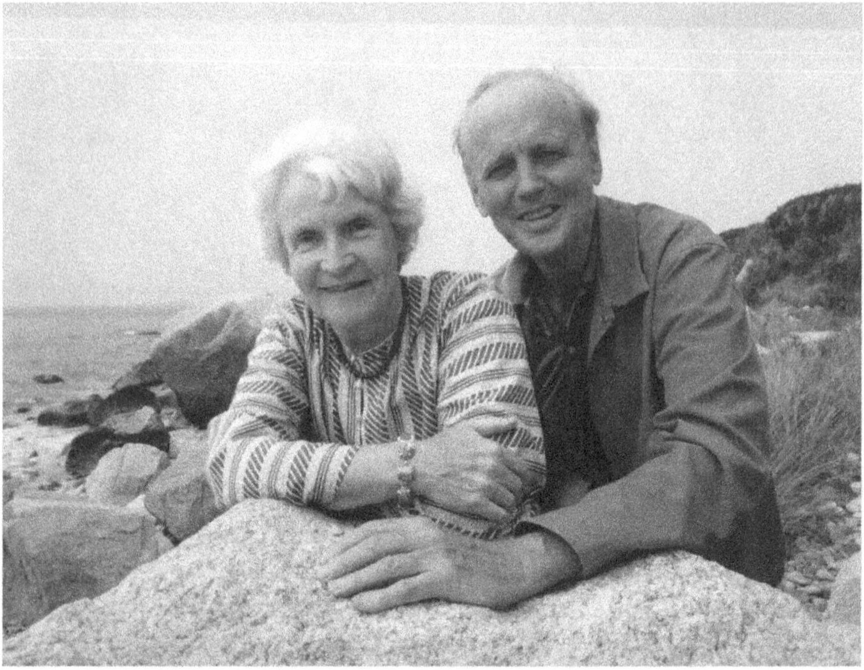

Olivia's parents: Amyas and Evelyn Perkins Ames

Although it is hard to be objective in describing one's parents, I must introduce my father. He was an unusual combination of qualities. Exceptionally gifted as a leader in his fields of business and the arts, he had a self-assured dignity that conveyed quiet power. He undertook all activities with intense focus, teaching us, his four children, to do everything to the best of our abilities and to always follow through. He could be demanding and a perfectionist, possibly some genetic traits left over from his two grandfathers, both of whom had been generals.

Ammie, as we called him when we reached adulthood, was easy to idealize, perhaps especially as his daughter. He was tall, athletic, strikingly handsome, and patrician in his bearing. Strong yet gentle, he was good-natured and deeply kind, with the emotional control of an old New Englander. He especially exerted that control over us because of our mother's sensitivities. He was very protective of her, guarding the stability of his family with fierce determination. If we crossed his vision of the happy family, he could flare with impatience and anger, but that happened only occasionally.

Even with all I've described so far, the picture of this man is far from complete. He was a devoted father who encouraged us whenever we showed the slightest interest in anything. For example, when I began identifying wildflowers, he gave me the gift of a flower press, sketch book, and set of colored pencils. He returned to the piano in his sixties and in retirement patiently practiced for two hours every morning until the latest piece blossomed under his fingers. He played Chopin, his favorite composer, as if playing to his beloved.

With his artistic sensibilities, he was, above all, an extremely gifted photographer. We might see him for extended periods lying flat on his belly in the grass, propped up on his elbows, holding his camera as he waited for the light to be just right or for the butterfly to land on a wildflower. Commercially published, *The Private Lives of our Natural Neighbors* was a collection of his photographs with accompanying essays that revealed his whimsical sense of humor and outlook on life.

Even with all his competence and success—*success* being a word he often used—one felt his sensitivity and tenderness. He had a shy streak, as if protecting (and also hiding) his inner world in the same way that he protected his family. I only saw him cry once, after a distressing episode during my mother's harrowing years with Alzheimer's.

Since my mother, Evelyn (known as Evvie), also appears in this story, I must introduce her as well. After all, whatever spiritual guidance we get—or don't get—comes initially from our parents. On Sundays during the World War when gas rationing severely limited any traveling, we sometimes had informal "services" in the living room where Ammie or Evvie played hymns on the piano and read us Bible stories. This was surely instigated by my mother. With minimal enthusiasm, she described herself as a lapsed Episcopalian, whereas my father identified himself as a Unitarian. Neither of them darkened the doors of churches except for weddings or funerals.

My mother grew up in Hartford, Connecticut, the daughter of my beloved Grandad whom I described earlier and her Danish mother whom we called Beep. My mother's life was nourished by this rich cultural heritage. Evvie, as I called her when I became an adult, was an intriguing combination of interiority and lively extroversion. This dichotomy was both a gift and a challenge. As a writer, she moved easily among an almost bohemian culture of writers and artists while also an engaging hostess to family parties or events connected to my father's public role in New York City's cultural life. Wryly, I sometimes thought of her as both a free-spirited poet and a reincarnated queen!

I have a treasured graphite drawing of my mother, the gift of an artist friend who did several drawings of her when she was a young woman. Evvie had blue eyes and light brown hair that in later years turned pure white with silver highlights. The drawing conveys her beauty and, with consummate skill, manages to portray the reflective, inward nature of her personality.

Evvie had her first breakdown in her early twenties and was institutionalized several times during her life. In and out of therapy, with occasional periods of depression, she was emotionally deep and complex. Although she could be overly self-absorbed, she had a strong personality and a curious knack for finding her way into friendships and occasionally intimate relationships with well-known people. My parents' marriage must have had its challenges, but the marriage was solid and loving, held in a loyalty that was apparent and inspiring.

She and I were unusually close as mother and daughter. While this can be a difficult relationship for many, we simply shared an uncommon love for one another. I was her first daughter, born after my two older brothers, Oakes and Ned. A couple of weeks after my birth, she plummeted into a post-partum nervous breakdown and was institutionalized for almost nine months. She told me several times how the memory of her newborn daughter was literally a lifeline for her. She imagined a golden thread connecting us. Our connection, she said, helped her to endure electric shock treatment and the terrors of a nervous breakdown and suicidal thoughts.

She returned to enter fully into family life. She was a gifted poet and writer with seven published books, multiple journals, and an extensive correspondence, often with well-known writers. As a girl, I was always struck by how my father protected her creative life. Across the pasture from our house, my parents had built a writing refuge for Evvie. We affectionately called it the *sneglehus*, the Danish word for "snail house." It was a tiny house, and being half Danish, my mother wanted to honor her ancestry. Besides the time she spent in the snail house, she also went off to writing retreats at places such as the MacDowell Colony and the Aspen Institute, sometimes for weeks at a time, something my father totally supported.

In contrast to my father's more reticent nature, Evvie was outgoing. She was curious about people and a gifted conversationalist, with an insatiable intellect and a lively sense of humor, delighting in telling a *risqué* joke. As the gracious hostess, she organized and presided over my parents' social gatherings.

Her emotional complexity, however, was not obvious in social settings; she was strong in many ways, sensitive and vulnerable in others, and something of a hypochondriac. I cherished our long, lively conversations, and in her later years, she began to confide in me about the anguish of her occasional depression. When Alzheimer's took over, the bright light of her personality gradually faded into the flat affect and silence of that frightening disease.

Together, my parents were a striking couple, very active in New York's cultural world because of my father's role as a negotiator for the arts, first as President of the New York Philharmonic and then Director of Lincoln Center. For me, as deeply as I loved him, in my young adult years I sometimes didn't know how to cross the boundary that I felt around him. We inhabited very different worlds. He was a public figure, moving among well known people, whereas I, now a therapist, had chosen psychology, a field that he recoiled from because of Evvie's history and her Jungian analyst whom he didn't like.

There was I, not only exploring new, little-known fields with strange names such as gestalt, bioenergetics, and psychosynthesis, but part of an alternative therapy collective with the somewhat flaky name of Greenhouse. I was now well into my inner quest and involved with a guru tradition—unbelievable even to me—and going off to India to a mysterious place called an ashram. This combination of my unusual professional life plus all my spiritual explorations created a kind of barrier between my father and me; he didn't know how to ask me about my world, and I didn't know how to talk about what was most important about my life.

I remember a time when I started to share something with him. My parents usually had a ceremonial gathering time in the living room before dinner. We'd all have a glass of Cinzano, a sweet Italian wine, as an aperitif along with some nuts or cheese on crackers. My father and I were there first. With drink in hand, he went to sit on the couch, and I was in the armchair to his right. I wanted to tell him what it was like to visit the Siddha Yoga ashram in the Catskills, about the beauty of the surroundings, the ancient chanting, teachings, and serene meditation hall.

I began to feel a familiar uncertainty about how to describe something that meant so much to me. Almost the moment I started to describe the ashram setting, I noticed how he looked down and slightly away. Subtle but clear to me, I sensed his discomfort, as if he really didn't want to connect with my words. How often I'd experience this subtle message! I knew this pattern not only from him but from others who were uncomfortable with my maverick spiritual life. In response, I could feel myself contracting. I too would pull back, feeling as though a fragile but important connection had been broken. For me at least, there was an invisible wall between us.

But there was no wall with my mother. She was always curious about my spiritual adventurings. She was a deep listener, as open and curious as I was, a kindred spirit. She wanted to understand what motivated people, their feelings, the depths of their lives. Years later, when I was deeply involved in Siddha Yoga, she would come to the ashram and participate in a two-day meditation retreat. In her later years, even when dementia was quietly infiltrating her inquiring mind, we would meditate when we were together.

On that sunny day when I was forty, the question remained: what was I going to give my dear father for his seventieth birthday? Suddenly, out of nowhere, the idea struck me: I had something important to tell him. That morning, feeling apprehensive, I found him at his desk in the music room. Hearing my own voice as if someone else were speaking the words, I announced, "Pa, I've got a gift for you, but it's not the usual kind. I think we need to be outside, at the edge of the meadow under the white birches."

He looked slightly puzzled but smiled and rose to follow me out of the room. As we paused for a moment in the front hall waiting to go out the screen door, I said, "I know this seems a bit mysterious, but let's walk up and sit for a few minutes so I can tell you what I'm thinking about."

"You've got me wondering," he replied, "but of course. Let's see what you're up to!" He laughed.

Somehow I had known instinctively that the row of white birches was where we must go. They were across the lawn and far enough away from the house for us not to be interrupted by the other family members gathered for his birthday. The birches were beautiful, standing like sentries at the meadow's edge.

I don't remember if we talked as we walked up the slope of the meadow to where the line of white birches marked its edge. I was scanning for a place to sit. It seemed very important to choose the right tree and a comfortable place in the grass. After all, he was seventy, and unlike me, he was not used to sitting on the ground.

As we eased ourselves down into the long grass, I reached out to take his hand and started to make light of what I was about to say. I noticed fleetingly that I'd taken his right hand, not the one with his signet ring and family crest. I was aware that my heart was beating wildly. *What do I think I'm doing? Where did this idea come from? Am I totally crazy? What in the world is he going to think?* A tumble of questions was vying for attention. My mind was racing, my heart pounding. He was looking at me with anticipation, waiting kindly.

"Pa, I know this is really unusual, but I suddenly had this idea that I wanted to share with you. It's kind of a present. Probably you would've thought I'd say this to Mom because she's a writer, the one always exploring philosophy and literature and all that. But something about this is just for you. Yeah, this is definitely unusual." I chuckled a little uneasily.

I hesitated, still wondering how to tell him what was in my heart. I felt as though I was on the edge of a tremendous abyss, an unknown space of unimaginable vastness. Aware of the thumping in my chest, I was barely breathing. Then I jumped into words.

"Pa, I just want to tell you . . . I just want to thank you for something really important to me. I want to thank you for everything that you've given me, all the invisible things, especially your love of beauty and the gift of spirit—especially that, the gift of spirit. And also . . . I want to tell you that I love you."

There was a tremendous rush of energy, a flood of love and relief, an indescribable feeling of breakthrough, like a huge wave breaking over me. I couldn't believe that words could have such an impact. I felt as though I'd crashed through some towering wall of ordinariness to find that the wall that had separated us—amazing discovery!—had no substance. I felt totally exhilarated and free.

Ammie lifted his head slightly. His eyes filled with tears. He put out his hand and laid it gently on top of mine.

"Oh my," he started and then paused. Sounding incredulous, he continued. "Isn't that something you'd say to your mother? But to me?"

His question, his surprise, hung in the air between us. "I understand how you might think that, given how close Ma and I are," I replied, "but this is something else. It's mysterious. I can't explain it. I just know it. And I just had to share it with you."

His face, with eyes still brimming, opened into a wide smile.

"Thank you. Oh, thank you," he said.

We stood up, hugged, and arms around one another, walked back toward the house, both of us silenced by what had just happened.

This encounter with my father may seem insignificant in the great arc of life, but for me, it was memorable and treasured. Breakthroughs invariably come when we take risks. I knew how easy it was to continue along with habitual patterns, accept the status quo, and not try to push the boundaries of experience. I had pushed the boundaries with this message. Yet it opened an ease-way between us and felt like some kind of karmic fulfillment.

In subsequent years, I felt our bond continue to deepen. There was no need for words to affirm it; I knew we both felt it. It was clear in little gestures of affection, in his eyes, in his words of appreciation. Out of respect for our different worlds, I didn't talk at length about retreats or teachers, but I felt greater ease sharing more than I had in the past. Without question, a profound shift had happened on his seventieth birthday.

Much to my surprise, another chapter to this story would unfold five or six years later. It happened in a most unexpected way. For as long as I can remember, I've been gifted with a lively dream life. I've had many so-called "great dreams," a term coined by Carl Jung, the eminent psychiatrist, philosopher, and mystic. Such dreams can be life-changing. They reverberate in memory as gifts from another dimension, beckoning us in ways that are often more compelling than waking life experience. Our dreams, which exist outside of time, sometimes return to our waking consciousness, asking for our attention.

The following landmark dream revealed an array of significant issues in my life—the role of my father and mother, freedom versus control, horses, water, and the overall mysteries of life. This dream happened a few years after my birthday gift to my father, but clearly the two events were intimately related.

In view of the fact that I was able to work on the dream in a therapeutic setting, it's important to place this experience within the context of my life. Already a practicing therapist at the time of the dream, I was in psychosynthesis training, a modality that includes working with subpersonalities—aspects of the psyche—as well as the spiritual dimensions of life. A few nights after I had the momentous dream,

Hob and I were both attending a training, and I asked Martha, the trainer, if I could work on the dream using guided imagery, a technique that accessed deeper, hypnagogic states, similar to the liminal states just before sleep. I'd already experienced the power of working in this way, surely amplified this time as I went to lie down on the floor in the middle of a circle with more than twenty other trainees as observers. I began by describing the dream.

"I am on a journey, climbing a steep incline in a beautiful countryside with farms and pastures. At the top, there is a horse farm where two gorgeous horses are courting, rearing, dancing around, and having a lovely time together.

"Down a slight incline, there is a peasant-like house and next to it a special little house for the children. It is made of wood and a little rickety with spaces between the boards so that the wind can get in. The mother of the house has knitted woolen ponchos for the children so they can sleep warm and protected in the hammocks that hang inside.

"Further along, I look down and see two great lakes, one feeding into the other, both fed from an endless source of water that comes down from the mountains. There I see a guide, a hooded figure surrounded by a flock of wheeling birds.

"Finally, down by the sea, I am in a room when my father hands me a very unusual object. It is a square block of glass or some kind of clear material. I see that a beautiful bird has been etched into the glass like the famous Steuben sculptures with etched designs. The bird's wings and tail feathers are spread open. Its head and beak look upward. The image is beautiful, exquisitely wrought. Most striking, the bird is luminous. It seems to be lit from within and radiates light upward."

Though beautiful and numinous, the bird was trapped in the glass—frozen, unable to fly and be free. The symbolism was utterly compelling.

After I shared the dream with the group, Martha came to sit beside me on the floor, covered me with a blanket, and began to ask a series of evocative questions. What follows are a few excerpts from a long and deep session that lasted almost an hour.

Martha: "Allow the image of the bird to reappear on your mind screen, and see if you can make contact with this bird. What would you like to say to it?"

After a pause, I began talking to the bird. "I want to set you free, but you are frozen there. You need to move, to be more windblown and free." I lapsed into silence, waiting for the imagery to unfold.

Martha asked quietly: "Would the bird like to say something to you?"

After another pause, I began speaking as the bird. "I'm part of you, and I'm longing to be free. You're looking at me but you're not nurturing me."

Martha: "Ask the bird how you might nurture it."

I spoke. "This nurturing has to do with expressiveness. The bird does not want to be an object that I'm looking at, separate from me. It's telling me that it needs to be part of my inner spirit so that it can manifest expressiveness in movement, in music, in art."

I again spoke as the bird: "I can manifest in still ways as well. I exist in that place you discover when you meditate, that's nowhere and everywhere. I might be invisible but I'm there too."

Martha: "How can you set the bird free? Trust your intuition. Maybe you will know, or maybe the bird will know."

I replied: "I could do that with the energy of my body. I'm focusing on that very hard, and the stuff holding the bird is beginning to melt away. The heat is coming from my inner energy."

At this point, I began to weep. I could feel the bird trying to get out at the same time that I was melting the glass. I commented that sometimes my expressive energy felt forced, compulsive, or striving in some negative way.

I continued: "The energy that the bird needs—that I need—is very steady and pure. It comes from the center of my heart, and the stuff is still melting. Except now the right side of my body, especially my right hand, is trembling, really shaking. That's the controlling side, the side my father always represents—the side that would keep the bird there, in the glass, just a beautiful, unmoving object."

While the bird was struggling to get free, the tension manifested as trembling in my body, a struggle between freedom and control. I said that I needed help from someone, and began to describe what unfolded next.

"She's here now. I'm getting help from the eyes of my maternal grandmother Beep. She very much represents the left side. She says I can melt the glass with faith, with believing, with the power of my inner energy focusing on what's holding the bird. She says the glass will just flow away."

After a long silence, I continue. "Now I'm holding the bird in the palm of my left hand. It's white now instead of clear as it was in the glass. It's very still. It's got dark eyes that are very knowing, very wondrous."

After a sequence in which the bird gathered strength with its new freedom, it noticed that my right hand is still shaking.

The bird speaks again: "I see that you're still trembling. I'm not going to take anything away from you. You're trying to control everything. You're trembling because you're in conflict. You're very masculine. You need that, but we can live together. I'll let you be, but I'm going to be very free to soar."

The dialogue between the bird and the right hand continued, the right hand symbolizing the masculine impulse to control and the spirit bird symbolizing the call to freedom. The right hand (also symbolic of the father) expressed its fear that the spirit bird (also me) would become a dreamer, a meditator, and disappear into some other realm.

The bird replied: "I'm not going to take anything away from you. I'm going to allow the masculine forces to be more gentle, more flowing, so the hand doesn't need to tremble anymore. This all has to do with being free, letting go, and trusting."

After another long pause, I said, "Well, the trembling has stopped. I feel very close to some resolution that has to do with bringing these two forces together. Now my focus is very much on my left hand because the bird is still there. I need to let the bird off my palm."

There was another very long pause. "Now I'm totally accepting of my left hand, and the bird is gone. I'm back to the earlier image where

I saw a guide—the hooded figure who came to help—who was surrounded by soaring birds and lots of sunlight. He reassures me that both of my palms can be open. The right hand doesn't need to be controlling, clenched and shaking. That feels very exciting."

During a silence, I began to experience very strong circles of energy in both hands. Martha invited me to explore the nature of that energy.

I continue to speak. "The energy is very strong and positive. It doesn't just come from inside me; it comes from somewhere else. It has to do with communicating and becoming a channel. If I try to grasp and hold onto it, it makes my body shake. I need to open to the channels and trust the energy that is outside of myself. I'm only a channel for it. Then my ego disappears, which is fine. Everything about the glass is the part of myself that wants to control, grasp and hold on. That's gone now."

Martha: "What's left?"

"Something that's very pure. I finally feel a resolution because I don't feel divided any more. I'm back to pure energy again—the energy of the bird, soaring and free."

At this point, I took my hands from under the blanket and very tentatively, my fingers met, tip to tip, until they formed a circle like a globe. For many moments, the hands rested in this position. The fingers, touching ever so gently, felt sensitive and awake, yet whole and totally complete. Then ever so slowly the palms came together into prayer position, eased down, and lay on my chest.

A powerful intrapsychic journey of this kind always needs to be integrated. Since almost an hour had passed during which I'd experienced other dimensions of consciousness and a long, unfolding story, including powerful emotions, I found it very difficult to bring my awareness back to the circle. I saw in people's eyes, sometimes through their tears, that the struggle between freedom and control was an issue almost everyone shared.

Truth to tell, I was unable to speak for the rest of the day. Because of the powerful and mysterious way that the imagery had unfolded, I felt an impulse to protect the sacred nature of the experience and not expend energy in interacting with people. I was in an altered state all afternoon and evening, having been blessed with the sacred gift of a dream image.

When I returned home, I drew the spirit bird, a drawing both spontaneous and free. I still have the drawing. There is the beautiful white bird on blue paper, forever a numinous image, radiating light. Its wings are extended to reveal the exquisite pattern of feathers as its head and dark eyes look upward into a vast, blue sky.

When I revisited this experience months later, I sensed that in spite of the depth of the guided imagery session, something was still unfinished. Perhaps, I thought, I could discover that elusive part of the dream through writing, which for me is an absorbing process, a form of spiritual practice. I had already experimented with receptive writing where I would choose a subject, invite my mind to be totally open, and start automatic writing.

With my father

In this instance, I chose to enter into an imaginary dialogue with my father. I asked if he could help me understand deeper meanings about his gift. For example, why was the spirit bird still encased in glass after our experience with the birthday gift?

He replied, "First of all, I gave you the gift of life—*inspirited* you in that way—by bringing your being into this world, with your mother, of course. I have always felt that there is something mysterious that lies very deep within everyone, but that my life, even with so many outward achievements, had not yet been spiritually fulfilled. I turned to photography, music, love of nature, and, of course, through my work in the world. Still, I sensed that there was much more—worlds that I had never known.

"You and I have often had trouble talking about these deepest aspects of life, yet I knew that the world of images and dreams allowed us to go places we couldn't go otherwise. Because you are my beloved daughter and I recognize your deep interiority and spiritual hunger, I gave you this gift of spirit to help you fulfill your own quest. With my gift, I trust you will be able to carry forward where I've been unable to go. That would be a gift to me as well.

"There is another important part to my gift. I've explained how spirit manifests in creativity, but it also includes the spirit that we bring to everything we do. Action in the world—service in any form—is a sacred gift. Even though this is not a usual way of talking about spirit, I wanted to give you my understanding about the place of work in the world. Through attention and love, all our actions can be imbued with spirit. Since our family legacy involves a long history of service and creativity, the spirit bird symbolizes all of these: music, beauty, nature's wonders, as well as actions imbued with spirit.

"With great love I gave the spirit bird to you. It's for you to find the freedom that is inherent in life's promise—to free the bird from within the glass and set us both free."

The receptive writing brought invaluable insights about my father's gift as well as about my birthday gift to him, for they were intricately connected. Both the imagery session and the receptive writing enabled me to bring the dream to completion. I couldn't help but marvel at the complex interweaving of our waking and dreaming lives. Even more, I felt how the presence of the spirit bird existed both out of time and far beyond the reality of one particular dream. It would forever be a precious gift from the depths of my dream world as well as from my father.

THE FAMILY TREE

For as long as I could remember, on my father's bedroom room wall hung a picture of the Ames family tree. With its hefty trunk and wide spreading branches, it was an impressive tree. Imprinted in my childhood memory, it was a symbolic reminder of my father's ancestral origins—and mine. Many stories were woven through the branches of that tree, and many of those ancestors were illustrious figures, sometimes appearing in my American history books.

The rose, the family symbol, was featured in the Ames family coat of arms. I had seen it engraved on shields and carved into the backs of Queen Anne chairs in a formal dining room. I imagined it on banners carried by knights and on flags flying from the battlements of English manor houses, perhaps during the War of the Roses, a name evocative of noble lineages, tribal power, and glorious battles righteously fought and won. How did all of that relate to my dear father's gold signet ring with a rose carved into the garnet at its center?

Periodically, I found myself wrestling with the implications of this legacy, particularly when people knew of my family and our illustrious history, and an otherwise desultory conversation began to heat up with excitement and curiosity. In myself, I would become aware of a cross rip of feelings, from pride to embarrassment. I didn't want people's ideas about my family to interfere with the ease of our friendship, something I treasured far more than my famous ancestors.

We all have stories about our family's origins, though they vary dramatically. I was struck when my therapist told me how fortunate I was to have all this known family history. She was the daughter of immigrants who had fled the Nazis. Under those terrifying circumstances, they were unable to bring any family records with them. Once her parents died, she knew only where her grandparents had lived, but nothing more. Her family history had been forever lost.

Her story deepened my appreciation for my family's extensive history. It also invited me to take a deeper look at the relationship between ancestral influences and how they had shaped me. I always felt a dissonance between my background and where life had led me. On one hand, there were all those accomplished, traditional ancestors, mostly public figures or entrepreneurs. On the other, there were my own adventures far into the worlds of spirituality, psychology, and consciousness. Those worlds could hardly have been more different.

When I looked at the family tree on my father's wall, the name William Ames appeared as the first name at the bottom of the wide, heavy trunk. He and his brother, John, had emigrated to Massachusetts Bay Colony in 1635, a story that came to life for me a few years ago when my British partner, Keith, took me to visit Pear Tree Cottage, the house in England that originally belonged to William Ames. How astonishing to find the original family house still standing. There have been renovations, of course, but the oldest part had been preserved.

When we arrived in Wyke Champflower, the tiny village just outside of Bruton in the county of Somerset, we found the house on a quiet road. As we stood by the front gate looking at the lovely yellow house beyond the pear trees, I was filled with anticipation and disbelief. At that moment, the owner spotted us by the gate and came over to ask if he could help.

When he heard my name, his expression broke into a wide smile as he extended his hand and invited us to come in to see the house. As we walked into the oldest section where the ceiling was lower, he gestured toward the fireplace. A huge timber formed the mantelpiece, and carved in bold letters into the rough-hewn wood was our family name, AMES—the work of my ancestor William Ames some four hundred years ago. A significant piece of my family history came full circle in that moment. I was amazed that such a meaningful relic from the past was there before my eyes, a connection across time.

To condense several centuries of history, William and John Ames, metalworkers by trade, left for the new world in search of new opportunities. An archetypal story of immigrants who succeeded, they started by establishing a hardware business. Over the centuries, the business expanded and eventually became world-famous for its tools, especially its wide range of shovels. By the nineteenth century, Ames & Sons was the largest shovel company in the world, located in the village of North Easton, Massachusetts. Shovels were the indispensable tool of the era—for railroads, the Civil War, and every other practical endeavor. The family business thrived.

In the long history of the family, a couple of particularly memorable stories stand out. The first was when President Lincoln asked Oakes Ames, then a Congressman from Massachusetts, to undertake the financing of the Union Pacific Railroad. Along with his brother, Oliver, they masterminded the massive project that built the Union Pacific Railroad, a major contribution to opening the West in the nineteenth century. While acknowledging the complexities of this groundbreaking endeavor, the fact was that the brothers and their descendants were gifted entrepreneurs and philanthropists. Thanks to the success of the shovel business and the family's sense of public service, they built many of the public buildings, which carry their names, in the company town of North Easton. Some were designed by the architect H. H. Richardson who, along with landscape designer Frederick Law Olmstead, helped the town become famous for all its historic landmarks.

Another historic figure was my great-great-grandfather, General Benjamin F. Butler. Many extraordinary stories surrounded this radical Republican (which is to say, in those days, an exceptionally liberal figure). When he was stationed at Fort Monroe on Chesapeake Bay during the Civil War, before Lincoln's Emancipation Proclamation, three runaway slaves sought refuge at the fort. Instead of returning them in their status as slaves, as dictated by law, he gave them protection and declared them "contrabands of war," bestowing the status of citizenship on them—the first time that happened in the history of our country. Through this creative interpretation of the law, General Butler set an historical precedent that had momentous implications toward civil rights for African Americans.

Besides General Benjamin Butler, who was later elected a Congressman from Massachusetts, another ancestor was General Adelbert Ames, appointed Reconstruction Governor of Mississippi by President Andrew Johnson. In that tumultuous chapter of our history, he stood out as a bold and radical politician, committed to improving the lot of Black Americans and their voting rights at the expense of his reputation with white Southerners. He was an early hero in the history of the Civil Rights Movement.

In my early seventies, on a visit to Scotland, I had an astonishing encounter that related to these ancestral connections. Keith and I had made the long trip northward across Scotland, then by ferry over to the island of Mull, and by another smaller ferry to the island of Iona, an ancient pilgrimage site that attracts people from all over the world.

On a grey day with intermittent showers and then sun and glorious light effects, we boarded a little tourist boat to visit the tiny island of Staffa, famous for its puffins, seals, and, above all, Fingal's Cave, a unique natural phenomenon. Our boat pulled up to a narrow cement pier, a challenge for even a seasoned seafarer because the long, slow swells kept the boat rocking as we carefully climbed down to the pier. We clambered up the slippery rock steps and then along a perilous path cut into the ancient rock formations with only a steel cable to hold onto, as the waves broke and exploded into spray a few yards directly below us.

As we came around the bluff, an unfamiliar, haunting sound of the sea became louder. We were approaching Fingal's Cave, a huge opening in the side of precipitous cliffs. The sea swells surged in and out, singing their song, variations on a theme, a haunting, mysterious duet between water and stone—a symphony of the sea. The sounds were mesmerizing—gurgling . . . slurping . . . sloshing . . . whooshing . . . whispering . . . rumbling like distant drums as the water caressed and echoed off the cavernous walls. I could feel the throbbing rhythms of sound in my body. A century earlier, Felix Mendelssohn felt it, too, and wrote "The Hebrides Overture," a symphonic piece that captured the sound of the ocean surging in and out of Fingal's Cave, a wondrous musical expression.

We picked our way cautiously along the narrow path that had been cut into the walls of the cave. Then we stopped, listening to the timeless music of the sea. I became aware of one other woman, for the others had already started back. Like me, she too was clearly transfixed by the sound. Neither of us wanted to leave. Reluctantly, in silence we carefully retraced our steps back to the narrow dock and our trusty boat, riding the waves as it waited for us.

When the boat turned and headed back toward Iona, I felt wistful to be leaving the island with its magical cave. A brisk wind came up. We alternately hugged the rail or huddled under the small canopy for protection from a passing shower. That's when I noticed the woman who'd lingered with me in the cave. We had silently shared that experience, and now once again, I sensed her sadness and felt drawn to reach out. I spoke above the sounds of the sea.

"Where are you from?" I asked, as she turned toward me.

"Mississippi," she replied.

"Oh, that's interesting," I said. "I've just finished a book about Reconstruction in Mississippi, and it's partly about my great-grandfather who was the Reconstruction Governor there after the Civil War."

She looked as though someone had lit a flame under her, hardly able to wait until I finished my sentence. She blurted out, "Adelbert Ames! I know all about him because I'm the daughter of the first Republican governor *since* Adelbert Ames!"

"Oh, I can't believe it!" I exclaimed, trying to take in the incredible coincidence. She continued, "Have you ever been to the governor's mansion in Jackson?"

"No, I've never been to Mississippi. My name is Olivia Ames," I replied, using my maiden name.

"I'm Angie Fordice. It's good to meet you. You really should come sometime because every governor has written their name and a message on a certain wall of the attic, and your great-grandfather's name and message are there.

I was always struck by that name, Adelbert. His portrait also hangs in the gallery alongside the other governors."

"Amazing! I just can't believe this, that we should meet out here in the middle of nowhere! What brings you to Scotland?" I inquired.

"My father died recently, and he hoped I would use some of my inheritance to make a pilgrimage to Scotland, his homeland. Here I am, traveling alone because I recently got divorced. It's hard sometimes, but I was curious to come. Dad got inaugurated in his kilt, surely the first governor to do it that way. He was elected in 1990 and served two terms, so I spent a lot of time as a child at the mansion and got pretty familiar with the history."

When the boat reached the pier at Iona, Angie and I continued talking as our fellow passengers congregated spontaneously, seemingly reluctant to leave each other after the bond of our shared journey to a magical place.

Nor was that the end of our connection. We corresponded and ended up exchanging the books we had both recently written. Hers was a lively, well-written account of growing up as the daughter of a governor. As for me, I marveled over the fact of how I seemed to bump into my ancestry almost anywhere, even in the most remote places on a little boat far off the coast of Scotland.

These were among many stories that could be woven into that family tree on my father's wall. For me, that familiar image came to life with my visits to my Ames grandparents at Borderland, the name of their estate in North Easton, Massachusetts. In 1910, Oakes and Blanche Ames bought up 1,200 acres of abandoned sheep farmland and built a stone mansion. It was modeled in the style of a grand English country house, and when my grandmother didn't like the architects' design, she fired them and proceeded to design the house herself, even learning the complexities of plumbing and electricity, still unusual for houses at that time. The house was entirely made of grey stone—floors, walls, and ceilings—unusual in New England but a fireproof solution for my grandfather's extensive library and rare book collection, especially in his field of orchidology. As a professor of Botany at Harvard University, my grandfather regularly traveled with Blanche into the jungles of Central and South America in search of undiscovered varieties of orchids. They were indeed exotic and unusual grandparents!

The mansion is imposing. Covered with ivy, it is three stories high with rows of tall, leaded windows and a huge iron bell that hangs on the roof. The bell had been brought back from Cuba as an impressive and practical addition to the mansion, mainly to call grandchildren back from their wanderings and to announce mealtimes. As children, we were intrigued by the bell. It took our full body weight to haul on the heavy rope to set the huge bell ringing across the countryside.

My grandparents' library was the centerpiece of the mansion. Stately and impressive, it housed thousands of books and was more akin to a university library than an ordinary home library. It was two stories high with a narrow walkway of thick glass that encircled the second floor to provide access to books stored higher up. As one entered the library through the wide doorway with its high, arching design, to the right stood a cylindrical case filled with Civil War swords, a reminder of the two generals in the family who were leaders in that war.

At first glimpse, one couldn't help but be overcome by the grandeur of the room and what it conveyed about my grandparents' dedication to books and learning. It smelled faintly of leather and mustiness. It was shrouded in a deep silence that made it feel almost like a temple—a temple to the intellect. I used to note wryly that our family house in Cambridge could have fit inside that library with a lot of space to spare.

At the center of the room stood my grandfather's imposing desk—stately, formal, and large as befitted the great room. I can visualize him there, bent over his papers writing his next contribution to some scientific journal. Or I imagine him sitting in the alcove, an extension of the library, bending over his microscope to examine the intricate details of some rare orchid.

We called our grandparents GrandB and GrandO, using the first letter of their names Blanche and Oakes. Surprisingly, her full name was Blanche Ames Ames, although she and her husband were not related. My grandmother was a monumental figure in our extended family, a powerful force whose accomplishments were astonishing. Besides being an inventor, author, cartoonist and brilliant artist of landscapes, portraits, and botanical illustrations of her husband's books, she was a passionate feminist, political activist, and leader of women's suffrage. She was once arrested for leading a protest demanding women's right to vote. She was quickly released, however, when the police discovered that she was the daughter-in-law of the governor. One of her political cartoons depicted a woman on a cross—a striking and unforgettable image. She was a Renaissance woman, a tower of competence, strong-willed and dominant with an outspoken, forceful personality. I admired her immensely, but I can't say that I loved her.

My earliest memory of the house was when I was four years old. I had been sent to stay with these grandparents when I contracted whooping cough. My sister, Joanie, had just been born. My parents wanted to protect her from catching my illness, so I was shipped away alone, a very sick child wracked with coughs, chest pain, and having trouble breathing. Separated from my family, overcome with homesickness, I felt abandoned in this huge, cold house with its drafty hallways and oversized rooms. I vaguely remember GrandB being there, but she was hardly a cozy grandmother. I can see her standing over me in the bathroom as she waited for me to "do my business."

As for GrandO, I don't remember him being there at all. Tall, thin, and quiet, he had a serious, even severe expression. He may have been a brilliant scientist, but he was profoundly introverted and shy. He ignored children unless perhaps they showed an interest in science. Frightened and sick, I have only haunting, desolate memories of a terrible visit.

Over the passage of time, I remember many family gatherings in this grand house with aunts, uncles, and cousins, various combinations of relatives who sometimes visited for as long as two weeks. Naturally, the mansion had a servants' wing, so there was plenty of help to accommodate the parade of family visitors. Although as a younger person I couldn't have articulated it, there was an air of formality about everything. I used to sit at the imposing mahogany dining room table and draw designs in the condensation on the silver water goblet at the edge of my embroidered placemat. Sitting to my right, GrandO once noticed my careless manners. He took the handle of his knife and whacked my elbow to teach me, without a word, not to put my elbows on the table.

As in many families, sad stories were woven through the branches of the family tree of those who suffered silently, eschewed family altogether, or stumbled through life carrying their hidden—or not so hidden—wounds. Although generalizations are debatable, people of white Anglo Saxon background (WASPs) can be reserved—cool, controlled, and somewhat distant—as though conditioned to maintain an invisible wall of protection from feeling too strongly or getting too close to others.

An exception to this was my Uncle Paschal, married to my father's sister. From Tennessee, he was a Southerner, open, warm, and welcoming. His soft accent, kindly eyes, and gentle manner contrasted to the family he had married into. In mid-career as a lawyer, he changed directions, went to Harvard Divinity School, and served as a minister for the rest of his life, a story that intrigued me.

After GrandB died in 1969, GrandO having died earlier, my father's generation of the family decided to preserve the wild lands of the estate for the public to enjoy and sold the property to the state of Massachusetts. Given the value of the land by that time, the price was a fraction of its actual worth. The 1,200 acres with its three lakes, wild forests, and elegant mansion were yet another philanthropic gift along with all those historic buildings in the town of North Easton. Now known as Borderland State Park, the beautiful estate is visited by thousands of people throughout the year, and the mansion, maintained exactly as it was at my grandparents' time, is open to the public one day a week.

From the Ames legacy, I internalized high expectations, assumptions of excellence, and the unspoken call to uphold the family's high standards in whatever one chose to do in life. From my perspective, that legacy rested on outward accomplishments—positions of leadership, railroads built, companies launched—excellence that could be seen and applauded. Naturally the stories of ancestral achievements were passed on, and although my parents did not put pressure on us children, their competence and visibility provided inspiring role models.

Where did my dedication to spirituality and the inner life fit with this legacy? Ultimately, I was grateful for the positive elements of my heritage—the assumption that you could do anything you chose and make a contribution by virtue of your heartfelt efforts. I dropped the oppressive parts—the attachment to over-achievement, the impossible standards, and, above all, the prevalence of judgment, that insidious compulsion to evaluate oneself and others by their social exteriors, which causes endless suffering.

GrandB played a paradoxical role in this saga. Because she and I had several lively debates on the subject of religion, I knew that she was a vociferous agnostic, opinionated, and the dominant force in any discussion. It was so different from my ways of wanting to be with people! I preferred conversations that connected me to others, where sensitivity was valued and my curiosity about people invited closeness. In contrast, she loved nothing more than a lively discussion and, better still, to prevail in a good argument. She simply loved to take on causes and people.

GrandB even took on President Kennedy. When she read *Profiles in Courage*, she was incensed that he had relied on Southern historians to write about her father, Adelbert Ames, the Reconstruction Governor of Mississippi. She wrote to Kennedy and asked him to "make some corrections of errata for your own sake as well as mine," instructing him to correct his "slanderous misstatements against Adelbert Ames." Kennedy replied that there would be no more editions of his book and declined her challenge.

Never one to take no for an answer, she set about to defend her father's reputation. In her early eighties, she began the research that led to an impressive tome titled *Adelbert Ames: 1835–1933: Senator, General,*

Governor. It was 602 pages long, filled with photographs of historical figures, maps of the Civil War, appendices of her correspondence with Kennedy, and other historical material. While she was writing the book, my father came to visit her and saw the long tables covered with dozens of books. He asked her how many pages she'd written.

"As of now, over 500 pages, but I still have more to write," she replied.

"Don't you think that's long enough?" my father asked.

She drew herself up to her full height, then slightly diminished with age, and said forcefully, "If Tolstoy could do it, so can I."

Nothing could stop GrandB's determination! She published the book herself and launched a campaign to make sure it got into both university and public libraries and was generally well circulated.

A couple of years later, I was getting my graduate degree in American history at Columbia University. My thesis advisor, having seen my grandmother's book, suggested I write my thesis on the same subject, my great-grandfather Adelbert Ames. He suggested I could check on the accuracy of the historiography in her book. No way! as my grandkids would say. I wouldn't touch that subject. From my training in historiography, however, I could see that GrandB had written a fine biography, perhaps slightly tinged with her bias but supported with extensive primary and secondary sources, impeccably researched, intricately footnoted, and written with authority. Later I heard from my thesis advisor that her book was admired by American historians as a valuable contribution to the field.

Although GrandB described herself as an agnostic, imagine my surprise when I discovered that she had written a Credo[4] with some startling statements that ran counter to that assertion. The list is composed of twenty-one items, each beginning with the statement *I believe.*

Given my discussions with her, several of her proclamations are astonishing:

4 See appendix for the full text of GrandB's Credo.

I believe in the Motherhood of God.

I believe in the blessed Trinity of Father, Mother, and Child.

I believe that God is here, and we are as near Him now as we ever shall be. I do not believe He started this world a-going and went away and left it.

I believe in the sacredness of the human body, this transient dwelling place of a living soul. . . .

I believe the love of man and woman is holy, and that this love . . . is as much an emanation of the Divine Spirit as man's love for God. . . .

Agnostic? I'm not so sure. I find her Credo stunning, evocative, and contemporary, especially once I let go of my aversion to her use of the male pronouns he and him to describe humankind, which equally includes womenkind. The remaining subjects in her Credo deal with right living, freedom, sorrow, death, and eternity. My grandmother, a woman of action, obviously had a contemplative side, a revelation to me.

The legacy issue faded in and out of my life, only surfacing when I encountered someone who knew certain family members or showed inordinate curiosity about my history. At these times, the familiar cross rip of feelings would surface. I would hide my privileged background. I didn't want it to separate me from others as it surely would, given my unresolved feelings about it. Nevertheless, a surprising and dramatic resolution to the issue would come years later when a friend in our Self-Ordination group made a proposal I never could have imagined, a story I'll tell later in this book.

THE SWINGING DOORS OF THE HEART

Given the underground stream of curiosity about the mysteries of life that flowed beneath the surface of my days, the early signs of my religious fervor were revealing. Let me distinguish here between "religious" as referring to traditional organizations of belief and "spiritual" as something beyond the individual self that is vast, ineffable, and sacred. Even if I didn't receive a traditional exposure to organized religion, I was fortunate that both my parents had spiritual inclinations. My father would have been surprised to hear those words, but my mother would definitely agree with them.

My mother, a poet and writer, was very attuned to people and the subtler dimensions of life—the beauty of the natural world and the role of art, music, and literature in uplifting and inspiring life. My father had a love of beauty, especially in the natural world, that was truly reverential.

Although my parents were not churchgoers, there was most certainly a Christian context for our family. As mentioned earlier, during World War II when I was six or seven, we used to have short Sunday "services" in our living room. We would not have gone to church anyway because of gas rationing, but the six of us—my parents and four siblings—would gather in the living room as they read us Bible stories, and we'd sing a couple of hymns accompanied by one of them on the piano. I particularly looked forward to the singing, and my favorite hymn lyrics were "Now the day is over, night is drawing nigh, shadows of the evening steal across the sky." I was always a lover of liminal times like dawn and dusk, and that hymn was like a lullaby, gentle and harmonious; I felt both reverence and comfort as we sang it. I loved those simple gatherings. They planted the seeds of loving to come together for a time set apart from the rest of life, and the Bible stories were vividly etched in my memory.

For my twelfth birthday, my godmother gave me a Bible. It had a deep red cover of textured leather, and its pages were paper-thin like no book I'd ever seen. I cherished it. At least twice I vowed to read my Bible from beginning to end—a twice-failed enterprise where I probably sank into overwhelm with all the strange names and dry facts, somewhere in Leviticus. During a zealous phase in early adolescence, I pricked my finger and made crosses of blood that crinkled the thin pages of my sacred book.

Along with this sacrifice and bonding with the divine, I had heroic fantasies about Jesus and how special I was to him and he to me. On the wall across from my childhood bed hung a little blue sign that read, "Jesus loves me." The luminescent letters shone in the dark, inviting and intriguing. Jesus was my comforter and inspiration as those letters shone brightly through the night. In my ultimate fantasy, I would make the winning goal in field hockey (I was a fierce competitor), and Jesus would be there, watching me in all my glory. Then, in a dramatic climax, he would take me as his bride. Such adolescent drama!

I spent a lot of time with that Bible, especially in the New Testament and the psalms. I read the 139th psalm countless times and even memorized parts of it. It was my favorite and would take on new meaning a few years later.

> O Lord, You have searched me and known me. . . .
> You comprehend my path . . .
> And are acquainted with all my ways. . . .
> Where can I go from Your Spirit?
> Or where can I flee from Your presence? . . .
> Search me, O God, and know my heart . . .
> And lead me in the way everlasting.

Though heavily excerpted, these were a few of my favorite lines. In retrospect, I can appreciate the immanent and transcendent mystery called "God" that permeated these lines and deeply pierced my young, searching heart. My religious background was also fed by singing in the choir of our local Episcopal church, as well as by attending chapel twice a week at boarding school. We were required to attend a local place of worship every Sunday.

Howard Thurman, modern mystic, my first spiritual teacher

I was seventeen when the presence of Howard Thurman burst into our family, touching especially my mother, my sister, and me. A close friend of my mother's had written a leading profile of Thurman for *The Atlantic Monthly*, and at my mother's encouragement, I ventured forth one Sunday and rode the subway, a long journey with three changes, to get to Marsh Chapel. Centrally located on the campus of Boston University and overlooking the Charles River, the chapel has two side-by-side Gothic doors—doubly inviting—above which rises a tall, narrow, three-paneled stained glass window. That first visit, I was excited, nervous, and overwhelmed. I'd never been part of such a diverse crowd of worshippers, not only the university students but adults of all ages, races, and nationalities. I remember thinking that it was like the United Nations, which I'd once visited, filled with wonder by the thrilling array of people from all over the world. The congregation at Marsh Chapel felt like that, too, especially for me, having been raised in the white, homogeneous world of North Shore Long Island.

By then, I knew something of Thurman's background. The grandson of a slave, his family, though impoverished, had been a refuge of love, faith, and courage. He had left home at fourteen to pursue the education unavailable to him in segregated Florida. He went on to become a professor of religion, the Dean of the Chapel at Howard University, the cofounder of a church in San Francisco, and finally Dean of Marsh Chapel. Always anchored in the spiritual ground of his exceptionally devout family, he went on to become a prolific author, poet, and mystic.

On that first Sunday as I sat looking at the Gothic architecture, stained glass windows, and wooden paneling, I was comforted by the familiar sound of the organ. Then Howard Thurman walked slowly through a side door and settled onto a high-backed chair below the pulpit. He was tall with noble bearing and a deep, quiet, compelling presence. I'd never seen a face so full of kindness and inexpressible depth. Sorrow seemed etched into his expression, perhaps carrying the weight of his enslaved forbears and all he had experienced in his own life. He radiated a strong, loving presence into which I felt immediately invited and embraced. When he began to speak, welcoming us to the service, I closed my eyes to feel more fully the deep resonance of that beautiful voice emanating something earthy, ancient, and reverent.

Between the different parts of the service, he'd return, moving slowly and majestically to the high-backed chair where he would sit, eyes downcast or looking out the stained glass window above his shoulder, clearly deep in meditation and prayer. When he rose for a prayer, he stood in silence, eyes closed, waiting . . . waiting . . . open . . . expectant

. . . no prepared words or formulaic prayers. His words arose slowly from his inner state. They were offered in his fully embodied voice that seemed to stream through him, charged with the holy. As though the mountains themselves were speaking, his words seemed to come from across time, from an ancient, infinite source that knew both great suffering and great love. Every utterance was suffused with heart.

I was transfixed, totally absorbed in the presence of this unusual man. I'd heard many ministers over my young years, but I'd always felt twinges of disappointment, hoping for something more, something unnamable. There were so many sermons and prayers—words, words, words—but mostly from the intellect, sometimes beautifully crafted but still coming through the dry sieve of the mind. I hardly knew what I was hoping for, but I always had this sense that there could be something more. I had wondered if I was the only worshipper who felt this disappointment, this longing. No one seemed to talk about it, but it was very real to me, a shadow moving in and out of my awareness as I attended various churches. Was this sense of something missing because of some deficiency in me? Or was there an experience of the mystery that these ministers simply weren't conveying or hadn't experienced?

These occasional ruminations of mine were totally silenced by Howard Thurman's presence. When he gave his sermon, he may have had notes, but he rarely looked down, and as with his prayers, all his words felt as though they were being born out of the moment, from deep in his body, from his heart. Again, the pauses. Again the rising and falling cadences of his voice, his obvious delight at the surprise of his own words—savoring, sometimes even singing them—all amplified by the expressiveness of his hands. His hands moved with elegance and grace like a dance accompaniment to his words. Occasionally his face would break into a radiant smile, or he'd be overtaken by his full-bodied, deep laugh laced with delight. I had simply never been in the presence of anyone remotely like this remarkable man. He was the embodiment of spirit.

Here were words again, but this time, when spoken by Thurman, the words felt suffused, inspirited by the Word. His words seemed to come both from beyond and from within —the mystery of the transcendent and immanent as one. Fully embodied, those words arose from one who had integrated all the joys and sorrows of life—the sorrows of his ancestral past and the inspiration of a life dedicated to spirit. As I listened, young, unformed, spiritually hungry, I became utterly still, held in the mystery of something new and powerful.

I used to wonder what might explain the mesmerizing quality of his speaking. In the final chapter of his autobiography, *With Head and Heart*, he ponders the subject of ego as opposed to what he calls the grace, visitation, or inspiration of that which is beyond ego, "that which at times is 'channeled' through the mind or which rushes through the swinging doors of the heart." I certainly had never experienced someone with such open, easily swinging "doors of the heart."

On that memorable Sunday and for many other Sundays during the rest of my time at boarding school, I ventured into Marsh Chapel to lose myself in Howard's presence. I kept a notebook into which I pasted the service program, the parts with quotations from him. I gradually got to know him during the receptions after the service. One Sunday my parents came, and for the first time in my life, I sat together with my mother and father in a church. Given their antipathy to organized religion, that event still amazes me, but it was the pull of Howard's reputation and the inspiring article that my mother's friend had written about him.

Without remembering the details of how their relationship developed, my mother subsequently became close to Howard. That was one of his many gifts. Many felt close to him, so wide and embracing was his loving circle. Not only had he visited her, but they carried on a long correspondence. She became very involved with the establishment of the Howard Thurman Listening Room at the Cathedral of St. John the Divine. How surprised I was when I read Howard's autobiography and found a photograph of my mother reading a tribute to Howard before a small gathering there for the dedication. After her death, among her papers I found a clutch of letters carefully wrapped together, bearing

Howard's distinctive handwriting.

From there unfolded the tapestry of how my life also became entwined with his. When I moved to San Francisco after college, I attended the church Howard had cofounded called the Church for the Fellowship of All Peoples—an interracial congregation intentionally designed to break through the barriers that separated people on the basis of race, color, creed, or national origin. Again I found myself in an unusually diverse congregation and for the first time awakened to issues of social justice as an integral part of one's spiritual life.

I was able to visit Howard in his book-lined study where a delightful array of little penguins—his favorite creature in the natural world—lined the sill of the wide windows that overlooked San Francisco Bay. It was during that visit when he told me that his favorite psalm was the 139th, as it was mine. I don't know why that touched me so deeply, but I had cherished and memorized parts of that psalm as a youngster. Now those inspired words felt like a shared treasure with him—my first spiritual teacher. Whenever I listen to the recording of Howard reciting that psalm, he is immediately present, along with a cascade of images from those early years of being in his presence.

Occasionally incorporated into one of the regular Sunday services at Marsh Chapel, Howard would perform a Dedication Ceremony—not a regular baptism but his way, as he put it, of dedicating a child's life to God. I had always been very moved to watch how he took the infant from the parents' arms and cradled it in his own, bending over as though beholding the most cherished being ever to enter this world. He then spoke the three verses of blessing—poetic, prayerful expressions from his Baptist background.

All those years ago as that seventeen-year-old adolescent from a nearby boarding school, I could never have imagined that I would be able to experience that beautiful ceremony with Howard with both our children—first Ethan and then Laura. In the mid-1960s, Hob and I moved near San Francisco to help start a school, and it was there that Ethan was born. Howard happened to be visiting San Francisco at the time and came to perform the Dedication Ceremony at the school. A small group of us gathered at sunset on a golden hillside under a great, spreading California oak tree. Ethan was five months old and dressed all in white. Howard was wearing his black robe. As he reached to take Ethan from my mother's arms, his beautiful face broke into a broad smile as he welcomed our firstborn and began to recite the verses, dedicating Ethan to a life of the spirit—to God. As part of the ceremony, the school's madrigal group, including Hob and me, sang several pieces, ending with the Bach chorale, "My soul there is a country, afar beyond the stars," one of our favorites.

Howard with Ethan after his dedication

What a marvel to watch our children's lives unfold from a treasured moment like Ethan's dedication. Aries-born with lots of fire and an adventurous spirit, he had a somewhat dramatic childhood. He was emotionally volatile with a hefty temper, but those qualities tempered with time, leaving his vibrant personality, compassionate heart, and passion for life shining brightly. Tall and slender, blond and blue-eyed, Ethan had an intensity, directness, and warmth that drew people to him. Exceptionally gifted with high school kids, he became a dedicated educator, teaching history and comparative religion. Later, his explorations with the entheogens (sacred medicines) further opened spiritual dimensions of his life that were striking and heart opening.

Laura's dedication took place in the little chapel of a neighborhood church in Cambridge, Massachusetts, where we had moved several years before. All our family occasions always included singing, and once again we sang Laura's welcome as our next-door neighbor, a concert pianist, played the organ. Once again, Howard received infant Laura into his arms. She was dressed in the long, intricately embroidered, white christening dress that had belonged to her Danish great-grandmother. Howard recited the prayers of the Dedication Ceremony, and Laura's life, like her brother's, was dedicated to the life of the spirit. That became evident at the early age of eleven and would lead to the dramatic archetypal story that she and I shared.

The last time I saw Howard was in 1979, two years before he died. When I was in my early forties. I had traveled to Oakland, California, to spend a week with Swami Muktananda, a Siddha guru from India. Baba, as he was known, was touring the United States to offer intensive meditation weekends that involved an initiation known as *shaktipat*, the awakening of spiritual energy. He was creating quite a stir among spiritual seekers, and I had already had my own subtle encounters with him, which I will describe later.

In the middle of that week at the Siddha Yoga ashram in Oakland, I went into San Francisco to see Howard. Besides catching up on the years since he'd been with us for Laura's dedication, I shared with him my impressions and perplexities about Muktananda. I described my powerful experiences with the ancient Sanskrit chanting, the devotional practices, and the vibrant community, all of which were presided over by this exotic, inscrutable Indian meditation master. To put it simply, I was feeling spiritually unhinged.

As we stood in the hallway outside his front door to say goodbye, Howard looked at me with a decidedly mischievous look in his eye and asked, "So, who is it going to be, the swami or me?" and he broke out laughing. There wasn't a shred of attachment to his question, but it reverberated with me. Finding resolution between my Christian past and my future ventures into Eastern contemplative practices would be my inner calling in the coming years.

In telling this story of my experiences with Howard, I've been struck by how alive these memories are, how they have reawakened the deep and precious bond I had with Howard, and the further realization that every aspect of our spiritual lives is timeless. Although that spiritual journey would lead me into two of the great wisdom traditions, Howard's influence will always have a unique, beloved quality to it.

What a mystery—how the lives of others touch us! I would be fortunate to spend a lot of time with enlightened teachers from other traditions, yet Howard holds a treasured place in my heart. A circle of love seemed to emanate from him, which invited and embraced whoever entered his life. Howard leaves an extraordinary legacy—more than twenty books, countless sermons and lectures, his dedication to inclusion and social justice, and the immeasurable impact of his ministry. A mystic and prophet for our times, he left a blazing trail of inspiration and love. I will forever be profoundly grateful that my life and our family's was so deeply touched by his great, loving presence.

PSYCHICS AND FINDHORN

Another phase of my devotional journey opened most unexpectedly when two events, several years apart, blew open my limited views of the world. From those earliest childhood days, I'd always been drawn to wonder about the unseen. Now, surprising new dimensions of those worlds unfolded before me.

In the first instance, my therapist suggested I might be interested in a reading with two well-known psychics, Wayne and Bella, who lived in Los Angeles but could "read" your life story from afar, asking only that you send a photograph and an object imbued with your karma. I was both intrigued and leery. How could they possibly do that? What was I supposed to believe—or not believe — about such a preposterous venture into psychic realms?

Despite my questions about this new venture, I chose a photograph and a *mala* made of seeds, which I had used for mantra repetition. Years earlier, I'd picked it from high off the wall of a shop that otherwise didn't carry items from the East. The seeds were a warm brown, about the size of a blueberry. To me, they were beautiful with their perfectly round, crinkled surface. I didn't know what kind of seeds they were and wondered why I was so attracted to this mala, the first I'd ever owned. Seven years later, when I became involved with Siddha Yoga, I learned that the mala was made of rudraksha seeds, sacred to Shiva (Shaivism being a tradition underlying Siddha Yoga,) and that many devotees were using this particular kind of mala. At the time, it was a wondrous connection for me.

I mailed off the two required objects to Wayne and Bella. About a month later, a package arrived in the mail with two audio tapes, more than two hours of information from the psychics. I was so unnerved by the prospect of hearing what they might have to say that I didn't listen to the tapes for several months. When I finally marshaled my courage, I listened with feelings of vague anxiety and heightened excitement. I was amazed that their reading challenged all my belief systems. I was invited to consider other realms of reality far beyond what we identify as consensual reality. They talked about my previous lives and how I was related, sometimes over lifetimes, to everyone from my husband Hob to my children, parents, and grandparents. They suggested karmic patterns between us that might account for our reincarnating together and the issues that dominated these relationships. They made the seemingly preposterous statement that my two grandmothers, Beep and GrandB, had been my twin daughters in a previous life! They even talked about my relationships with other, nonhuman forms of being. The reading was mind-blowing. Although I couldn't accept everything, many things simply sounded right, and as I listened, there were familiar echoes, distant but beckoning. Although I tend to be open to unusual phenomena—perhaps at times overly credulous—I also have a cautious side. I took notes on the tapes, put them away in a file, and inwardly shelved the impact of what I had heard. All this information sat in a back file of my mind, waiting for some kind of affirmation, possibly from another source. A few years later, that affirmation came in the most unlikely way.

In the mid-'70s, I began to hear intriguing descriptions about an experimental New Age community called Findhorn located in northern Scotland. How wonderfully mind-bending to hear that this little community—only three people at first—started because of the channeled guidance of two women, Dorothy Maclean and Eileen Caddy, who regularly received guidance from other dimensions. Along with Eileen's husband, Peter Caddy, the three of them had been on a spiritual path for some time. They trusted the guidance and the art of manifestation, as they called it. That meant not only the gifts of receiving channeled information but the ability to transform that guidance into form.

Courageously listening and following the information coming to them, they moved in 1962 into a caravan (what Americans call a trailer) on a forbidding part of the northeast coast of Scotland. Dorothy and Eileen's exceptional psychic abilities allowed them to be aware of many invisible dimensions of reality, inconceivable to most people. Their next step followed from Dorothy's ability to contact the nature spirits, or *devas*, as she called them, a term from Indian culture. She could intuit and hear the spirits of the plant world. Through that unusual gift, the plant spirits guided them to start an experiment in manifestation by planting a garden. A garden—what an unlikely way to begin! But they followed the guidance.

Despite the hostile environment with its rocky soil, cold climate, high winds, and generally inclement weather, the garden began to flourish. Seemingly a miracle of nature, flowers, plants, and organic vegetables grew to prodigious size. No one had ever seen a phenomenon remotely like the Findhorn garden. It became a magnet. The stories began to spread, and gradually people started coming from all over the world, not just as curious tourists but to settle there and join the community.

In 1977, when the community was still relatively small, I had an opportunity to hear Peter Caddy give a speech in which he described the background of their unfolding experiment. How could anyone not be intrigued by the unlikeliness of it all! Afterwards, when I met both Peter and Eileen, I decided to experience this phenomenon for myself. It combined easily with my periodic visits to a beloved Scottish family member who lived in Glasgow.

A couple of months after hearing Peter's talk, I found my way to this remote little community. I was filled with anticipation when I finally reached the village of Moray in northern Scotland and checked in at the welcoming center. Under an overcast sky with a brisk north wind, typical of the weather there, a couple of other visitors and I found our way to our accommodations. We were assigned to a caravan, the primary form of accommodation in those days. The word *caravan* sounded more inviting to me than *trailer*, as we called them at home. Having never been in one, I was taking in every detail as we climbed the three steps up to the door. The interior was far more spacious than

I could have imagined, a warm and cozy home for the week as the wind continued to whistle outside.

As newly arrived visitors, the next morning we were immediately incorporated into Findhorn's way of life. The expanding community could only work with the help of everyone who arrived, and furthermore, that would be how we would learn about the philosophy of this experimental community. I was assigned to work in the gardens. Our supervisor gathered ten or twelve of us into a circle and invited us to join hands. This struck me as a bit unusual, but I had heard from Peter's talk how every activity at Findhorn was preceded by a ritual of attunement. There I stood, holding the hands of two strangers while the supervisor explained that we would observe a few moments of silence to attune—first to oneself, then to our fellow workers, and finally to the task at hand. The intention was to bring our energies together so we would work with love. This reverential moment of gathering was repeated before every activity.

As a gardener for many years, I was happy to find myself among the flourishing, abundant plants in Findhorn's famous vegetable gardens. All the rows of dark, luscious soil had been carefully cultivated with not a weed in sight, and every vegetable displayed nature's exuberance. It was all very striking compared to our modest, though much-loved, vegetable garden at home. I settled onto my knees and got ready to plant the flat of tomato seedlings that had been entrusted to me. At that moment, I heard a voice over my shoulder.

"Let me show you how we ease the soil open and slip the seedling in. The soil is filled with microorganisms, and we don't want to disturb them too much. We do everything mindfully, with care, understanding that the soil, the plants, and everything has consciousness."

The supervisor knelt beside me. She took my trowel and very gently created a narrow opening in the soil. With tender hands, she placed the delicate seedling into the waiting soil. I instantly saw the difference between how my approach had been overly aggressive with its "get the job done" attitude, whereas her approach had been sensitive and caring toward every aspect of a simple task.

Life at Findhorn was predicated on the shared belief that we are guided by spirit and that everything, even physical objects, is imbued with its own spirit—a perspective that invites us to treat everything with love and respect. At the end of the morning, our supervisor demonstrated how to take care of our tools. In our garden back home, I'd never cleaned a trowel so lovingly. She handed me an oily cloth to protect the metal from rust, and I rubbed that blade until it shone! It was such a seemingly small moment, yet it, too, characterized the spirit of Findhorn.

I also spent several days working on the building called Universal Hall, still in the earliest stages of what would be the first large meeting space for the growing community. I sensed the excitement around this project, but I was apprehensive about my work assignment because it involved carpentry. I had only the most rudimentary skills. As always, we started the day by coming into a circle to attune to each other and the job. Standing quietly and feeling the warmth of our joined hands helped to quiet my nervously beating heart.

My first task was to help assemble the scaffolding that would provide the structure for our work. I'd never wrestled with heavy rods, cold pieces of steel that fit together to form the structure. Nor had I ever had to go up and down ladders all day to reach my work position, a narrow board suspended from the scaffolding ten feet above the ground. Even with my initial anxieties, because of the spirit of working together, I gradually felt held by my coworkers as if we were part of something larger than ourselves that was supporting all of us. After a while, my nervousness dissolved, and I felt quietly triumphant for overcoming my fears. I delighted in my newfound building skills.

We mostly worked in silence, but occasionally there would be a little flurry of conversation. At one point, a fellow carpenter named Hans told us about the preliminary stages of building the Universal Hall. Hans was tall, physically strong, and Nordic-looking with a full, light brown beard. In his gentle accent, he explained that before the cement for the foundation could be poured, the design of the building had been laid out with stakes and cord. The design phase had been completed, he continued, but then everything stopped. None of the orders for materials came through. A specified kind of rock wasn't available. Obstacles to the project appeared everywhere. The whole project ground to a halt. People at Findhorn knew, he told us, that something was misaligned—off in some way—and that universal forces were blocking the building's further progress.

I paused to listen, sensing that another Findhorn mystery was about to be revealed. Then I heard Hans say the names of Wayne and Bella, two psychics from California. I nearly fell off my perch on the scaffolding. *Wayne and Bella! My psychics!* It seemed that they had been invited to Findhorn. *To do what?* As my mind raced, I felt precariously balanced, not only high on the scaffolding but between the reality of standing there with my hammer and another reality of psychic readings.

I was incredulous as Hans went on with the story. Shortly after their arrival, Wayne and Bella were invited to the building site of Universal Hall to see if they could discern what had blocked its progress. After meditating at the site and walking its perimeters, they diagnosed the problem. The design of the building was laid out several feet off the "ley lines" in that area.

Hans paused with the story, knowing that probably some of us weren't familiar with the term. Ley lines, he explained, are subtle lines of energy that flow in patterns across the Earth's surface. Early peoples, far more attuned to subtle energies, could sense these flowing patterns crisscrossing the Earth. Where the ley lines intersected, they created powerpoints. Places like Stonehenge, Avebury, and the great cathedrals were built at these sacred places, as well as countless other examples such as sacred earth mounds, holy wells, abbeys, churches, ruins, and other prominent landmarks.

Wayne and Bella's psychic attunement to the ley lines affirmed that the layout design of Universal Hall needed to shift several feet to the northwest to align with the energies of the land. Once the stakes and cord had been repositioned, almost immediately, everything related to the building's construction opened up and began to flow effortlessly.

When Hans finished speaking, it took me a while to process the implications of his story. I rejoiced that the Findhorn community was so receptive to subtle dimensions of reality that these influences affected much of what happened there. During my visit that week, I met fellow travelers, people who trusted the invisible influences that are so much a part of life, even if unconscious or ignored by many. The Findhorn story and my visit propelled a leap in my consciousness about the mysteries of our world. Everything about Findhorn reminded me of my childhood where I, too, had sensed invisible presences and subtle mysteries. I had wondered then why people didn't talk about them. I still wonder why skepticism about invisible phenomena is so embedded in Western culture. At Findhorn, however, something precious and affirming had found completion.

My time at Findhorn blew open the doors of devotion in wondrous new ways. There was a community of like-minded people who chose to attune to the spirit of everything in life. The thought form of love pervaded the community.

On one of my last evenings, about ten of us gathered in our caravan for a sharing circle, as was the custom for visitors. We were sitting very close to one another in our cozy caravan as that north wind continued to blow. Starting as always with the group attunement, we went around the circle, reflecting on our week's experiences and how we might integrate our insights into life at home.

Findhorn was love in action. Having spent the week steeped in the atmosphere of that unique community, the experience became embedded in my memory and continued to influence my life in surprising ways. For years, my work in the Findhorn gardens inspired how I worked in our family garden. I experienced new levels of reverence for all the plant beings. How I handled the soil, transplanted seedlings, and weeded the garden were all imbued with Findhorn's philosophy. I devised my own rituals for inviting subtle energies into the garden. I repeated mantras with each planting and created a little stupa of stones to honor the spirit of the plants. Findhorn was now a part of our garden.

Beyond the garden influences, I've pondered the mystery of the ley lines and how that view of the world might relate to Findhorn's place in the evolution of new groups dedicated to living in harmony with the Earth, each other, and consciousness. Not only does the Earth have its networks of energy, but the science of quantum physics reveals the boundless interconnectedness of everything in the universe, including even our individual thoughts. Everything matters because everything is interconnected. One could say that quantum reality is composed of an infinite, intricate pattern of ley lines—interdependence and connection being one way to describe the nature of the universe.

When one accepts this vision, the impact of the Findhorn experiment radiates into the quantum universe. For over half a century, this vision has been reverberating beyond time and space, far beyond that small settlement on the north coast of Scotland because that is the nature of subtle energy in a quantum reality. Findhorn's principles continue to have a significant impact, not only through its original vision but through its ongoing evolution, as with educational programs that reach people around the globe. Whenever individuals, small groups, or communities seek to live more enlightened lives dedicated to love in action and compassion, they will help to bring more light into our troubled world.

TIBETAN CONNECTIONS

Who would have believed that such a seemingly inconsequential moment could have led to such a surprising series of events? It was the fall of 1973. I was walking along a residential street in our neighborhood with my daughter, Laura, then five years old. I had heard that there was a Tibetan Buddhist Center on this street and was curious to see which house it was. I knew nothing about Tibetan Buddhism, but as we walked along, I found myself ruminating about where I was in my life and my initial explorations into spiritual traditions.

At this time, I was in my mid-thirties, a young mother with two children—Ethan, eight years old, and Laura, three years younger. We lived in a brown shingled house on a dead-end circle in north Cambridge. We had recently completed a major renovation to expand our very small house, having added a family room extension into the garden and raised the roof. That bold step had transformed our former attic into a stunning space with windows all along the east and west sides. The room was like a secret aerie, hidden among the treetops where we could watch the abundant bird life and the antics of our resident squirrels.

Hob and I had already ventured into several of the spiritual traditions that had recently migrated from their Asian origins to America. We'd briefly experimented with Transcendental Meditation, a guru tradition from India headed by the Maharishi, a colorful figure often photographed with famous people, especially the Beatles who were dedicated followers. We'd moved on to still deeper practice in the Zen tradition referred to earlier, a stepping stone to Vipassana, a form of Buddhism in the Theravada tradition primarily from southern Asia. More commonly known by the name "insight meditation," Vipassana would become Hob's primary spiritual path from which he never wavered for the rest of his life. We had been sharing in Vipassana practice, having started to meditate together most mornings, but I continued to have this gentle, deep longing for something more. What exactly could that have been? I couldn't have been very articulate about it then, but the longing was connected to my wise child's message about being free. It also arose from a subtle movement of the heart—a devotional impulse that is part of all religious traditions.

Those were some of my ruminations as Laura and I found Upland Road and began looking for the address I had in hand. Soon it appeared, a rambling Victorian house on the north side of the street with a porch leading toward the front door. We climbed the three steps to the porch where Laura noticed a bulletin board with a poster on it. She was drawn by the photographs of perhaps twenty Tibetan youngsters. It was hard to tell how old they were, maybe about eight to fifteen years old. At the top of the poster in large letters was the name of an organization—Tibetan Aid Project.

I read aloud the short statement at the bottom. The Tibetan children wanted to find a pen pal with an American youngster. Hopefully, the sponsoring family could help with the Tibetan child's education by sending a modest annual donation. While I was reading the description, Laura was scanning the faces in the poster, and after a few moments, she said, "I want that one," and pointed to a boy who seemed to be around twelve years old. His name, we learned later, was Konchok Gurme Sandup.

That's where the story began. For several years, Laura and Gurme had an occasional exchange of letters, and I sent a contribution to the family to help with his education. Then their correspondence lapsed, but by that time, I had my own contact with Gurme's father, Zoegyam. I kept sending the annual donation, and occasionally a little package from them would arrive in the mail with a gift. One time, the gift was a square of cotton cloth, deep yellow, on which was stenciled the imprint of a mandala, a sacred, usually circular image used for meditation. Another time, it was a simple necklace of braided twine with little bits of coral and turquoise woven into a medallion. Each gift seemed very precious to me, something lovingly chosen to thank us for our help with Gurme's education.

Five or six years went by. Zoegyam always wrote a thank you letter, translated into English by Gurme or one of his five brothers. One year I received a letter from Gurme explaining that he was going to attend the Institute of Higher Buddhist Studies in Varanasi, India, and would no longer be able to write. I continued to make our annual donations, however, figuring that the brothers would be needing help with their education as well, or maybe the money would help pay for Gurme's studies at the Institute.

With these periodic exchanges with our Tibetan family, a tapestry of connection was being woven. About the same time, in 1977, I had been profoundly inspired by Lama Govinda's book *The Way of the White Clouds*, given to me by my beloved older friend Jean who periodically fed my spiritual inclinations. That's when I first read about the Kulu Valley, one of the most spectacular areas in northern India, now home to several Tibetan refugee settlements. In those same years, I also discovered the dramatic art of the Russian mystic Nicholas Roerich, many of whose paintings were inspirational portrayals of the Himalayas. He had lived in this same area, the Kulu Valley.

I became transfixed by his mystical paintings with evocative titles such as *Warrior of Light*, *And We Do Not Fear*, and *The Most Sacred.* I'd never seen an artist whose work portrayed the longings of my own heart. Among my favorites was *Star of the Hero* depicting a shooting star cutting a path of vivid light through the night sky, with a man meditating in the lower corner of the canvas and dark, looming mountains behind him. I was fascinated by another painting titled *Stronghold of the Spirit* with soaring mountains, yellowish sky, and a monastery clinging to the mountainside that rose up beyond the frame of the painting.

I spent hours with these inspiring images, seeding my imagination with hopes of one day visiting the Kulu Valley, home to Roerich and several well-known lamas I'd heard about. With his soaring, inspirational images, Roerich had somehow portrayed the longings of my own heart—that subtle longing for freedom that I only vaguely understood at that time in my life, although it had been present in my heart since I was a little girl.

Imagine my delight when I learned that Zoegyam, his wife, and five of Gurme's siblings lived in Bir, a Tibetan refugee community in the Kulu Valley. I began to dream of going there and meeting Gurme's family after all these years of connection. I dreamt of spending time, maybe in retreat, in the incomparable beauty that Roerich's paintings had depicted, near this family of whom I had grown deeply fond.

More years went by. I began to have the feeling that somehow, sometime my path would cross with Gurme. Was it wishful thinking? Was it an intuition? The possibility was a like a very fragile seed planted somewhere deep within my heart.

Meanwhile, Gurme graduated from the Institute, disappeared for long retreats, and was ultimately granted the honorific title of lama, or spiritual teacher in the Tibetan Buddhist lineage. His name was now Lama Gursam. I no longer heard from Lama Gursam, but his father, Zoegyam, and I continued to be in touch. I kept sending financial support for the brothers, and modest as it was, Zoegyam always expressed deep appreciation, sometimes accompanied by another little gift, which arrived in a package displaying exotic stamps and Tibetan writing—always intriguing.

Some thirty years after Laura had first chosen this young boy from the Tibetan Aid poster, I received an email announcing that Lama Gursam was coming to teach in the United States. My premonition that we would one day meet took on a new possibility. When? Where might that happen?

Soon after, I learned that he was coming to New England to teach in a remote little village called Lincoln, Vermont. I was stunned, almost unable to believe the announcement as I read it. How could it be possible? Lincoln was just over the mountains from our family house in the Mad River Valley. Our view looked west, and if you looked slightly to the south beyond Mount Abraham, you would be looking toward Lincoln Gap, a steep, winding mountain road that led through an opening in the mountains to that little village after which it was named.

Now it was November, and that perilous road was closed for the winter. After an exchange of emails trying to arrange our meeting, I set out one overcast November morning to drive over the Appalachian Gap, the other way over the mountains to the west. I was filled with anticipation. I wondered what it would be like to finally meet this person who had had such a unique role in my life for almost thirty years—a connection with the other side of the world, a collection of letters translated into idiomatic English, the little gifts that carried the mystery of this distant tradition.

I got halfway up the mountain pass when the car in front of me went into a careening skid and spun off the road into a ditch. It wasn't a serious accident, but it was a dramatic warning that the road was slick with ice and not passable. I returned home, tense from the dangerous driving and near accident, disappointed that I had been turned back from this historic meeting.

The next day I set out again, and this time I arrived safely in Lincoln. I parked in front of the modest Town Hall, an unprepossessing building that seemed a totally unlikely place for a Tibetan lama to be teaching. This was all so incongruous. I felt as though I was living in a dream. How could he have come to this tiny village just over the mountains from our family place, a second home in the mountains of Vermont? What was he like? Would he speak enough English for us to communicate? I was filled with questions, anticipation, and incredulity.

I walked into the main hall where someone greeted me. I wasn't planning to attend the whole day because I was then practicing in a different tradition, and I had always been a bit daunted by the complexity of the Tibetan path, having once explored the tradition by spending a week at the Nyingma Institute, a Tibetan Buddhist center in Berkeley, California.

I explained to the welcoming woman that I had a more than ordinary reason to be there and asked if I could meet the Lama before he started teaching because he was expecting me. The woman disappeared through a door at the back of the large, sparsely decorated room. What a stark, unwelcoming space, I thought to myself as I waited, filled with anticipation, my heart pounding. A few minutes later, Lama Gursam came through that door and walked into the big, barren room.

How do you greet a lama you've never met, especially when you've had this unusual relationship for over thirty years? How would he greet me? Would he shake hands? I knew that many male lamas refused to touch women. What would he say? What would we talk about? A tumble of questions went through my mind.

Lama Gursam was dressed in the traditional crimson robes of a Tibetan monk. His black hair was pulled back in a ponytail from his wide forehead. He was coming toward me with an infectious, broad smile, his open, welcoming expression inviting me instantly into his warm, heart-centered presence. He extended his arms and we met in a hug.

Lama Gursam at our first meeting in the early 1980s

Disbelief, delight, excitement, wonder—a torrent of feelings swirled within me. Who was this man, this lama? What was the shared karma that had brought us together and then kept us in touch on and off for so many years? We talked for about fifteen minutes about his family, his training, his initial invitation to teach in the United States, and his teaching schedule. He mentioned that he would be teaching in Somerville, Massachusetts, in the fall. When he learned that I lived in the next town, he invited me to consider attending those teachings. I couldn't believe it. Once again he was showing up to teach in the next town. It struck me as another utterly impossible coincidence. And so began the unlikely path to our reconnecting again, not through letters this time but in person.

In Somerville, he taught about the Seven Points of Posture and breath awareness practices. Another year, he came to Brattleboro, Vermont, for a day of teachings on Green Tara. Again, I attended. Gradually I seemed to be drifting toward the Tibetan Buddhist tradition. Over the next few years, Lama Gursam made several trips to India for retreat and to visit his family. Although he was mainly affiliated with a Tibetan Buddhist center in Maryland, he seemed to be a peripatetic teacher, moving among various centers in California, Texas, and along the East Coast. Eventually, I lost track of his email and wasn't able to keep up with his whereabouts.

Many years later, after a long foray into a devotional tradition from India, I was in my seventies and practicing Tibetan Buddhism. I had connected with a new teacher, a woman named Lama Willa. She had spent twelve years living and training in a monastery in New York state and had completed two of the traditional three-year, three-month, three-day retreats in the Tibetan tradition. With the support of her students, she founded her own center in 2012 in Springfield, New Hampshire, called Wonderwell Mountain Retreat Center where I began to attend residential retreats.

Once again, I was startled to read Lama Gursam's name in the latest newsletter. He was coming to Wonderwell, my favorite retreat center. Five days before it began, Lama Willa announced that Lama Gursam would be coming to co-teach with her, the last retreat in a five-year

Dzogchen training. I couldn't find words for my astonishment at this latest unfolding of events that kept reconnecting us. How could the universe have set up such a wondrous pattern?

I began signing up for his retreats from then on, every time incredulous at how our entwined karma kept weaving this unlikely pattern that had started with my daughter's random choice of that young boy from a poster all those years ago and continued with his international teaching and his becoming an honored teacher at the meditation center where I, too, returned many times to be in his presence—a blessed journey that had spanned almost fifty years and continues to this day. That is one of life's mysteries. Seemingly insignificant moments can unfold into stories we could never have imagined.

With Lama Gursam after his retreat (2023)

THE NIGHT ON MOUNT ABRAHAM

It was only a brief reference in a book, so I was initially mystified by what prompted me to act on it. I was in my early forties, about the same time that I had read the landmark book *The Way of the White Clouds*. Again, because I've always been a voracious reader, I was inspired by something I had just read, a fragmentary reference to a nighttime vigil. A nighttime vigil—that's the phrase that captured my attention. The American philosopher William James had spent the night in a vigil on Mount Marcy, the highest mountain in New York state. I remembered nothing about what happened to him, only that he had spent a night in vigil, a word that I found strangely captivating. I associated it with the Christian tradition and vaguely remembered that Jesus had spent nights in prayer during his forty-day retreat and that this was referred to as a vigil. More than its religious connotations, however, I was primarily intrigued by the prospect of spending a night in meditation on a mountain.

Family home in Waitsfield, Vermont

It was summertime in the 1970s. Hob, Ethan, Laura, and I were vacationing at our family gathering place in the Mad River Valley in northern Vermont. This much-loved vacation place had its beginnings before I'd even met Hob. At the time, he was teaching at Columbia University in New York City and used to drive over six hours on Friday nights to spend ski weekends in this stunningly beautiful valley with the Green Mountains to the west, rising to over 4,000 feet. At that time, there was only one ski area, Mad River Glen, its trails carving designs into the mountainside. It was one of the first places I learned to ski. I was an eager fourteen-year-old, awed by the precipitous beginner's slope and the motto for the area that read, "Mad River: Ski It If You Can." I already had wonderful memories of this valley where eventually two more ski resorts would be added—Sugarbush South on Mount Abraham and Sugarbush North on Mount Ellen.

Hob fell in love with the valley, and even though he was still a bachelor, he made the bold decision to buy eight acres of cow pasture from a local farmer. Not stopping there, he invited an architect friend to design a one-level house that he described as Japanese Swiss since it combined elements from both cultures with its walls of windows to the outside and its pleasing simplicity.

We started to spend our summer vacations at the house. By that time, we'd put in a pond with trout, ideal for swimming in summer and skating in winter, as well as a garden filled with vegetables and flowers. As the one who initiated the garden adventure, I called on our neighboring farmer to rototill the hard scrabble meadow. In his distinctive Vermont accent, he announced to me that nothing much would ever grow there. Undaunted, I added organic fertilizer and fresh manure from local farms, and with all my loving attention, a prolific garden appeared, including in that first year every gardener's nightmare—an overabundance of zucchini, fat as baseball bats and numerous enough for my kids to make a fort with them. Nature had taught me my first lesson!

That summer, in August, nearing the time of the full moon, I found myself first absorbed and then totally captivated by the account of

William James having spent a night on Mount Marcy. I began to fantasize about challenging myself in the same way. I would spend the night of the full moon on Mount Abraham, the highest mountain of the range that we looked out on every day from dawn to dark, that beloved skyline of mountains—Mount Abraham, Mount Ellen, and Stark Mountain—rising from south to north, leading toward Camel's Hump, another majestic peak in the line of beautiful mountains. I'd climbed these mountains at different times and knew what a wilderness lay in those forests. The wild and free side of my nature was calling.

It was a blessing that Hob and I were both spiritual seekers by then, sharing a Buddhist tradition. We had a tacit understanding, never really discussed, that we would support one another in retreats and various forms of training. Hob plunged into the world of retreats, attending three-month silent retreats of sitting and walking meditation from dawn to dusk. But spending the night alone on a mountain was a somewhat different undertaking. Was it even a wise idea? Nevertheless, he supported me in my venture.

The chosen day arrived. That morning I walked out to the front terrace and looked across the valley to the mountain range where Mount Abraham to the south stood out as the highest peak. I'd climbed it from Lincoln Gap in the south but never from the east. I'd ascended the mountain many times in a chair lift because this was also the Sugarbush ski area. Because I had decided to spend the night near the summit, I had estimated that it would take me about an hour and a half to climb. I had decided to semi-fast and assembled only a small snack of dried fruit, nuts, and water. I put a flashlight, sweater, windbreaker, and ground cover into my backpack. There were no cell phones in those days, but I checked the weather in our much-used little brown weather box. When you pushed down the plastic lever on the front, the crackling voice of the weather forecaster came on with the latest forecast, somehow simpler than waiting for it on the radio. The forecast announced that it would be clear with a full moon, with a storm coming in but not until later in the morning the following day.

It was late afternoon when I drove across the valley, left the car, and started climbing up the wide access trail that led to the top of the mountain. I was experiencing both excitement and flickers of anxiety.

Am I crazy to be doing this? We all know there are bears, bobcats, and who knows what else in these forests. I'm seeking wilderness and solitude, but I'm a woman alone on this vast mountainside with no means of communication. What if? . . . What if?

I continued to climb, breathing heavily as I ascended, taking in the wild beauty around me—the stands of maple, birds calling in the trees, the late light filtering through the leaves, with an occasional opening where I caught glimpses of the valley now far below. As the views into the valley became more distant, I began to feel how far I'd left behind the familiarity of that welcoming valley, how far I had ascended into the mountain wilderness.

Just before sunset, I reached the uppermost reaches of the mountain and found an open rough meadow filled with grasses and wildflowers. Settling in on a ski run wasn't exactly the wilds of Mount Marcy, I thought to myself, but to me it felt very remote and wild up there. I took my time deciding where to settle for the night. Finding the right place felt like an important decision—practical and sacred. My intention was to meditate on and off and be with whatever else unfolded in the night. I had absolutely no idea what lay ahead, only the sure sense that I would do this vigil on Mount Abraham.

Because the summit of the mountain was behind me to the west, I couldn't see the sunset, but once I'd settled into my place, I watched the fading light turn distant clouds into rosy hues. It was a beautiful, clear, warm August evening.

As darkness crept over the eastern sky, I became aware of a vague uneasiness. At first I couldn't identify the source until suddenly the uneasiness bloomed into primal fear, waves of fire surging through my body. I realized that it was about my back, which felt totally exposed and vulnerable. I was overcome with feelings of urgency. I needed to do something to protect my back—to protect myself. I had never experienced anything like that before, feelings so primal they were almost animal-like in their rawness.

I remembered that I'd seen a hay bale somewhere at the edge of the meadow, presumably to protect skiers from some dangerous obstacle. Propelled by the fear, I carefully picked my way back to where I'd seen the bale and then awkwardly hauled it back to my place. Because of the way the meadow rose sharply above my little piece of level ground, the hay bale provided just the measure of protection I seemed to need.

By now the darkness of night had descended. Then a glow of light appeared to the east over the Northfield ridge, a precursor to the rising moon. I'd never before watched a moonrise with such a sense of anticipation. First just as an aura, then as a sphere of light, very large when low on the horizon, it felt like a living presence, providing me company high on this remote mountainside.

The night sky became as much a part of the vigil as meditation with closed eyes. The brilliance of the moon obscured the stars around it. I marveled at the changing display, returning to the moon over and over again as my focus, my refuge. Aside from the occasional flashes of concern over what might be in the darkness of the forest to my right and left—those bears, bobcats, or whatever else—I settled into a calm and exceptionally alert state, grateful that I had found deep peace amidst challenging circumstances.

Sometime around 1:30 in the morning, the first clouds started to drift across the face of the moon. At first, the cloud patterns were intriguing, but gradually as the cloud cover thickened and moonlight flashed out less and less, I realized that the weather predicted for later was starting to come in. The hardest part was losing the light of the moon. How attached I'd become to that source of light! I'd lost a companion, an anchor. Now, the darkness was heavy, obscuring all that I'd been able to see before.

Then came the first drops of rain. It was unbelievable how quickly the weather had changed. I put on my windbreaker with its hood, but it didn't take long for the rain to get heavier and saturate my clothes. I realized I had no choice. At about 2:30 in the morning, I gathered up my things, bowed to my seat, and started down the access trail. With the darkness and the driving rain, I knew it would be a risky descent, but I had made an irreversible decision. The storm was now in full force. With a hard rain falling and a rising wind, I picked my way slowly and carefully down through woods and meadows, the access trail only faintly lit by my flashlight.

I knew I had to be exceptionally mindful of every step, rock, root, or slippery place that could take me down. Fierce determination guided me. I must not fall! I must just keep going, steady and sure that I would make it down safely. I was soaked to the skin with rain coursing down my face, but I hardly noticed. Fully aware of the dangers of descending the mountain in the dark with high winds and pouring rain, I felt a determination unlike anything I'd ever experienced before—an iron will of attention to every step, every breath, every glimpse of ground under my feet.

After all those hours on the mountain with its ever-changing beauty and challenges, I finally got to the bottom of the trail. Relieved and exhausted from the effort, I faced a strange, surreal experience to find where I'd parked my car. It was like moving from one reality to another, going from the treacherous descent through wilderness to the ordinary act of unlocking and getting into a car. Even more surreal was my arrival home about 4:00 in the morning to my sleeping family in the dry and familiar comfort of the house. The night in vigil was over, but it would take time and reflection to understand why it had been such a memorable experience.

In the mystical traditions, one finds references to the role of vigil, time set aside for solitude and practice, often in a remote place. I was reminded of the desert fathers of early Christianity, Tibetans on long retreat, or Father Bede Griffiths, my husband's primary teacher, who as a young man had spent a night in prayer and meditation in his own room. The word vigil suggested a dive into deeper levels of practice, a leap into the unknown, an exploration and time-honored part of the inner journey.

Choosing to be alone in the wilds of Mount Abraham felt in itself like an immense challenge, moving into the unknown through an immersion in the natural world. I had no idea what might happen that night, but I felt the strong call to climb that mountain and spend the night up there, knowing that negotiating the unknown is one of life's central challenges.

Strangely, coming up against that primal fear of being so exposed and vulnerable was one of the revealing events of that night. We all know the many facets of fear but facing and overcoming this animal-like fear felt like a triumph. Yet another gift of the vigil was surrendering to the unexpected reality of having the storm drive me from my sacred place and back down the mountain before the night was over. Even though it was a fairly accessible trail, that descent was another level of challenge. With the darkness, driving rain, and wind tearing through the trees, I was assaulted by the elements but had to remain steady. The power of my attention was in overdrive, amplified dramatically by the circumstances. Because it was such a wild scene, I developed a superpower—to use my grandkids' term!—that I hadn't known I had. Because the descent was so perilous, that intensity of attention was exhilarating.

Many years later, I looked for an account of William James' experience during his night on Mount Marcy. I laughed aloud as I read. What a difference between my fantasies about his vigil and the facts of what actually happened! In July 1898, James was fifty-six years old and had started out with a guide and a friend to climb Mount Marcy. They spent the first night in a hiker's cabin in Panther Gorge, along with a group of youthful climbers. When James was unable to sleep, he walked out into the night to the brook that drains the gorge. As the moon rose, he experienced a life-changing epiphany, numinous and transformative. He tried to describe it in a letter to his wife a few days later, how he had entered a state of "spiritual alertness." The beauty of nature and his love for his wife and family expanded into a boundless experience of oneness.

That night in Panther Gorge was the turning point in his intellectual life. He had experienced a spiritual opening, not as a concept but as an inherent part of human consciousness. It led to his most famous book,

The Varieties of Religious Experience. When I first read the brief reference to his vigil, I knew nothing about his epiphany or what followed. For me, the inner call to vigil had come from my associations with the word.

My experience that night on Mount Abraham stood out as a landmark in my spiritual journey, combining my choice to move toward the unknown to spend a night alone in the wilderness, expose myself to danger, confront my fear, and finally deal with the dramatic turn in the weather. In retrospect, it was empowering to meet the challenges that arose, whether external or within my own mind/heart, and to discover the superpower of my heightened attention in the descent through the storm. Before that night, I could never have known that whatever had called me would lead to those revelations.

AN UNLIKELY ENCOUNTER

I don't know where the term *wisdom treasures* came from, but I found myself using it to describe those precious bits of inspiration that appear in books, spiritual teachings, or conversations with a friend. It was my habit to write down these treasures on note cards so I could keep my practice inspired and use them in future teaching. Little piles of note cards were everywhere—next to my meditation seat, in the bookcase under my altar, on my desk, on my bedside table, and so on. Eventually they contributed to my second book, *Aging with Wisdom: Reflections, Stories & Teachings.*

Like some jackdaw—a bird methodical in its search patterns and famous for collecting shiny objects—I, too, was a collector. The habit, now a longtime friend, comes from that quiet longing of the heart to explore the mystery in which we live, to keep lighting the flame of devotion to something greater than myself, to absorb the wisdom of others, and, above all, to remember the sacred dimension of life.

A few favorite books fall into the category of wisdom treasures. Foremost among them is *The Way of the White Clouds: A Buddhist Pilgrim in Tibet* by Lama Anagarika Govinda, a book given to me in 1977 by my beloved elder friend Jean. She knew about my spiritual search and periodically would give me a book or article that supported it.

Lama Govinda, German by birth, had first traveled to Sri Lanka, then called Ceylon, to study with some of the leading Theravada Buddhist teachers. When he later traveled to India to participate in a conference, he began hearing about various lamas in Tibet who taught within the Mahayana tradition. Eminent among these teachers was a lama named Domo Geshe Rinpoche. Highly respected and loved, this lama had thousands of devotees. The honorific geshe is given only rarely to those most dedicated practitioners who have completed many years of study and meditation practice. The title is somewhat analogous to a Doctor of Divinity but far beyond that in attainment. Domo Geshe was furthermore regarded as fourth in succession of importance to the Dalai Lama with whom he had a close association.

Lama Govinda traveled widely in Tibet with his partner, Li Gotami, a pilgrimage that lasted almost two years and inspired him to write *The Way of the White Clouds*. At that time, Tibet was a remote, mysterious country rarely visited by Westerners yet full of cultural richness and unfamiliar practices, all overlaid with a cloak of mystery. The book, first published in 1970, became a best seller among spiritual seekers, given the explosion of interest in Eastern mysticism. He tells the story of a life-changing encounter, a story that riveted my attention and started a new chapter in my search for an enlightened teacher.

Drawn by curiosity, Lama Govinda continued his travels to Sikkim with hopes that he might meet this remarkable lama. Here, the unfolding story takes a turn into the esoteric mysteries of the Tibetan tradition. As Lama Govinda tells the story, when he first heard about Domo Geshe, he was told that Vairocana, one of the archetypal forms in the Tibetan tradition, was reported to have said this about Domo Geshe, then called Lama Ngawang:

> Even in this age of strife and spiritual decay there are some saintly men, and among them in this very country of Tibet there lives a great hermit, whose abode is in the Southern Wheat Valley. His name is Lama Ngawang Kalzang. I shall request him to go forth from his retreat into the world and kindle the flame of the Dharma in the hearts of men.

Lama Govinda learned that Lama Ngawang had been meditating for twelve years in various caves and retreats in the mountain wilderness of southern Tibet. Apparently, he then descended from the mountains into the Domo Valley, known for its wheat (Domo means "wheat") and started Dungkar Gompa, the Monastery of the White Conch.

Subsequently, through an extraordinary vision described in great detail in Lama Govinda's book, Lama Ngawang received that superior authority, which in Tibet is ascribed only to Tulkus, those perceived to be the living embodiment of the Bodhisattva ideal. It's significant to our story that this includes the power to direct their future rebirths according to the needs of practitioners.

This remarkable vision, also seen by many of Lama Ngawang's disciples, plus the intercession of the State Oracle of Lhasa, inspired the Lama to leave his life of retreat and his time at Dungkar Gompa to devote the rest of his life to bringing the dharma not only to Tibet but to the world at large, regardless, as he said, of caste, color, or creed.

This was the mysterious background to the eventual meeting of Lama Govinda with his guru. He found his way, including a life-threatening journey through an historic blizzard, to a large monastery where Domo Geshe was in residence. After making a formal request to meet with Domo Geshe, he finally found himself in the presence of the renowned master. When Domo Geshe laid his hands on Lama Govinda's bowed head, Lama Govinda perceived "hands whose lightest touch sent a stream of bliss through one's whole being, so that all one had intended to ask vanished like smoke into blue air. Merely to be in this man's presence seemed to be enough to dissolve all problems . . . like darkness in the presence of light."

Among the many teachings that Lama Govinda received from his guru, one stands out for its relevance to what has become an archetypal experience for many Westerners—how does one reconcile the exalted view that these teachers are supposedly "enlightened" with the thoroughly unenlightened behavior that so many of them fall into?

Given what was to unfold for me, I was struck by what Domo Geshe said to Lama Govinda in their first meeting:

> If you wish for me to be your Guru, do not look upon my person as the Guru, because every human personality has its

> shortcomings, and so long as we are engaged in observing the imperfections of others, we deprive ourselves of the opportunities of learning from them. . . . It is not the robes, nor the body, nor the words, that make the Guru, but that which lives in him of truth and knowledge and light (*bodhi*). More he possesses this, and more his outer conduct and appearance is in harmony with it, the easier it is for the Chela [disciple] to see the Buddha in his Guru. Therefore, he should be as careful in his choice as the Guru is in his acceptance of a Chela.

Deeply touched by the presence and obvious spiritual attainment of this Tibetan monk, the encounter led to a dramatic change of direction in Lama Govinda's journey. Although he never lost touch with his Theravada roots, he now began practicing within the Tibetan tradition, eventually being ordained by Domo Geshe and given the name Lama Anagarika Govinda.

His book, filled with wondrous stories about his pilgrimage throughout Tibet, provides an extraordinary introduction to a country about which little was known at that time. While describing the experiences of this extended pilgrimage, Lama Govinda also shares deeply about his unfolding spiritual practice, guided by his guru, which he wrote about further in his book *Foundations of Tibetan Mysticism*.

The inevitable time came when Domo Geshe made it known that he would soon be leaving his body. He was seventy-two, physically old but still vigorous, spending most of his time in meditation and study except for the many hours he spent meeting with his followers.

"But there is no reason for you to feel sad," he told his followers. "I do not forsake you, nor my work for the Dharma; but instead of dragging on in an old body, I shall come back in a new one. I promise to return to you. You may look out for me within three or four years."

Those close to Domo Geshe knew that he spent the nights in sitting meditation, never lying down or losing control over his body but in the highest form of meditation practice, a state of continuous *samadhi*, an entirely different level of consciousness. He gave instructions not to be disturbed, and after ten days when his attendant went into his room, he found Domo Geshe still sitting motionless on his seat. Only when they held a mirror to his face did his followers realize that he had stopped breathing. "He had left his body during his meditation and had consciously passed over the threshold between life and death or, more correctly, between one life and another. He had left his body, before death could snatch it away from him, and directed his consciousness towards a new germ of life, that would carry on the impetus of his will . . . of the attainment of his ultimate aim and the fulfillment of his Bodhisattva Vow."

And so it happened that about three years later, the signs of his predicted rebirth began to unfold. A baby boy was born in Gangtok, Sikkim, whose mother died shortly after childbirth, as had also happened with the birth of Shakymuni Buddha, considered a sign in the Tibetan tradition that a highly attained reincarnation had been born.

Much like the story of His Holiness the Dalai Lama's recognition of his rebirth, as depicted in the film *Kundun*, this little four-year-old boy gave clear signs of his true identity. He protested when his father called him *pu-chung* (little son) and declared that his name was Jigme (the Fearless One), the same name uttered on that very day by the Oracle at Lhasa who had been consulted in the identifying process.

When a delegation of monk officials came to Gangtok following the Oracle's vision of the house, garden, and even specific trees, as they entered the garden, the little boy ran toward them, calling out, "Father, my people have come to take me back to my Gompa" (monastery). Incredibly, he addressed each of the monks by the same name he had used in his former incarnation.

When the monks laid out a large assortment of ritual objects, including several from his previous life, the little boy immediately picked up those that had belonged to him in his previous reincarnation even though brighter and fancier ones lay before him.

On his journey from Gangtok, Sikkim, to Dungkar Gompa in Tibet, his monastery in his earlier life, the party met the Amchi, the

Tibetan doctor who had treated Domo Geshe in his last years.

"O Amchi," the little boy called out, "don't you know me? Don't you remember that you treated me when I was sick in my previous body?"

All these signs were witnessed by several people and confirmed without doubt the authenticity of his rebirth. Furthermore, it became clear that he hadn't forgotten much of his previous knowledge. Not only was his education more like a rehearsal of what he already knew, but he presided over large gatherings of his former devotees, carrying out complex ritual activities even though he was only a young boy, now a recognized Tulku named Jigme Ngawang Kalzang Rinpoche, or more commonly, simply Domo Geshe Rinpoche—the same name as his previous incarnation.

Fast forward to 1959 and the invasion of Tibet by the Chinese. In these terrifying times, vast numbers of people flocked to Domo Geshe, not only to seek his solace and protection but to become part of the struggle to liberate their country from the Chinese. For being such a well-known, eminent figure, Domo Geshe was eventually arrested by the Chinese and thrown into prison. With ceaseless efforts to break his spirit, the Chinese subjected him to forced labor sixteen hours a day, torture, a starvation diet, and solitary confinement in an airless, dark cell.

He survived, although his health was permanently damaged. In 1961, word came that under diplomatic pressure from the government of India and the personal intercession of Prime Minister Nehru, he had been released from prison and the prospect of sure death. Because he had been born in the town of Gangtok in Sikkim, a few miles from the Tibetan border, India claimed he was an Indian-protected citizen. Although Lama Govinda's story goes no further than this epochal event, Domo Geshe's story was to take a thoroughly unexpected turn in a most unlikely place halfway around the world.

Here I must pick up the thread by telling you about Margot, a close friend of my mother's, soon to become a beloved friend of mine as well. Then in her sixties, Margot was a striking figure. Tall with noble bearing, brilliant white hair, and a powerful, ebullient presence, she had been born into a family involved with the Anthroposophical tradition.

Margot was steeped in these universal teachings from a young age. She read widely in philosophy and religion, and became a lifelong seeker, unusual for someone of her generation.

One day, shortly before a trip to visit one of the four Acharyas (Sampradayas), eminent spiritual leaders in India, Margot went to Bloomingdale's to find a new suitcase. While perusing one of the many piles of suitcases, she was surprised to see two Tibetans apparently also searching on the other side of one of the piles. She looked. She looked again, trying not to stare, but was mysteriously drawn to one of them. She experienced a moment of immediate recognition. Who was this Tibetan, slight of stature, composed, emanating a deep calm? How was she to understand this instant recognition?

A hearty extrovert and not one to hesitate in an unusual social situation, Margot went around the piles of suitcases and introduced herself. She asked who they were and what brought them to New York City. The one to whom she was drawn answered in awkward English, "My name is Domo Geshe."

Domo Geshe Rinpoche

That was the beginning of an unlikely story. Learning that Domo Geshe and his attendant had no place to stay, she invited them back to her spacious apartment. Margot's moment of recognition awakened some mysterious and ancient bond that she had with this gentle Tibetan. Domo Geshe became her teacher and guru for the remaining years of her life until her death at the age of 102.

Lex and Sheila Hixon, a couple who had also met Domo Geshe, found a place for him to live in a hidden valley deep in the Catskill Mountains of New York, which became a refuge for those who found their way to him, including His Holiness the Dalai Lama with whom he had a close connection. Domo Geshe was a hidden teacher. He never gave public teachings, only individual spiritual guidance to those with whom he had the bond of guru and disciple.

Meanwhile, about this time, having practiced in the Vipassana tradition for about five years, I had just finished reading Lama Govinda's book. I had been intrigued and deeply affected by his description of meeting this eminent, highly realized guru, his initiation, the guru-chela relationship, Domo Geshe's remarkable death, and then the identification of his reincarnation.

The whole sequence of events had awakened in me the seed of longing to find an enlightened teacher. I was incredulous when my mother then told me the story of Margot's meeting Domo Geshe in Bloomingdale's of all places—the holy man whose previous incarnation had been the central figure in *The Way of the White Clouds*. That meeting had totally changed the inner world of Lama Govinda's life. In turn, simply reading his story had deeply stirred me, setting in motion a curious unfolding of events.

My first impulse was to contact Margot and find out how I might find Domo Geshe and ask to meet him. Over the next two years, I tried several times to call Ann, his devoted assistant who managed the place, also called Dungkar Gompa after his previous monastery, and who protected the hidden way of life Domo Geshe had chosen to follow.

"No, a meeting won't be possible because Rinpoche is in poor health right now," Ann told me.

The next time I called, she responded, "No, it won't be possible to meet him now as he is traveling in India."

There was no invitation to call again, no meeting in spite of my efforts. I didn't give up, but something else interrupted my search, something unexpected and perplexing.

THE GURU APPEARS

Although I hadn't given up my hope of meeting Domo Geshe, by then one of my colleagues, a devotee of Swami Muktananda, had taped a photograph of her guru on the filing cabinet in the front office of Greenhouse, the name of our psychotherapy collective. There it was, this mysteriously compelling image of an Indian swami. Dressed in the orange of a renunciant, he looked directly into the camera with penetrating eyes that seemed to radiate some kind of spiritual power. Referring to this poster as her Baba's *shaktipat* photo, she explained that he had done many years of intense practice, described in his autobiography, *Play of Consciousness*, and that he was a renowned master of energy with the power of awakening that spiritual energy in those who sought initiation with him.

Still hoping to meet Domo Geshe, I was dubious about my friend's enthusiastic embrace of this mysterious Indian guru. I was even vaguely uncomfortable with the word *guru* when applied to this Indian master, whereas I hadn't doubted anything about the relationship that Lama Govinda had described as a disciple of Domo Geshe. What was that difference? Did it matter? I recognized the shadows of doubt in my own mind and wondered why I felt hesitance about this Indian guru but not about Domo Geshe whose devotees also referred to him as their guru. Little did I know how much this discrepancy would play out in the coming years.

My friend described how thousands of people were flocking to Swami Muktananda at his two large ashrams, one in India and another in the Catskills not far from Domo Geshe's place. There were also dozens of Siddha Yoga centers around the world. Siddha Yoga was the name of this tradition, a somewhat confusing name in the West where most people associate the word *yoga* with hatha yoga. The name conveyed a way of life that derived from the siddha tradition. The word *siddha* referred to highly realized masters and historically to the eighty-four mahasiddhas of India and Tibet.

In contrast, I knew that Domo Geshe had no formal center, only a main house with several outlying cottages in a quiet valley in the Catskill Mountains. There were no programs and no public teachings, only the individual relationship of the teacher with a small number of students.

Then, out of nowhere, I had a landmark dream—unbidden, unsettling, demanding.

I am in an unfamiliar place, part of a gathering where people have come to meet a spiritual master. He is sitting on a raised seat so everyone can see him. I don't go forward to meet him, but somehow he appears right in front of me, looking directly at me, holding my gaze.

Then suddenly, he is gone, dematerialized, vanished. Nothing. Only an empty seat.

Moments passed. Then in an invisible flash, he reappears. Still looking directly at me, he is laughing—laughing a full-bodied laugh as if simply delighting at his own play and what I might make of it.

What was this dream trying to tell me? It kept pushing into the front of my consciousness for weeks following, like an insistent intrusion yet somehow uplifting because of his playful disappearing act and all his laughter. Was the dream about his powers or to show me that life is a play of consciousness? Might this have been my first meeting with him?

I continued to ponder the dream until finally I spent a week in Muktananda's presence. The week was riddled with a play of opposites. I was put off by the hustle of the ashram scene, utterly in contrast to the silent retreats I'd done in the Vipassana tradition. Muktananda, with his dark glasses and orange hats, looked more like a jazz musician than a Siddha guru. I felt awash in unfamiliarity yet wept openly when I first heard the haunting music of the Rudram, an ancient chant sung every morning. I felt strangely moved by the beauty of the devotional practices, the repetitive rhythm of the chants, the waving of Arati lights, the beauty of everything. But then I was put off by the noisy meditation hall,

all kinds of sounds and movement unleashed when Muktananda moved through the darkened hall giving shakipat with his sandalwood-scented peacock feather wand. Yet when he came to me, I dropped into a timeless state—the deepest, totally thought-free, most expanded meditation I'd ever experienced. Vastness. No sense of the body. Total stillness. Beyond, totally beyond.

I learned that Baba's own spiritual journey, which unfolded from his years of intense practices, involved two traditions—Vedanta and Kashmir Shaivism—the latter being an esoteric tradition from north India, similar in many ways to Tibetan Buddhism.

As I ricocheted between troubled reactivity and blissful experiences, I remained in this perplexing situation, trying to figure out all the cross-currents of my experience yet knowing that "figuring it out" was only a mental obsession that ultimately wouldn't resolve anything.

Shortly thereafter, I was visiting my friend Jean, who had originally given me Lama Govinda's book. It was a fall afternoon with wind-blown leaves brightening her lawn with golden light. We were sitting on her sunporch, a glassed-in room with a row of African violets lining the window ledge that looked out over her garden.

Jean was telling me about how she had gone to the local Siddha Yoga ashram to attend a program and how perplexed she'd been by Muktananda whom she had met briefly during darshan at the end of the evening's program. A committed Christian her entire life, she couldn't understand why this very unusual Indian swami had affected her so deeply. Now late in her seventies, Jean was living with cancer, and I sensed the urgency of her questioning.

"So I called my friend Harold Talbott," she explained to me, "because with his lifetime of practice in Eastern traditions I thought he might be able to help me. I asked him if any of his teachers knew anything about the swami."

At that moment, the phone rang. Jean answered it. She glanced over at me with a surprised expression and whispered, "It's Harold." After a few moments of conversation, she hung up, turned to me, and said, "Harold apparently spoke with a Tibetan teacher named Dudjom Rinpoche. He told me that Dudjom is one of the leading Tibetan teachers currently teaching in the West, a remarkable and very highly regarded lama. When Harold told him about my questions, the Rinpoche replied, 'Muktananda is a world teacher, a great master. He is the reincarnation of one of the eighty-four mahasiddhas in the Tibetan tantric tradition.'"

How unbelievable it was! A synchronicity beyond belief! I was with Jean when she got this message, one that was particularly significant for me too. Dudjom Rinpoche's words startled me. They linked Muktananda with Tibetan Buddhism and thereby provided a bridge between the two traditions, Vipassana in which I'd been practicing for five years and Siddha Yoga, this devotional tradition from India about which I was still ambivalent. Since I was still deeply devoted to my Vipassana practice, I was amazed to hear an eminent Buddhist teacher indicating the connection between Buddhism and this eccentric Indian swami.

Even though I continued to harbor some persistent doubts in the far recesses of my mind, I was gradually drawn into this devotional tradition. The Vipassana tradition emphasized working with the mind, a deep exploration of the most subtle permutations of one's own mind-body process. Although I'd done many retreats, as soon as I read Lama Govinda's book, I recognized my longing to find not only a highly attained master but the longing for a more devotional practice. I could hardly articulate exactly what that might be, only that I experienced a yearning of the heart that hadn't been met by my Vipassana practice.

I had also been riveted by Lama Govinda's experiences with his guru Domo Geshe Rinpoche. Whatever his extraordinary state, his impact on that world was filled with mystery. Furthermore, I longed for the possibility of a teacher-student relationship that might guide my practice in the ways he had described.

My connections with the Siddha path continued to deepen and led to a major turning point in our family's life. Both Hob and I were involved in the new field of transpersonal psychology as well as our respective meditation practices. We decided to take the leap of going to India to attend the international Transpersonal Psychology Conference to be held in Bombay, as Mumbai was then called. The conference, "Ancient Wisdom and Modern Science," was a forum for exchange between new paradigm scientists from the West and spiritual leaders from the East, attracting explorers of consciousness such as Fritof Capra, Rupert Sheldrake, and Stanislav Grof, along with eminent spiritual leaders from various Eastern traditions, including Sufi Sheiks, Taoist Master Chungliang Al Huang, Benedictine monk Father Bede Griffiths, Mother Theresa, and Swami Muktananda, to name a few.

After this life-changing week when we experienced some of the most innovative, brilliant leaders in the fields of transpersonal psychology and mysticism, I returned to the ashram in Ganeshpuri for the rest of the month before returning home for work. Our daughter, Laura, who had accompanied us to India, was attending the international school at the ashram in Ganeshpuri about two hours from Bombay.

For Laura, it was a month of healing. Recently, Hob and I had been concerned about her. She suffered from an unusual endocrine condition that had stunted her growth and arrested her development in every respect. Although thirteen years old and in eighth grade, she looked about eight or nine. The smallest girl in her class back home, she was being teased, ignored, and excluded from the cliques of young adolescent girls. The humiliations that she silently endured battered her self-confidence and sent her spiraling downward. We would only discover later how much she had been wrestling with hidden pain.

When she got to the ashram school, however, she was surrounded by kids of different ages from an assortment of countries. The educational environment was based on the teachings of the yogic path with emphasis on the cultivation of qualities such as kindness, generosity, acceptance, and even including the rather startling saying, "See God in each other." They were learning Sanskrit and were easily memorizing the ashram chants, including even the longer, scriptural ones.

When we returned to the ashram from the conference, we found Laura happy and flourishing. She was now being called Purnima, the name Baba had given her. The name meant "whole" or "complete," traditionally evoking the image of the full moon. Sometimes when Indian women heard her name, they hummed with a kind of loving delight. I loved her name for an additional reason. After several difficult years at her previous school, the name implied a sense of wholeness as well as the possibility of healing because she was now in a school that honored who she was regardless of her temporary physical challenges.

For me, the rest of the month was filled with new experiences and the inspiration of ashram life—days structured around meditation, chanting, and *seva* or service, the assigned jobs that helped with the daily running of a large, international community. The Siddha Yoga ashram was situated in a small village called Ganeshpuri in a valley about two hours from Bombay (Mumbai). The original ashram had been founded by Muktananda's guru, a mysterious, wandering yogi named Bhagavan Nityananda who had had many followers. Over the years, with Muktananda's ever-growing number of followers, a sprawling cluster of buildings gradually appeared on the rolling hills of the ashram grounds.

The symbolic center of the ashram was the temple to Nityananda, called his samadhi shrine. A large, unadorned room with his silver embossed statue at the far end was the setting for chanting and worship services twice a day and a pilgrimage site for countless followers who arrived at all times of the day and night to pay their respects to their guru's statue. From the simplest country folk to formally dressed dignitaries, devotees flocked to this place as they came forward and dropped into full *pranams*, bowing until full length on the floor in front of the statue. To the devotionally inclined Indian, a statue was not an inert object but was imbued with the spirit of the guru. Devotees believed that they had come into the living presence of their guru, and their every gesture displayed that reverence. Even for me, with no background in this kind of devotional practice, it was easy to imagine a kind of force field around the statue.

Such is the power of the mind to create whatever we choose—a phenomenon that I watched in myself with a certain degree of wonder.

How did I ever get here? I sometimes wondered. Mysterious karmic connections seemed to be the inevitable answer. Surely the skeptical Western mind would summarily dismiss that explanation, but how can one disprove the inexplicable feelings of instant connection with someone newly met or other intimations of previous lives? I often felt that I belonged more to the devotional, mystical nature that is part of Indian culture than to secular, materialistic American culture with its skepticism toward anything mysterious, invisible, or spiritual.

The ashram was an incomparably beautiful place. Next to the samadhi shrine was the courtyard where the guru came each morning so that devotees could sit in his presence and go forward for *darshan*, a moment of personal connection perhaps to ask a question or simply meet in silence. With spreading shade trees, the courtyard, paved in white marble, was a quiet, cool refuge from the relentless heat of the Indian sun.

Beyond the courtyard lay extensive gardens filled with exotic plants, flowers, and trees, crisscrossed by paths leading to secluded places for quiet reflection. One path had a series of statues of Indian saints. Another led to a secluded hall where one could meditate at any time of day. Wherever one walked, there was a symphony of shifting fragrances from the wide assortment of flowering bushes and plants, the heavenly smell of jasmine here and there. At the farther end of the property rose a steep hill called Tapovan that one could climb for a view over the whole ashram complex, across the valley to the river and Mount Montagni, an impressive mountain with several caves occupied by seriously dedicated, long-term yogis whose cooking fires one might see when darkness fell.

How I loved the pre-dawn dark. Along with other ashramites who had risen as early at 3:30 a.m., I walked through the darkened gardens to the meditation cave, a room beneath the ashram's main building that was always open for meditation. Once my eyes adjusted to the dark, I would see the two large photographs at the front of the spacious room, one of Muktananda's guru Swami Nityananda, the other of Baba—the same photograph that my friend had taped to the filing cabinet in our front office.

After meditation, silent, dark figures moved along the garden paths on their way to the dining room where hot chai, a sweet, gently spiced tea, was being served. I stood in the silent line, looking up at the stars, their brilliance softened by the Indian air, heavy with heat and traces of early morning cooking. I felt a deep inner quiet, a sense of wholeness, and abundant gratitude for the gifts of this way of life.

We stood in silence outside the samadhi shrine, that revered place where the lilting song of the sparrows flying in and out of the open windows serenaded us as we waited in the pre-dawn dark. An hour and a half of chanting followed morning tea, an immersion into the power of large group chanting. After a long scriptural chant, there was a sequence of melodic chants with accelerating rhythms accompanied by a harmonium, tambouras, violins, and flutes. By the time we emerged from the chanting hall, the sun had risen, and the adjacent village was awake. Four hours had passed—the most sacred part of the day. I felt as though I'd come home.

Occasionally, a few of us would skip the early morning rituals. Well before dawn, we'd walk to the river about a mile beyond the ashram complex. We'd pick our way in the dark across the riverbed, mostly dry at that time of year, and find the hot springs, often used many years previously by Nityananda to ease his arthritic pain. Out of respect for Indian custom, we'd bathe in our long skirts, sinking into the healing, hot springs where we'd soak, sometimes in the company of a few other Indians. Still dark outside, we'd talk in whispers or remain silent, looking up at the stars and the night sky. I'd look up to Mount Montagni and see the yogis' fires, while the nearby Nityananda temple came alive with the sounds of the 5:00 a.m. chant, the sound of bells and drums drifting our way. At times like this, I felt as though I'd come home to something ancient and familiar deep within, accompanied by feelings of wholeness and freedom. I was inexpressibly happy. Warmed by the healing waters and surrounded by the faint outlines of the Indian countryside, I was in a state of grace. Personal boundaries dissolved into the profound stillness and mystery of the pre-dawn darkness as waves of gratitude washed over me.

This first visit to the ashram was a time of deepening practice and occasionally startling revelations about the inner life. Purnima and I went on several short pilgrimages to sacred sites, including a most memorable one to Nasik, one of the sites of the Kumbh Mela, a periodic gathering of millions of pilgrims. I will tell that story later. The week after our return, Purnima made a pronouncement that would rock my world as a mother.

Wearing my first sari on my 45th birthday (India, 1982)

DOORWAYS TO DEVOTION

Reflective by nature, I used to wonder where my feelings of longing might have their origins. Perhaps many spiritual seekers share this longing—an intuitive sense that there is something vast and mysterious, an ultimate freedom that beckons. Particularly during the years when I was practicing Vipassana meditation, those feelings flickered here and there, not as a dominant issue but a presence, as though a tender place in my heart was calling. Something was missing in my practice. It would be fulfilled once I started practicing in Siddha Yoga, a devotional tradition from India. That path would become both the fulfillment of my spiritual seeking and the initiation into the darkness of disillusionment.

When I began to explore the origins of my devotional impulse, I was surprised to find where it led. I trust that these reflections will also resonate with others. Of course, we are all unique beings with our particular propensities. Nevertheless, it's illuminating to recall the Indian tradition and its description of the four yogas or four paths to awakening. These four descriptions can apply to all spiritual traditions—*karma yoga* (the path of action), *bhakti yoga* (the path of devotion), *raja yoga* (the mystical path), and *jnana yoga* (the path of the intellect.) Everyone tends to have a dominant path, but often a spiritual path combines elements of all four. I identify primarily with *bhakti* and *raja yogas* but always sense the dance of all.

How, then, does this tender path of devotion unfold in one's life? As I described earlier, I carry a world of memories from my early years during the Second World War when we had to ration gas. I played alone for countless hours in the woods behind our house. I always felt the mysterious company of presences. I wasn't alone. Not only did I feel the presence of trees but also of the little creatures—chipmunks, squirrels, rabbits, and birds—that were part of my wooded neighborhood, along with other kinds of presences or spirits.

As a child, I sometimes called them fairies, a term peremptorily dismissed by most people except those who are intuitives and sense the spirits of plants, animals, and so on. That's just the word they use openly, without embarrassment, to describe invisible presences. Those who might be embarrassed are the skeptics who are enchained by the materialistic, scientific paradigm, unable to conceive of anything that can't be seen, measured, or analyzed. What a loss, for wondrous realms lie beyond intellectual prisons. Materialists miss knowing about intuitives, psychics, channels, the quantum reality of physics, and countless other modalities that access unseen, mysterious worlds, now recognized as part of the emerging new consciousness.

Whatever one may believe, I know that those carefree hours spent alone in the beauty of nature contributed to a lifelong trust in the invisible. I was fortunate to have a natural openness and curiosity about other invisible phenomena such as psychic events, premonitions, dreams, crop circles, and many other mysteries that are a natural part of the human experience.

We know that young children often live closer to the mystery. They haven't yet been conditioned by society's dictates and religion's strictures. Perhaps that accounts for the enduring love for William Wordsworth's famous poem, "Ode on Intimations of Early Childhood," especially the following excerpt:

Our birth is but a sleep and a forgetting;
The Soul that rises with us, our life's Star,
Hath had elsewhere its setting
And cometh from afar;
Not in entire forgetfulness,
And not in utter nakedness,
But trailing clouds of glory do we come
From God, who is our home:
Heaven lies about us in our infancy!

The phrase "trailing clouds of glory" probably explains why people are so mesmerized by newborns and infants. We sense something inexplicable about them that touches us—a purity, innocence, and openness pervaded by a spirit that hasn't yet been obscured by the ego-self, which becomes increasingly conditioned by family, schooling, and culture until that original purity and spirit are veiled.

I look back with appreciation at how the seeds of loving connection were nourished by growing up close to nature and having parents with a reverential attitude toward the natural world. Both parents drew our attention to beautiful cloud effects, pointed out the moon's cycles, or invited us to delight in our linden trees when radiant with bloom and humming with bees. I dare say they were both unacknowledged pantheists in how they loved the world of nature and conveyed that to us.

Age 7 with pet rabbit

My heart warms with memories of all the creatures that were part of our family—always two dogs (talked to and treated like people), guinea pigs, gerbils, chameleons, fantailed pigeons, rabbits—all these in addition to whatever creature one of us might have rescued, particularly my second brother, Ned, a biologist by nature who collected everything from wounded birds to snakes. Memorable among these was Smokey, a baby pigeon abandoned in its nest on the balcony of our eleventh floor New York apartment, who became a full-fledged family member. We took Smokey in and plied him with medicine droppers of warm liquid until, from a homely featherless body, he grew into a handsome pigeon who rode around on our heads or shoulders, traveled back and forth from the city to the country as we did, and was a dearly loved feathered friend, a full family member.

I have loving memories of another rescued friend, a baby robin that had fallen out of its nest. We four children instantly mobilized to dig worms—dozens of them—to feed its prodigious appetite. There was an urgency and dedication to saving this little being's life that stirs me when I think about it. We gave it so much care! Finally came the poignant moment when it was old enough to fly off and join its flock.

In my early adolescent years, we moved to a home on the North Shore of Long Island. Historically called Linden Hill, it had a magnificent stand of mature linden trees, two pastures with gentle hills, and a small red barn. As a passionate lover of horses, I was responsible for caring for our two horses. When I turned eleven, we got Cara, a stolid part-Morgan horse, a very ordinary horse whom I dearly loved. A second horse, a Thoroughbred named SeaSaw, was given to us to care for in her retirement from the racetrack. She stood seventeen hands high (that's big!) and had a gorgeous chestnut coat that gleamed gold in the sun. I was thrilled that she was related to the famous racehorse Sea Pirate. Since her dam was named Sawdust, she was named SeaSaw.

I spent many hours in the barn caring for the horses and also a goat and chickens. I loved the smell of manure and freshly mown hay, the dusty atmosphere of an old barn, and the company of scurrying mice and the lilting song of the swallows. There was also an old cider press that we brought out in the fall when our apple trees were heavy with fruit. Nothing compared to the hard work of manipulating the heavy metal handle to press out the juice and drink the ambrosial, fresh apple cider.

I remember feelings of deep communion with the horses. On winter nights when the temperature plummeted toward zero, I'd walk up the driveway from the barn to the house carrying their feeding bucket, boil water to mix into the bran—their favorite grain—and carry the steaming bucket back down the driveway to the welcoming smell of the barn. I would be rewarded with Cara's nickering. She knew what was coming. Then I would hear the satisfying sound of both horses munching and snuffling with pleasure as they ate their warm bran supper.

With Cara

Riding Cara bareback and backwards!

One might wonder how this litany of family animals might relate to the development of my devotional nature. I look back and appreciate how caring for animals awakened a unique form of love. We open to the spirit of the animal, sense their energy, intuit their needs, and may often find ourselves talking to them in the secret language of loving. Surely there is nothing like the unconditional love of dogs. I truly believe that these early experiences of unconditional love plant a precious seed that remains for life, that forever draws us to animals.

All of these creatures, a treasured part of our family life, cultivated a particular form of love that was open and free of the inevitable complications of human relationships. That plus the love of nature, rescuing the lives of wild creatures, caring for them, whether wild or domesticated, all involves reciprocity. The loving doesn't flow only in one direction—us toward them. Something subtle in their presence returns to us. All of it involves the cultivation of connection and care. All is nonverbal, although we talked incessantly to our dogs, even played with nonsensical words and names. How heartwarming these examples are! The connections are intuitive, a deep, felt sense of loving.

To complete this picture of how the influences from my childhood nurtured my devotional nature, here are two more examples. The first may be totally surprising, whereas the second was a natural unfolding of the devotional life.

When we moved to Cambridge in the mid-'60s, the south side of our house had an unkempt garden but a protected, sunny spot. I began to cultivate dahlias, a favorite flower with its different shades of color from deep purple to yellow to the rarest one, an orangey-apricot colored flower of the so-called dinner plate size. The enormous blooms filled me with wonder. Their tightly patterned petals unfolded from a center point, radiating out in perfect, overlapping circles like a floral replica of the *sahasra*, the crown chakra, or the thousand-petaled lotus of the yogic traditions. To make a thought-provoking connection, when the crown chakra opens through spiritual practice and eventual enlightenment, this energy center at the top of the head opens, thereby unifying individual and universal consciousness. This accounts for the halos in Christian iconography and the topknot, or raised hair mound, in portrayals of the Buddha—mystical connections indeed!

Unlikely as it may sound, I worshipped these miracles of nature. I wrote a poem to them, "Ode to Dahlias" (see Appendix). Over many years, I created beautiful arrangements for tables and altars. I gave away thousands to friends and curious people passing by. Each year in the fall, we dug up the tubers, stored them away from the freezing winters, and replanted them in the spring. I never bothered to fertilize the dahlias. They were thriving on their own. One year, my favorite orange apricot-colored dahlias grew and grew until, incredibly, they reached the second story window. I was lured onto a ladder to reach the highest blossoms and cut the heavy blooms so the plant wouldn't buckle under their weight. That moment was immortalized in a photograph to accompany an article in our local newspaper. The saga of the dahlias was truly amazing, akin to the Findhorn gardens.

Here is one further observation about these dahlias. When we behold something beautiful, the experience of duality between the object and ourselves dissolves. There is a moment of unified awareness, always a form of grace, where we may become momentarily flooded with wonder, delight, and love. No wonder that beauty transports us. The flower is beautiful, yes, but our experience of beauty lifts us beyond duality into Oneness. The momentum of the mind ceases, and we experience spaciousness and freedom—sacred moments.

It may seem like an unlikely leap from a flower's beauty to my being drawn to practicing in devotional traditions from the East, first Siddha Yoga and then Dzogchen in Tibetan Buddhism. In thinking about this devotional stream in my life, an image arises from my childhood. In early April, I would be thrilled at the sight of the first blossoms on one particular apple tree. I had a special relationship with that tree. It stood next to the pasture shed, its branches arching over the shed roof. I'd climb onto the pasture fence and from there up onto the almost flat roof. There I'd spend solitary hours reading under the gentle protection of the branches.

The promise of spring was in the air. More and more flowers opened until the whole apple tree was a magnificent display of white blossoms tinged with pink and, like the linden trees nearby, humming with the sound of bees.

My mother captured these moments in a poem called "Give Her April," which appeared in her first book of poetry. The book is divided into five sections. The poem appears in the third section called "Of Life That Must Be Freed." Given the theme of longing for freedom that pervades my story, these words are particularly meaningful. So indeed is the poem. Even though I was only a girl at the time, my mother saw me.

Give Her April

Don't call Olivia now. Leave her alone.
She's lying out on the shed roof in the sun,
The apple branches—still unleafed and bare—
Scrawling their crooked shadows on her hair,
Leave her: April will soon enough be gone.

Sun-warmed and wind-cooled, wrapped in midday peace,
She's reading the legend of the Golden Fleece,
The story of young Jason and the Argonauts
Sings like the sun in her close-budded thoughts.
She would never hear you calling: she is in ancient Greece.

Nor would she hear it if experience said
That few quests end as the Greek heroes' did:
Her faith and sureness are like the magic bough
Breaking through unknown seas on Argo's prow.
(Remember, remember, her own quest may succeed.)

Don't ever call her to you—let her know
She may stay out till sun and moon are low;
The apple branches—still unleafed and bare—
Will be in blossom soon, and she be fair;
All you can do is give her April, now.

My mother, Evelyn Ames

Like that apple tree, the signs of devotion throughout my life blossomed into fullness. As I think back, images of devotion start to unfold, some of them from meditation centers or ashrams in the United States or India—the incomparable beauty of call and response chanting accompanied by an ensemble of musical instruments; the ceremonial waving of votive lights to express devotion toward a sacred image; meditation centers where everything was done with loving attention; beautiful flower arrangements, inspiring artwork, the aroma of incense; the aspiration to live with mindfulness, leading to gentler, slower life rhythms; chanting introductory mantras before undertaking any project, much like at Findhorn except the chanting was in Sanskrit; and finally, the deep calm of the meditation hall, the heart of every center or ashram.

These examples further invite the subject of pilgrimage, a journey undertaken with a spiritual intention. My most memorable pilgrimage involved four of us, devotees living in the same ashram in India, who decided to go to Nasik, an ancient pilgrimage site on the Godavari River many hours from where we were living. In fact, each of my trips to India would be a form of pilgrimage, a return to the country that felt like home to me, a country whose culture was saturated with devotion. Come into any temple or sacred place. Devotees entered, their hands in *namaste* as they carried garlands of marigolds, waiting to come forward to the altar or statue to make their offering and then drop into a full-length *pranam*, an extended bow of reverence. How many times I, too, performed that ritual—the joy of surrendering to the deepest sources of love, whether within or without. The ultimate place of pilgrimage will always be one's own heart.

PILGRIMAGE

My memories of our pilgrimage to Nasik to visit a little-known teacher, reputedly a siddha or highly attained master, returned through a photograph that stood in a corner of our living room bookcase. Like many things around the house, familiar and unchanging, I hadn't really looked at it carefully for a long time. Something made me pick it up, like a distant treasure from the past.

Laura, age 13, at Swami's cottage

A young girl looks directly at the camera. She stands in front of a peach- colored bungalow, her figure framed by the faded blue shutters and screen door that perfectly match her loose Indian blouse with its pattern of little flowers at the yoke. In her hands she holds a modest clutch of variegated roses wrapped in newspaper, an offering she has just bought from a street vendor to bring to the person she is waiting to visit. With her light brown hair braided and pinned up across the top of her head, she looks at me, her mother with the camera, with the open, trusting smile of a girl to whom life has been kind. I notice that she has applied red sandal paste at the space between her eyebrows to mark "the third eye," a bindi, a symbolic reminder in Indian custom to cultivate one's spiritual vision.

This was my daughter, Laura, who had recently received the spiritual name Purnima, joining the many devotees who had spiritual names, including her young friends at the ashram school she was attending.

Noting the angle of her shadow against the house in the photograph, I remember now that it was still early in the morning, just after sunrise. We had just spent the night in a *dharamsala*, a public guest house that provides modest accommodation for travelers in India.

The night before, my heart sank as we entered the place. The evening breeze scattered the dust and refuse that lay in corners. The halls carried the stench of filthy latrines. As I flipped on the naked light bulb hanging from the ceiling, Purnima cried out with revulsion as several huge beetles scuttled noisily under the bed. Trying to model an equanimity that I was not feeling, I pretended to be unconcerned.

"We'll figure something out," I announced with conviction. I couldn't deal with the beetles right away.

I looked around the room—at the dirty stone floor, the wall by the mirror smeared with sandalwood paste left by women applying makeup, the two wooden beds with their thin straw pads with grimy covers. Ordinarily I welcomed simplicity, but the dirt and the wildlife unnerved me. I started by killing the mosquitoes that were drifting in the unscreened window.

"Don't worry, we'll do what we can with this place," I prattled on mindlessly as I continued to ponder the problem of the beetles. They were far too large and armored to step on. What was I going to do?

As Laura sat on the bed, her legs drawn up under her, I struggled inwardly between my excitement at being on pilgrimage in India—this land I already loved so deeply—and the reality of the moment. This is no big deal, I told myself. I'll just do what I need to do. I refuse to pay any attention to my aversion to this place.

Aversion—the word reminded me of the teachings. Since we had spent the last few weeks living at the ashram, steeped in the practices and teachings, I noticed how much they had come to permeate my thinking. Still, the beetles were retesting my resolve. With multiple legs, they were dark brown and armored like little tanks scuttling around our room. Distractedly, I thought about the first precept, the intention to practice *ahimsa* or nonviolence. I was living in the land of Gandhi, wasn't I? It was not a good time to kill beetles whose home we were visiting for a couple of nights.

I went down the hall, ferreted through the trash, and found a large jar, a possible way to catch them and carry them outside. But after several skirmishes, accompanied by Purnima's litany of revulsion, I accepted that we would have to co-exist with beetles for the night.

It was a long, restless night. The street noise continued into the early hours, a typical Indian cacophony of loud voices, rumbling vehicles, and harsh, metallic music—probably a wedding. They were renowned for going on until dawn with ruthlessly amplified music invading the night for miles around. I drifted between ragged wakefulness and troubled dreams.

I welcomed the morning and the shaft of bright sunlight that flooded through our window. We had left the ashram before dawn the previous day, and already it seemed as though days had passed. Right from the start, I had been struck by our somewhat unusual entourage. That was mainly because of our beloved friend Leonard. In truth, we had never known him as Leonard. We had always known him as Mahadev. Our guru had given him that name, a Sanskrit word meaning "great one" or "great god," an apt name to describe the extraordinary courage with which he met the progressive, debilitating disease with which he lived. He was quick to tell people that he had long outlived his prognosis, an extraordinary fact that he attributed to the mysterious, intercessory power of our guru.

Since his teenage years, Mahadev had been living with muscular dystrophy, and now, in his late thirties, he was in a wheelchair, a most unusual sight in rural India. Yesterday morning, even though it was still dark, a group of curious onlookers had clustered around the bus to watch the extraordinary maneuver of lifting Mahadev's largely inert body up the stairs of the bus and into the front seat.

In addition to Purnima and me, the fourth traveler was Joe, also known as Govardin. He had joined us as Mahadev's personal assistant. He was tall and physically strong, a gentle, thoughtful man who would have been grateful, I thought to myself, to spend the rest of his life in long, solitary meditative practice. He, too, had a dharma name, a common practice among students committed to a guru. Asking for a spiritual name signified not only one's devotion but also reminded one that there is a larger perspective than the personal story that gets attached to a birth name. The name Govardin means "the cave of the heart," and although I scarcely knew him, I was struck by the deep inner quiet that pervaded his presence.

We had spent six hours on a hot, crowded bus traversing the state of Maharashtra to reach the town of Nasik, a place of pilgrimage with many ancient temples and holy places in its environs. It is also one of the sites for the Kumbh Mela when literally millions of seekers stream in from all over India to spend a week or more participating in continuous worship, ritual, and ceremonies.

We, too, had come to visit the sacred sites around Nasik, but our primary reason was to meet a swami named Prakashananda who lived quietly on the outskirts of this central Indian town. Only a handful of Westerners had found their way to his door. He had visited our ashram and was known to give generously of his time and wisdom. In Indian culture where the goal of self-realization is assumed to be the purpose of human life, it is considered a blessing to meet exceptional teachers. Even though we had come to India to spend time with Muktananda, we also wanted to make this pilgrimage to Nasik to meet another much-loved swami who was reputed to be a siddha, a highly realized master of meditation.

There were rumors that Baba had invited this swami to be his successor. The swami had refused, apparently saying that he did not want to give up his commitment to his small coterie of students to become the head of a vast yoga network that was rapidly spreading across Europe, South America, and the United States. He did not want to become a "hotel guru."

As we left the dharamsala and headed off into the noisy, crowded street, I noticed how many people turned to take another look at the slightly hunched, bearded man in a wheelchair, his tall, quiet attendant, my thirteen-year-old daughter, and me. I walked beside Mahadev's chair, feeling protective, remembering our meeting several years before.

It had been in the late 1970s on my first trip to an ashram in the States to meet the charismatic Indian guru informally called Baba. Wherever he went, he seemed to create a stir. At that time, many people began to explore the meditation traditions. He was acclaimed for being not only a master of meditation but also for his power to awaken profound levels of spiritual energy in seekers who came to him. I had initially been puzzled, even put off, by the ashram scene that he presided over—the many people, the Sanskrit chants, the Indian cultural overlay, his eccentricities. On the other hand, I couldn't deny that I was deeply affected by Baba's presence. I loved the chanting and meditation, all taking place in an exceptionally beautiful place, all touching me in unexpected ways.

I met Mahadev in the midst of this confusion of responses. I was still living with the question from several days before when Howard Thurman had asked me, "So which will it be, the swami or me?" Mahadev listened deeply, accepting my confusion. He seemed like a refuge in this wildly stimulating scene. He chuckled and laughed, childlike and wise at the same time, radiating warmth like an open fire and stability like a mountain. Our bond was instant and deep. He became like a brother to me, a beloved friend, the person I gravitated to whenever I returned to the ashram. And so it was with Purnima too. She invariably went to find him. For him, as he once said, she was the daughter that he never had. Shortly after our pilgrimage, these words would take on new meaning.

As we followed our directions through one winding street after another, I noticed that I was feeling exceptionally buoyant and happy, a welcome shift from my agitation and doubts of the night before. I loved the noisy chaos of Indian street scenes—people, animals, and vehicles proceeding in total disorder; shouting, singing, distant chanting and temple bells; the assault of smells, from flowers to burning dung, cooking food, and other exotic smells, including the stink of sewage in the open gutters.

Finally, we reached the landmark that took us off the street onto a beaten path across an arid field. The wheelchair bumped and twisted over the rutted Indian soil. The sun had just risen above the distant hills, illuminating ahead of us a small grove of trees, their leaves limp, almost lifeless from the ruthless sun. A simple, peach-colored adobe bungalow stood to the right of the trees where the path was leading.

Even though it was only 7 a.m., it was a relief to be invited by the swami's assistant into the dark, cool room. As my eyes adjusted to the shadowy interior, I became aware of a spare room that had only a large altar at one end and beside it a long, webbed plastic lawn chair, obviously the place where the swami would sit. We settled onto the stone floor while Joe maneuvered Mahadev's wheelchair into position.

A door opened. An old man appeared wearing the orange of a renunciant, the faded cotton garment draped loosely around his body. He walked serenely with mindful steps.

"Good morning, and welcome," he said with a strong Indian accent. As he settled himself into the green and white lawn chair, we answered with a little chorus of "good morning" and then silence.

My attention had already wandered to his elaborate altar, typical of those who worship in the *bhakti* tradition, the devotional path of practice, one of the major spiritual traditions of India. It is called the path of love, claimed by some to be the easiest way to self-realization. The altar was adorned with large pictures of Indian saints and deities, some actual photographs and others the garishly colored paintings typical of much Indian religious art. In every picture, the image had been anointed with *kumkum*, the red paste applied as a form of ritual worship, lending a slightly tawdry, messy look to the whole arrangement. There were also fresh flowers, several candles, and an incense burner from which a plume of smoke arose.

I struggled between two worlds. To my Western eyes, the altar was garish, culturally inaccessible, vaguely outrageous. Who was this man who now rested quietly, utterly at home in the deep silence that pervaded his room? Apparently, he experienced no need to speak, even though the four of us had finally arrived after a long, arduous trip to visit him.

How did I ever get to this moment? What questions would I ask him anyway? Who was he, and how did one know if a person was a siddha? Enlightened, they said, supposedly established in an illumined state that can deeply touch the receptive seeker. I'd already received initiation from another swami, supposedly enlightened. We'd traveled far to experience the presence of this man, hear his teachings, see what might happen. Once the door of spiritual longing opened, the impulse was to open it wider.

A siddha—I loved the word and didn't know why, perhaps because it evoked images of a freedom that I had fantasized about even as a child. That child, four or five years old, wanted to lose herself in the inexpressible beauty of the world. A dreamer, she wanted to leave her body, fly out and away from the suffering she experienced and saw all around her but which no one seemed to talk about. Why didn't they? Why didn't someone talk about the mystery of it all—why we're here, what it's all about, where we're all going? I was a child wrestling with impossible questions, trying to fit the pieces of a puzzle together, the impossible assortment of pieces scattered like fallen leaves in random patterns, beautiful, helpless, torn away from their home on the way to death.

As my mind chattered on, throwing up questions and challenges, I noticed that my heart was beating hard, disturbing me and the palpable serenity that pervaded this room. No one had spoken since the swami's initial greeting. There was just silence . . . silence gradually becoming comfortable . . . finally still like a forest pool on a windless day . . . reflecting everything in a flawless mirror . . . no leaves, no irregular pieces, no thoughts . . . only an endless, open moment.

"They've come from Ganeshpuri," the swami's assistant, Harinam, said quietly.

"Ah," said the swami, a murmur of appreciation.

"Why don't you introduce yourselves?" Harinam continued. Words seemed invasive in the stillness. Mahadev spoke first. Then after a short silence, Purnima spoke up.

"My name is Purnima," she started out, using the spiritual name Baba had recently given her. "I'm thirteen and I've come to India with my mother."

The swami gestured to her, beckoning her forward. She handed him the bouquet of roses, which he accepted with a nod and a smile. He was a warm, twinkling presence. His face was craggy and unshaven. He looked at Purnima with all the tenderness of a grandfather meeting a beloved granddaughter.

She sat on her knees in front of him. He reached out his big, gnarled hand and took one of hers.

"I know you," he said enigmatically, looking directly into her eyes. After a long pause, he repeated it. "I know you."

My mind stopped on the brink of an unfamiliar abyss. Then came a waterfall of commentary. *What's that supposed to mean? Why was he greeting her that way? Was it because she was the youngest? Was I supposed to read some mystery into those words? Was he saying that he knew her from another lifetime?*

I felt as if I had been catapulted into another dimension of reality where the world, as I ordinarily knew it, had slipped into the unfamiliar. Nothing looked or felt quite the same anymore. How had I ever ended up in this semi-darkened room with its exotic altar in the company of an inscrutable, kindly old man who treated my daughter like his own? I was excited and troubled simultaneously. I trusted, and then I questioned.

This was India where the division between the visible and invisible worlds seemed to dissolve in an instant, where people believed, perhaps too easily, in things the rational mind couldn't possibly understand such as remembered lives or synchronous meetings or visions—the mysterious, even the miraculous, woven into a seamless, sacred whole. This world of stories, myth and ritual intrigued me, pulled me into its gentle embrace. I felt like a child being gathered into the welcoming arms of the Great Mother, Bharat Mata, Mother India.

This was also India the land of paradox where appalling poverty, squalor, and sudden violence shattered the images of rural serenity, natural beauty, and sacred places; a land of extremes that shook the mind out of its complacency; a land where the battle between darkness and the light was represented by the dance of Shiva, the archetype of creation and destruction, his wild dance portraying, finally, the ultimate order of the universe.

During the next three days, the swami orchestrated our visit. We sat in his little room, listening as he wove stories, teachings, and homilies into an effortless stream of talk. We joined the devotees who came for evening chanting. He suggested the places for us to visit—the cave where Sita and Ram hid out in the epic story of the Ramayana; sacred places along the Godavari River; shrines and temples, especially Trimbhakeshwar of which he said, "You must visit that ancient temple and meditate there."

After a dramatic drive that took us north from Nasik, a landscape startling for its steep, mountainous outcroppings, we arrived in Trimbhakeshwar. This ninth century temple had been built over one of India's natural jyoti lingams, a place where nature in her exuberance erupts from the ground in the form of an abundant spring that continuously bubbles over three stone protrusions called lingams because they resemble the creative, phallic form that symbolizes Shiva. This was sacred ground. This was sacred water—a great mystery perpetually unfolding before the vast stream of pilgrims who journeyed here to experience it.

I approached the railing that kept the pilgrims at a discreet distance from the holy place that was tended by three Brahmin priests. I leaned closer and saw the water bubbling up and spilling over the rock protrusions, the Mother in her abundance, creating the wellspring of the Godavari River, one of India's many sacred rivers that farther downstream at Nasik was one of the scenes of the Kumbh Mela where millions of pilgrims and holy ones came to worship every twelve years. This was the Source—the headwaters of a great river, the Goddess emerging from the earth in the form of water to nourish the land and inspire worship of the sacred in this form.

I moved away to allow other pilgrims to come close. I found a dark corner of the temple away from the crowds and sat with closed eyes. Even as I was aware of the agitated noise of an Indian temple, I dropped into a deep state of meditation. All sense of limitation and separateness dropped away as the mind became absorbed by the deep silence that underlies the restlessness of the ordinary mind. Gone. Gone beyond.

So deep was the holiness of this temple, of these moments, that had someone announced that I should die at that moment, I would have accepted it as another part of the mystery that permeated this place and willingly left my body to dwell in the peace of death.

After a while, I opened my eyes again to the temple scene where pilgrims moved slowly through the dusky light to make their offerings, drop to the floor in full pranam, and express their devotion in timeless rituals. How was it that I felt so at home in this place, sitting in that darkened corner, watching the play of brilliant light streaming in the open windows? Fleetingly, I noticed the warmth radiating in the center of my chest and remembered having heard once that the ultimate place of pilgrimage is one's own heart.

The pilgrimage to Nasik and Trimbhakeshwar ended the next day when we returned in the early morning to thank the swami and say our farewells. By that time, I was aware of how comfortable I now felt in the swami's presence and with everything around him—the garish altar, his dilapidated plastic chaise lounge, and the crepuscular light that contributed to the dreamlike feeling of the place. The four days had been a magical time filled with surprises. From traveling with Mahadev in his wheelchair to the Indian countryside with its dramatic rock protrusions, to the visits with the swami, to the temples, I felt suspended in a timeless state, filled with grace.

Shortly after the pilgrimage to Nasik, we were scheduled to return home to the United States, which at this point seemed as far away as the moon. We'd been immersed in a totally different lifestyle through living at an ashram, which was like a subculture with its own forms and practices, utterly different from life at home. Furthermore, we were in India, a country so different and challenging that it invariably elicited very strong opinions between those who loved the country and those who abhorred it, who were simply unable to tolerate the chaos, poverty, and suffering.

For Laura, then thirteen years old and still a young teenager who had already been involved with Siddha Yoga for several years, one might well ask how this story began for her and how she ended up in this tradition. She began coming with me to the evening programs at a center near us in Cambridge. Musically gifted, she loved the chanting. The pleasingly melodic chants were accompanied by a small assortment of musical instruments, usually a harmonium (a small keyboard), along with various other instruments such as guitar, flute, and maybe a violin. The chants were call and response, making it natural to follow the lead chanter and respond with the melodic lines, all of this in Sanskrit, an easily transliterated language. The chanting was beautiful, even mesmerizing, as it invited one to turn within and absorb the beauty of these ancient chants.

Furthermore—and unusual for a meditation tradition—families with children were very welcome. There were special programs for the children, and one would often see clusters of kids not only playing the hand cymbals in the chants but happily hanging out together. Laura was very much a part of these groups.

Laura was only eleven when one evening in darshan she went forward on her own to ask Baba if she could attend a meditation intensive. There were no intensives for children at that time, so she would be the only child participating in a weekend of talks, chanting, and long meditations. Her intention was striking for one so young. She hadn't said anything to me about it; she had simply proceeded independently.

Gradually she, too, became involved in this spiritual community where she felt welcomed and secure, a vivid contrast to her school. It was at that first intensive that Baba gave her the name Purnima—a beautiful name, I thought, because it seemed to promise a wholeness that she desperately needed to reclaim.

When Hob and I decided to make our first trip to India to attend the Transpersonal Psychology Conference, we already knew there was an international school at the ashram that she could attend during our month's stay. She wanted to come with us for by now, she loved this community and knew some of the people who would be there. The ashram school where she felt accepted and appreciated was a welcome change from her school at home. After only three weeks, she was thriving. It was in that last week before our return when she announced, "Mom, I don't want to go back home with you next week. I want to stay here as long as I can. Can't I finish my school year here? Please?"

"Well, this isn't exactly a surprise," I replied as a wave of anxiety flared through my body. How would I ever decide between my protectiveness as a mother and at the same time wanting to respect her request. This conflict had just rocked my world as her mother.

"I somehow knew you'd ask," I said, "but we've only got a few days left. If you stay, it will involve a lot of rearranging of things, and I don't know if it can all be done in time."

"Mahadev could be my guardian," she continued. "You know how much I love him, and I know he'd really watch out for me. We already hang out together a lot. Also, I'm sure we'll be able to find someone who'll be coming back in June when monsoon starts who could bring me back with them."

"Let's see what we can do," I told her. "I'll also have to talk to Dad about it. And you know his worries about Siddha Yoga, the guru, the whole scene here. We'll have to see what happens."

"Okay, Mom, but I really want to stay. *Really*!" she said emphatically. She hugged me enthusiastically and then disappeared up the path that led to the ashram school that she had come to love so much.

Her determination was striking. I wanted to support her, young as she was. But nothing quieted my turbulent feelings at the prospect of leaving her alone in India, even if Mahadev was to be her guardian. At thirteen and such a young thirteen at that, I ricocheted between excitement and anxiety, carrying the worries deep in my body where a mother holds the mysterious, incomparable bond to a daughter. I envied her being able to stay yet pushed away the questions that haunted the edges of my attention. *What if she gets sick? Or homesick? Or if something unforeseen happens?*

I reassured myself by knowing what a welcoming and safe environment the ashram was. There were many hundreds of devotees from America, Europe, and Australia, and it was a well-run spiritual community with a fine medical clinic, healthy food both Western and Indian, and daily schedules organized around chanting, meditation, and *seva* (the jobs that everyone had to help with the running of the ashram). I knew how much I had felt embraced and supported by the community. That was very clearly how Purnima felt as well.

As I started to rearrange plans, I noticed how much I was replaying the history that led us to this point, trying to reassure myself that all would be right with this decision. Now obviously happy and at home, she was blossoming in this spiritual community. She loved the school and had many friends, not only other youngsters but older people as well. Why should I have any doubts?

By a series of events that seemed to unfold seamlessly, I managed to reach Hob by phone in New Delhi where he'd gone to do further healing work with a remarkable Bengali woman who had treated his painful post-dysentery symptoms while at the conference. Hob always threaded his way carefully through the spiritual traditions we'd explored together. By nature, he was fiercely independent, often counterdependent, and particularly leery of people in positions of power. Baba certainly fell into that category. Hob's skepticism was hard for me, for he kept finding ways to relentlessly question and judge the path of devotion that was now the organizing principle in my life.

In spite of his judgments and maybe because Laura was now also involved, Hob occasionally accompanied me to various ashrams. To his consternation, Baba would single him out of crowds and make a point of telling him where he'd last seen him. This disproved Hob's contention that Baba couldn't possibly know all the devotees who were drawn to him. At the plenary session of the Transpersonal Psychology Conference, Baba was one of the keynote speakers, and when he entered the vast hall where 500 people waited, he walked up the aisle and stopped by Hob, took both his hands, and looked at him very directly. Granted, Hob stood out. He was in a wheelchair due to his temporary disability, but once again it proved to Hob that Baba was making a point of connecting with him.

When Laura, now called Purnima, went up to ask Baba if she could finish the year at the ashram school, he affirmed her wish but said that she needed to get her father's permission. Somewhat to my surprise, when I finally reached Hob and explained the situation, he readily agreed. He already knew what a positive experience she was having at the school. All the pieces for her finishing the school year in India had now fallen in place.

It is sunrise, just after the early morning chant. A little group of us are gathered in front of the ashram gate to await the bus that will take me on the first leg of the long journey home. Mahadev, lighthearted and merry, sits in his wheelchair, the center of this animated circle of friends gathered to see me off. Purnima stands beside him, her hand on his shoulder. I stand by her other side, holding her hand. She is dressed in her favorite blue punjabi with its pattern of white flowers, her light brown hair braided and pinned in a crown on top of her head, her bare feet in thongs.

Where are my words? Anything I say sounds disembodied, hollow. I feel suspended between worlds—between ashram life, my spiritual home, and my other life back in the States, as distant and unreal as if it were a novel, the story of someone's else's life. I feel as though part of me has already left; another part can't bear this leaving. If I had any choice, I'd stay here indefinitely.

"Mom, I'll write you a lot. Don't worry about me. We'll be fine," Purnima says, speaking already as one of this little family of friends who have become deeply, inexplicably bonded.

"I know you'll be fine, but it's really hard to go," I reply as I hear the belching, bouncing sound of the bus coming around the corner of the rutted country road. Hurriedly, I move around the circle, hugging each friend. I can hardly breathe by the time I get to Mahadev's big, inert body.

"Goodbye, Maha. Take good care of Purnima She's your daughter now."

And then to Purnima, my eyes brimming with tears, "Goodbye, Purns. I love you so much. This is wonderful. I'm so happy for you, but I can hardly bear to leave."

"Goodbye Mom. I love you too. A lot! I'll be fine."

She holds on to me long and hard, pressing her head into my chest. I can feel the pressure of her braids against me and the soft cotton fabric of her punjabi.

How can I be leaving? This is unbearably painful.

Everyone helps to wrestle the bags up the steps as I climb onto the bus and to a window on their side.

"Goodbye!" "Have a good trip!" "Goodbye!" Then there are a few moments of sign language through the window as the bus starts to pull away. I'm still struggling to breathe, flipping wildly between laughter and sobs, my body heaving with a violence of feeling I've never experienced. In the core of my being, I feel as if something is being torn away from me. My heart is breaking open with grief and love.

The bus rounds the corner where the side road forks to Vajeshwari, the next village with the goddess temple. We visited there just a couple of days ago. We'd climbed the wide row of steps to the little temple with its image of the goddess bedecked with garlands of marigolds, offerings from the devotees who traveled to this oasis of devotion. I remember thinking that in Vajeshwari, as in all Indian temples, there is a sense of disarray—flowers dropped from offerings, bits of trash, devotees talking, the heavy smell of incense—yet in spite of it all, an atmosphere of devotion transcends the unlikely chaos.

Between the convulsions of feeling, I start humming the devi chant from the temple. "Keep chanting . . . keep chanting . . . just keep chanting." I propel myself into the words, passionately coaching myself through the tumultuous feelings.

I'm on my way home.

A SEA OF DOUBTS

The phone rings, startling me. I resent that the phone is ringing at all for I'm in Vermont for the long weekend. I am totally immersed in the annual ritual of planting our garden—a silent, mysterious process of reawakening my relationship to the earth after the winter. Long, quiet hours working the earth, smelling the damp soil, planting seeds, transplanting seedlings, hearing only the call of birds, the sound of insects interspersed with the silence of the remote Vermont mountainside.

The metallic ringing violates a sacred space. Hob and I have been home from India for four months, long enough to be deeply reinvolved with our lives yet still in touch with India through frequent, enthusiastic letters from Purnima.

"Olivia?"

"Yes."

"This is Jack Kornfield."

"Jack! How did you know we were here? How did you ever find our phone number?"

I'm stunned that Jack is calling. He is my husband's primary meditation teacher, and we haven't seen him since the previous winter in India where our paths had crossed several times.

"Hold on, I'll get Hob," I say.

"No, I wasn't calling to speak with Hob. I wanted to speak with you."

"Oh." Inexplicably, I feel a stab of concern. Is it something about the tone of his voice? What could he possibly want to talk to me about?

"Yes," he continues. "It's about what's going on at the ashram in Ganeshpuri, information I thought you should know because I remembered that your daughter is still there."

As I stand by the window, leaning on the high sill, looking out over the pond, images of the ashram begin to flash across my mind—the courtyard with its cool, white marble and shade trees and cascading flowers, the acres of exquisite gardens, the deep dark of the meditation cave, the sound of ox carts and shrill voices from the street outside the ashram walls. In seconds I seem to be standing in two realities at once.

Jack's voice continues. "I was talking yesterday with some good friends of mine who have been living at the ashram with their two teenage daughters. A few weeks ago, the daughters began telling them about what was going on, especially with the girls living in the teen dorm. It seems that night after night, these young girls are being summoned to Baba for sexual exploitation."

Now I'm hearing only pieces of his account of sexual encounters, flagrantly numerous, some with girls as young as thirteen or fourteen. His friends left the ashram within twenty-four hours after hearing these stories.

I listen in a panic of disbelief as Jack's steady voice goes on. A fire suddenly rages around my heart and then spreads through my entire body like rapids of molten lava, a meltdown in my gut, a volcano at night, rivers of fire coursing down its slopes, ears roaring, heart pounding so loud, I struggle for the next breath, the next thought. I feel as though the world is dissolving around me.

Jack's voice continues with the same steady assurance.

"I thought you should know all this because I was concerned for your daughter's safety."

I struggle to reply. My voice sounds strained and distant as if coming down a long, desolate tunnel of anguish.

"Oh no, Jack. I can't believe it. That's just incredible. Baba? How could he, a siddha? He's surely beyond that kind of thing. I mean, are you sure? That just doesn't seem possible!"

"I know. They're very disturbing reports, but I knew you would want to know."

Questions race through my mind. Baba's reputedly a siddha, an enlightened meditation master, established in a supreme state of consciousness, they say. How could he be interested in young girls? Given such exalted states of consciousness, why would anything physical even appeal? It doesn't add up. How does Jack know for sure? Teenage girls have vivid fantasy lives. How do I find out for myself?

"Jack, I'm so stunned, I don't know what to say. I just can't put the pieces together. I guess I've got to do something, but—"

"I know. It's very distressing, hard to believe, and painful what people must be going through. But let me know if I can be of any further help."

"Well—" I hesitate. "Thanks for calling." I hardly recognize my constricted, hollow voice as we conclude the call with the usual pleasantries.

I hang up the phone and stand frozen, looking intently out the window, blind to the beautiful mountainside in front of me. I struggle to contain the fires of disbelief and fear raging through my body. I'm vividly aware of the realities at war within me. What am I supposed to believe now?

Jack is a highly respected meditation teacher, one of the leading Vipassana teachers in the West, a reliable, well-intentioned source. But Baba's a siddha. Then come the echoing words—sexual exploitation, young girls.

Now I feel a wave of anger at Jack for being the one to bear this news. Images of Ganeshpuri struggle to displace the seamy images. I see Baba sitting on his dais in that supremely beautiful courtyard, sitting before a crowd of people—people from all over the world, thousands of them, Indians, cosmopolitan ones from the cities, humble ones from the neighboring villages, scores of devotees from around the world. Baba pours out love and guidance, wisdom and inspiration, playfulness. How could he be fooling around with young girls?

What about Purnima? That's why Jack called, yet my first reactions aren't about her. I trust somehow that none of this could be touching her. She's protected because she's still pre-adolescent and looks like a nine-year-old girl. She *must* be all right. And besides, she'll be coming home in a few weeks anyway.

Struggling to calm myself, I open the door to return to the garden. How will I ever explain all this to Hob? He's been leery about this path ever since I first became involved. He and I have shared so much between our training in psychology and meditation, yet with my commitment to this devotional tradition, our paths have diverged. I am aware of my racing thoughts, and a memory surfaces. I remember how Phil, one of our colleagues, had volunteered a surprising comment. "Hob has a peek-a-boo heart," he had said. It was a thought-provoking observation about this husband of mine. Hob adored Ethan and Laura but didn't express his love verbally. He shared his love of music as he sang lullabies to them before bed, accompanying them on his guitar. Or he would burst into song on our family car trips, sharing his musical passion as we sang rounds together; that is, until one of us messed up our favorite, the challenging one, "A sad and weary traveler was weary from his wandering." With his tendency to be judgmental, Hob would make a sharp correction, and the three of us would collapse into disappointed silence. Other times, he lovingly taught Ethan how to fish or shared his love of literature with Laura, long readings where he impersonated the characters with delight and impeccable accents. Becoming a father at forty-two had challenged him, yet I could see how much he loved our children, this man with his peek-a-boo heart.

I came back to the reality of Jack's profoundly disturbing call. *I must find out the truth of what's happened. I must talk to a senior swami. I'll also write to Swami Chidvilasanda, formerly Malti, Baba's translator, now one of his two successors. I will ask for a private meeting when she returns from India to the ashram in the Catskills.*

But there's still a deeper struggle. How do I hold two such divergent, warring realities? First are my experiences of Baba—the beautiful, powerful practices, the chanting, this beloved community, the deepening of spiritual life. And then there is the looming, dark shadow of rumors, violations, violence. How can they both be true?

I was determined to face this crisis head on. The next time I was at the Catskills ashram, I met with one of the swamis as well as talked with senior teachers and many trusted friends also struggling to understand. Beneath the surface of this sprawling, beautiful ashram, there was an undercurrent of distress with many devotees trying to sort through rumors that didn't fit their perceptions of the path. Everyone was as troubled as I was by the stories, as well as by an article that appeared in the *CoEvolution Quarterly*.

I was not alone in finding it almost impossible to decipher the official explanations for what had happened. The swami had said something about esoteric Tantric practices, which Westerners wouldn't understand. The most repetitive response was, "Don't listen to the rumors, but trust your own experience." This was a very indicative statement. There was a lot of emphasis given to "experiences" in this devotional tradition. The awakening of kundalini was the heart of the initiation, and many of the practices focused on nurturing and amplifying that ineffable, sacred energy. The most common word in this community was *shakti*, a reference to this subtle energy and how it manifests in practice and daily life. As a result, countless people were often having very memorable experiences.

In all the programs, every talk was usually crafted around the telling of at least one thought-provoking, sometimes truly dramatic story about the guru—spiritual awakenings, meditation experiences, or seemingly impossible occurrences. This view of the meditative path was almost diametrically opposite from the Vipassana tradition where a central teaching involved non-attachment, including to any kind of meditative experience or mystical opening.

I'd never forgotten an interview with a well-known teacher, famous for her direct, painful confrontations with us when she saw any signs of attachment. When I shared one of my first mystical revelations during a meditation, understandably profoundly affected by it, she cut my attachment to shreds. Tears poured down my face. I was shattered that something so precious could be torn away from me.

When I wrote to Chidvilas, a shortened version of her swami name, she replied immediately, saying that we should meet when she returned from India. The time arrived, and I found my way to where her office was located. As in any guru tradition, an aura of mystery surrounds the guru and their immediate associates. Some combination of tradition, mystique, and the devotion of countless seekers heightens the intensity around them.

I feel the charged atmosphere as I wait for the appointment. As successor to an internationally celebrated guru, Chidvilas is also treated with great respect. The hallway, restricted to only specified visitors, hums with the earnest bustle of her assistants. People speak in hushed voices. Instinctively, I watch carefully to decipher the protocol of the carefully orchestrated environment.

Her first secretary summons me. Aware of being nervous, I've already imagined this moment many times and rehearsed how to ask the questions that might put to rest the appalling allegations against Baba. As I walk in, Chidvilas remains seated behind her desk. She greets me with the warm equanimity that characterizes her role as Baba's translator. I notice the sunlight streaming across her desk and the willow tree framed in the window that looks out to a courtyard beyond. On the walls hang several large photographs of Baba. A lavish display of yellow roses adorns a table, and the space smells faintly of incense.

Even though she has recently been designated a successor, a rare and remarkable honor in Indian culture, I'm struck by how young she looks. Dressed in the orange of a renunciant, her head is closely shaven, the black hair beginning to grow back from the shaving ceremony, part of her initiation as a swami only a few weeks earlier. Still in her late twenties, she is a beautiful woman whose presence conveys self-assurance and authority. She had already traveled the world and had extensive experience as Baba's translator.

She takes the initiative and rescues me momentarily from the dilemma of how to start a difficult conversation. She thanks me for writing about my concerns and proceeds to talk about Baba, about his greatness and power, about the countless people he has touched, about her unbounded love for him. Based on her devotion, on scripture, on the irrefutability of his worldwide impact as a rare master of meditation, she provides a formidable defense of Baba.

She pauses, and I start to reply. "Yes, but I'm still concerned about everything I've heard."

"Of course, around a great siddha there will always be rumors," she continues. "Their power is misunderstood. There will always be people who misinterpret the mysterious actions of a siddha. The problem is their limited vision. The most important thing is not to let your faith be shaken. Trust your own experiences, not the gossip. Baba's greatness is beyond measure. That's what you should never forget."

As she continues to extol him, my questions seem to dissolve. All I hear is her extraordinary respect and devotion for him. In an earnest, touching way, she reveals her gratitude, even awe, toward the one who had trained her since she was a girl.

She speaks, too, of her brother, appointed as the other successor, expressing her great affection and respect for him. He is even younger than she, barely twenty years old, "a very old soul," she explains as if to account for his being given the name Nityananda—the name of Baba's guru and a famous *avadhut*—a reference to the greatness being born in her brother even at this stage of his young life.

Chidvilas's unflinching faith and easy responses assuage my worst fears. Of course, Baba couldn't have sexually exploited young women, I reassure myself. How could he, not only given the state of a siddha but also my experience of him as the most powerful, supremely free, and liberated being I'd ever met.

Toward the end of our meeting, she starts talking about one of her exceptionally able assistants named George Afif, the tall, striking Lebanese man who is her bodyguard, always in her presence, clearly the alpha male in the ashram, having authority even over the swamis.

"He's a beautiful man, isn't he?" she asks rhetorically, speaking to me more like a sister than a guru's successor. Her words reverberate between us, a peculiar observation from a renunciant swami. A few years later, these words would come back to haunt me, part of this unfolding story.

Immediately after leaving her office, I began to remember the other questions I had intended to ask. How could I have forgotten? What happened in our meeting? Had she exerted some hidden power over me, or was it the power of projection inevitably at play around a powerful figure? I felt both exhilarated and uneasy, vaguely aware that I had accepted her explanations because they corresponded with what I desperately wanted to believe. In another corner of my mind, I was unconvinced, doubtful, and troubled. How indeed do we hold these opposing forces, such differing interpretations that pull and tear at each other in a mighty, internal struggle?

A DRAMATIC AWAKENING

Occasionally, messages in our lives seem to drop into the deeper recesses of our psyches, awaiting that moment when we will need them. I had received one of those messages at a talk by Ram Dass, well-known and much-loved luminary who brought Eastern philosophy and practices to the West. I remember sitting among a thousand people in a Boston University gym as he talked about his guru, Neem Karoli Baba, and other extraordinary teachers he'd met during his travels in the East. To paraphrase his words, "It's always important to understand the difference between the teacher and the teachings. The teacher may be giving talks filled with wisdom, scriptural references, and humor, but look carefully at how they're living. Are they living the teachings, or is there a discrepancy between the two?"

I had fallen into that perplexing space between the guru and the teachings. The depth of my inner life on this path had held me in my love of the practices. Fortunate to have practiced almost six years in the Vipassana tradition before I'd gotten involved with Siddha Yoga, I continued to meditate more in that tradition with its emphasis on open awareness than with use of a mantra, the basic practice of Siddha Yoga. Despite my doubts about the rumors surrounding Muktananda, I still felt dedicated to the devotional dimension, pulled toward practices that inspired my inner life and opened realms beyond the limited self such as chanting, scriptural recitation, and various ritual practices. These continued to flourish at the deepest levels of my being, untouched by the surface stories of what may have happened.

How does one describe this ineffable process? Was it compartmentalizing, rationalizing, or dissociating? Or was it all three? Despite my years of psychological training, these questions fell more into the murkier category of one's faith or belief—perilous territory as I would eventually find out.

Almost eight years had passed since Laura was thirteen and had spent her spring semester at the ashram school in India. It had been late May when I received the call from Jack Kornfield with the alarming stories about Muktananda's involvement with young girls in the ashram. I was shattered by the news, incredulous at first. It was only three weeks until her scheduled return. I took solace in the fact that she still looked like a little girl. Whatever the situation with Muktananda, I lived with that uneasy rationalization until she arrived home from India, radiant and happy.

Now she had started talking about her intention to spend a gap year serving on staff in India before her junior year in college. I was excited for her at the prospect of that kind of immersion in the ashram culture that I, too, had come to love so deeply. Meanwhile, having made an uneasy truce with the shadow side of Siddha Yoga, I continued to practice, teach, and do retreats.

In the month before Laura was to leave for India, an astonishing sequence of events started to unfold. We had gone to the Catskills ashram along with Elena, my niece by marriage. Elena was in her late twenties, having married my nephew a couple of years earlier. She was a tall, statuesque woman with blonde hair, blue eyes, and a warm, ready laugh. When we first met, she told me that she had always been a "sensitive," someone particularly susceptible to the subtle influences around her—in other words, psychically very open. She also said that she had been a sleepwalker as a child, sometimes interpreted as happening due to a state of non-ordinary consciousness.

During the weekend of intensive practice, Elena started going through an exceptionally extreme manifestation of a powerful kundalini awakening. This heightened state, utterly compelling and dramatic, was to continue for about three weeks, although that timing, which was to become significant, was something she couldn't possibly have known then. Since I'd already been part of this tradition for some years, I'd heard many talks and taken courses that described the potential power of the practices that we were all engaged in. Siddha Yoga emphasized the centrality of one's meditative experience. This was both a source of inspiration and a lure into attachment, an obstacle on the path. Nevertheless, because I was steeped in the teachings, I was well prepared to deal with what was about to unfold with Elena.

Such amplified experiences were sometimes an integral part of this path of yoga, a combination of the emphasis on energy practices, the centrality of the guru—especially someone like Muktananda and his successor, Gurumayi, who could awaken kundalini in their devotees—and the ashram environment itself, a cauldron of intensity fired by many hundreds of devotees and the cumulative force of their devotional practices.

Elena experienced a classic awakening reminiscent of the early mystics who were sometimes taken over by the power of spiritual energy that totally disrupted ordinary life, like the spiritual ecstasies of Theresa of Avila. For Elena, this involved many of the classical signs such as the involuntary physical movements known as *kriyas*, as well as rapidly changing hand *mudras*, the inability to eat, cascades of laughter, and an inordinate sensitivity to all spiritual stimuli, whether the scent of incense, religious photos, or the sound of chanting. To Purnima and me, who accompanied her through these next days, Elena was clearly possessed by a powerful force over which she had no control. Although she was in a state of ecstasy all the time, some manifestations of the kundalini energy were exceptionally dramatic. For example, Laura and I had to hold her, one of us on each side, as we went down the *darshan* line approaching Gurumayi. Elena's body began to undulate like a snake, a dramatic manifestation of the kundalini, a spiritual force that is symbolized by the undulating, snake-like energy as it rises up the spine.

Once the three of us got through *darshan* and into the outer hallway, Elena's body was seized by a paroxysm of overpowering energy. With volcanic force, her whole being erupted in a primal scream, a soaring, searing sound of unimaginable intensity. An instant later, she was reveling in laughter, totally surrendered to the process that had taken her over.

For two full days, this extraordinarily powerful display of kundalini continued, completely possessing Elena's life. Laura and I stayed with her, trying to provide our grounding and steady presence. We knew that when a devotee was having a particularly powerful kundalini experience, Baba would give them something sweet, which, though counterintuitive, seemed to calm the energy. So Laura and I plied Elena with cookies and fruit. There was nothing more to do than honor the power and mystery of this spiritual energy as it played through Elena's being.

The day after we returned from the ashram, Elena called and asked if she could come over. She explained that she couldn't tolerate the intensity of her apartment. The energy there was too strong because of all the practices she'd done there. Unable to sleep, her husband had removed all the photos of the guru and had tried to hold her still throughout the night to keep her body from its spontaneous movements. She was in the full force of a spiritual emergency, the term recently coined to explain overpowering spiritual experiences that seriously interfered with one's functioning.

Elena had hardly walked in our door and started down the hall when she dissolved into peals of laughter and called out, "Who's there behind me?"

Her body was being pulled backward, arching sharply as if in an upside-down cobra posture, pulling her toward the high back shelf where there was a photograph of the Indian saint Ramana Maharshi. She couldn't even see the photo behind her although the force of spiritual energy emanating from the photo was apparently initiating her movements. Clearly she was in an extraordinary state of consciousness, in realms beyond time and space, possessed by ways of knowing the ordinary mind can't begin to comprehend. Presumably, her altered state was responding to the invisible forces emanating from that photo of a great saint.

Ammie, with Evvie's photo behind him.

Then came another dramatic moment. As Elena walked by a bookcase with several family photographs, she paused to look at a photograph of my father. In the photograph, by his right shoulder, was a smaller photograph of my mother. At that time, my mother Evvie was in a nursing home on Long Island, severely diminished from Alzheimer's. She was suffering through a terrible phase of the disease where she—once a writer, poet, and lover of words—could no longer speak. The only sound she made was a heart-rending wail as if crying out to the world in agony over what she couldn't say. It was unbearable to hear. The wailing sound of her suffering cut to the very core of one's being.

Elena had never met my mother. Now she stood before this little photograph of Evvie within the larger photograph of my father and started to speak. "Your mother is talking to me. She is calling to you. She wants you all to come to her, now."

My mind began to race. *What's going on here? Where's Elena getting this message? Was my beloved mother about to die?*

"What do you mean?" I paused and then continued. "Maybe I could go in three weeks or so," I replied as I quickly scanned through the next weeks, casting about for when a trip might be possible.

"That's too late," replied Elena. "It's got to be very soon, within the next two weeks at the most. And she wants *all* of you to come."

I was at the edge of an unfamiliar abyss. *What am I supposed to believe? Am I supposed to follow what she's saying? What does she mean by "all" of us? How many family members would that be? Can I trust her words?*

There was her conviction, compelling and incontrovertible. For me, everything seemed to be moving at an accelerated speed. I couldn't keep up with the crosscurrents whipping through my mind.

"Okay," I said. "I guess I can go the weekend after this, but I'll need to contact the family. Geez, my father and the whole family?"

"She's very clear," Elena added. "She wants everyone to come. And I'm supposed to come too."

I stood there beside Elena, transfixed by what she was saying. They were powerful words—something between an invitation and a command. How was I ever going to explain this to my father who was not remotely interested in this world of clairvoyance, spiritual crisis, and channeling?

In those first moments of Elena's channeling, I was momentarily paralyzed in a vice of indecision. *Do I trust this or not? How can I possibly call my family, especially my father, and suggest a meeting less than two weeks away? Based on what?* Then the inner shift occurred and released me from the hold of the vice. I chose to trust a very subtle movement in my heart that said, *"Just trust!"*

Astonishing to me in retrospect, within mere seconds I went from indecision to decisiveness and followed that inner command to call my extended family. With Elena's non-ordinary states of consciousness, it was becoming clear that she was open to information totally unavailable to those of us in ordinary reality. Clearly, Elena was both clairvoyant and clairaudient, and part of her intense spiritual possession included the channeling of my mother whom she had never met. I couldn't believe what was happening.

While Elena was still with us that day, I started making the calls. With my inner balance feeling rather precarious, I started with the key person and called my father. I simply said to him that I had the strong sense that we should go see Evvie and soon—in fact, the weekend after next. I didn't say anything about Elena. I didn't describe anything that had been happening. I tried to keep my explanation simple and heartfelt because, of course, it was. He listened quietly. Then, without hesitation, he accepted my explanation and agreed to go. Maybe it wasn't so surprising, I reassured myself. All of us knew that given the stage of her illness, Evvie could die at any time. I went on to call my two brothers, my sister, and the niece and nephews who lived close enough to go to Long Island. With relief, I completed the assignment dictated by Elena's astonishing role in the midst of a family she hardly knew.

A few days later, still a week before the proposed gathering with Evvie, there was another startling event that involved Elena. I had already planned to hold what I called my Menopausal Ritual, an event that unfolded directly in response to my memories of my mother's harrowing experience with the medical community when she was going through menopause. In those days, when women were menopausal, doctors routinely prescribed hysterectomies. Unbelievably, they were pathologizing menopause, a totally natural process in middle-aged women, admittedly sometimes with challenging but manageable symptoms. Routine hysterectomies had become a fashionable practice even though there was no clinical evidence to indicate taking out a woman's uterus.

My mother was fierce about wanting to keep her womb. At the time, I was only a teenager, but she shared with me her conflicts with one doctor after another. She simply refused to follow their directives. As a woman who loved and listened to her body, she had no troubling symptoms and trusted her good health. She went from one doctor to another in search of one who would support her. Ultimately, she prevailed, a hard-won victory given the power of the medical establishment.

I vowed to myself that when I reached her age, I would go through menopause with ease. Furthermore, I decided to celebrate this very significant life passage with a menopausal ritual with a group of women friends. The evening would include introductions, a short chant and meditation, storytelling, affirmations around aging, and the exchange of gifts. I invited everyone to bring an object to give away, something that conveyed positive attitudes toward older women.

That evening, thirteen women gathered in our living room for a celebration of this universal women's passage. The youngest in the group was Laura, then just twenty-one, my sister Joanie, several friends and colleagues, and most memorable of all Harriet Robey, our honored Elder, my first cousin once removed. A long since retired psychiatric social worker, very unusual in her generation, Harriet was also an author, a vivid and high-energy presence. At that time, Harriet was ninety-five and blind. She hadn't been out for an evening in ten years, and she was thrilled to be included.

There was a heightened sense of excitement as we gathered. None of us had ever experienced a menopausal ritual before. We were all on the edge of the unknown. Laura and I had spent a lot of time preparing the space, setting up an altar, bringing in flowers, and blessing the space with the scent of incense.

We gathered in a large circle. I was in front of the altar with Laura on my right and Elena on my left. As I welcomed everyone at the start of the ceremony, I began to explain the origins of this ritual and how much my mother would have loved to be there, but she was in a nursing home on Long Island, far from Cambridge.

Then something cataclysmic happened. The moment I mentioned Evvie's name, I was aware of a shudder coursing through Elena's body, and out of her mouth came the unearthly, horrifying sound of my mother's wail. The sound cut through the air like a sword. My sister started to weep because she knew this sound all too well. Instinctively, Elena and I reached for each other's hands while everyone froze in disbelief, waiting for someone to explain what was going on.

Everyone in that room was a kindred spirit, even the one woman that I'd never met. Elena had insisted she should be there. She explained that of course the group should include a stranger—a way of bridging our ritual to the wider world. By this time I was fully accepting the guidance from Elena's clairvoyant state. Still, it was a shocking moment.

I explained about Elena's exceptionally powerful spiritual opening the previous weekend, how she was in a heightened state that included both clairvoyance and clairaudience, and that incredibly, although she had never met my mother or known about my mother's wails, her non-ordinary state had mysteriously connected the two of them and literally brought my mother's presence into that room. The rest of the evening and subsequent ritual was saturated with the power of this incredible event.

Nor was this the last of Elena's impact on the people around her. Another remarkable chapter was about to unfold.

OVERWHELMED BY STARS

About the same time as Elena's powerful spiritual opening, I had my own unexpected experience of non-ordinary consciousness. It happened in a matter of moments within a dream. The experience totally shook up all my ideas about reality. Who am I—really? Am I this person with a name, various roles, and a life story? What is consciousness anyway, and where does it reside within me? There was a waterfall of questions—the same ones, now more evolved, that dwelled in the heart of that little girl who just wanted to be free. The dream seemed to point to dimensions of consciousness I'd read about but never expected to happen to me.

I am in an underground room gathered with a group of friends who share an interest in Jung and his teachings about transpersonal psychology, the collective unconscious, and self-realization. These were highly charged, forbidden subjects at the time, considered subversive and dangerous to the powers that be. Presumably, it was a religious organization of some kind.

It is nighttime when we gather in a basement room, seeking privacy and safety. There is one small window high up in the cellar wall which we have covered with a cloth to hide the room from any passersby on the street. During our meeting, I happen to glance up toward the window, instinctively checking for our safety, when I notice that the cloth has slipped slightly. Someone's eyes, staring intently, appear above the cloth, peering into our underground hiding place.

It is the moment of discovery. Terrified at the prospect of what might come next, my consciousness explodes out of my body, shooting up through the ceiling and out of the building altogether, propelled like a rocket into outer space.

Darkness everywhere . . . catapulting into space . . . gone, gone beyond . . . a great, vast silence . . . until seeing the stars . . . stars everywhere . . .

darkness, vast space . . . surrounded by stars . . . millions of stars . . . space . . . infinite . . . timeless. . . .

There is no knowing how long this lasted, but very slowly, a shred of consciousness starts to return, though still accompanied by feelings of terror at the vastness, the space, and the overwhelm of stars. But still the palpable experience of descending . . . descending into space below . . . descending slowly, then more rapidly until my thundering heart woke me up. Eyes opened, but still there were stars. Waves of terror subsiding . . . the contours of the darkened room slowly coming into focus.

I was back in my body. Then in my forties, I was well aware of the surprising ways that life can provide the next step of our awakening. The dream certainly had that impact. Having been a student of Carl Jung's writings, I knew he would have called it a "great dream," a landmark experience as real as this consensual reality. The dream continued to resonate over time and beckoned, asking for attention.

Sometime later, memories of the dream suddenly resurfaced, triggered by a brief reference in the book I was reading. These words jumped off the page: "An underground church whose members were sworn to secrecy." The book was titled *Paradoxology* by Miriam Therese Winter, a Catholic nun who was exploring the quantum theories of contemporary physics through the lens of her Catholic faith. The arresting title combined the words *paradox*—two contradictory statements—and *doxology*, a term from Christian liturgy.

The author was writing about her friendship with a Czechoslovakian nun named Ludmila, another devout Catholic who, in the spirit of Vatican II, was experimenting with new forms of worship. These two nuns had met at a conference, and although living in very different social and political worlds, they shared the same passionate commitment to explore new liturgies. It was a bold departure for both.

In reaction to the restrictive policies of the state-sponsored religion, Ludmila had started an underground church—an invisible entity, a secret gathering for worship. Participation was against the law. For twenty years, Ludmila and the other members of the clandestine community lived with the threat of being discovered, threatened with imprisonment and even death.

Miriam and Ludmila didn't share a single word in common, but they were deeply bonded through their passion for freedom of worship, each leading an underground church, one within a relatively free society and the other in a society oppressed by hostility and fear. My heart had started to pound as I read about the issue of freedom and freedom of worship. I stopped reading, momentarily lost again in the power of the dream.

Where had it come from? What might be its roots in some unconscious part of my psyche? Why this dream at this time? I began to recognize a pattern in my life that surprised me. I realized that both my work and my spiritual path had led me into territory that many among my family and friends found hard to understand, surely judged, and may have regarded as unacceptable given their more traditional values. I knew some members of my family were worried about me.

For example, in the 1970s, both Hob and I had been training in the new therapies and incorporating them into our work with clients and groups. They were therapeutic modalities such as gestalt, bioenenergetics, psycho-motor, sensory awareness, and for me particularly the psychospiritual tradition known as psychosynthesis. I remember struggling to explain in a few words what it was and why it had so captivated my interest. Oh dear! It was just too subtle, complex, and close to my heart to find any adequate explanation. I also did not know how to talk about the power of Siddha Yoga, the devotional tradition from India in which I had been deeply involved for many years—a path of meditation grounded in the traditions of Kashmir Shaivism and Advaita Vedanta, a guru tradition.

How could I ever explain all that to someone who had no knowledge much less any interest in Eastern spiritual traditions? In a secular, materialistic culture rooted in individualism, many a person might wonder how anyone could get involved in a guru tradition. When asked about what took me to India six times, I threaded my way with careful language, saying a little but not too much, finding words that would connect, not alienate, always aware that I was in tender territory.

During that period of my life when I was invited to teach in the new field of behavioral medicine, people would ask, clearly incredulous, what I was doing teaching meditation, yoga, and cognitive therapy to outpatient groups in a hospital setting. Some were hesitant, dubious, and clearly perplexed. Our patients had been referred by their doctor to try this unorthodox approach to healing their stress-related illnesses. As the word slowly got out through studies, media coverage, and books, interest in mind-body medicine eventually took off, especially as the word *mindfulness* became part of mainstream culture.

In the early 1980s, however, the term behavioral medicine having first appeared only in 1977, those of us teaching the clinics were forever cognizant of how trigger words such as *meditation* and *yoga* could alienate some patients. So we cloaked those words in careful, more medical-sounding terms such as "relaxation response." Or in the case of yoga, we called it "stretching exercises."

While teaching in those pioneering years, I was forever searching for the words that would create bridges to skeptical patients who had been referred by their doctors but really didn't want to be there; that is, until they started experiencing the benefits. They often had revelatory experiences, almost unable to believe that something so seemingly simple as sitting still and turning one's attention within could lead to such freeing, heart-opening experiences. Several of them returned to their religious roots or sought out the burgeoning number of meditation centers that had sprung up.

Nonetheless, I was always aware of the delicacy of language and how I had to tread carefully with people who were suspicious of anything that sounded the least bit "spiritual" or mysterious that couldn't be scientifically proved or didn't fit their materialistic, secular worldview. I wearied of hearing the dismissive words "that sounds so New Age" or "how woo-woo."

Sometimes I was challenged outright. How well I remember the first class I taught after being hired. Knowing that yoga stretching was part of the program, most patients came informally dressed, but this well-dressed lawyer in a three-piece suit, obviously straight from work and uncomfortable at being there, raised his hand and in a challenging tone of voice asked, "So tell me in one word, what is the point of this ten-week course?"

I was momentarily startled, but after a moment's pause, I replied, "Balance—finding balance in your life."

I doubt he was thrilled with that answer, and I am not sure anything would have softened his prickly resistance. Our group never saw him again.

My out-of-body dream experience expressed the ways in which I have needed to be both sensitive and vigilant about what I could and couldn't say. Depending on the person, I sometimes felt a flash of anxiety, almost dread. People who have no knowledge of meditation or yoga, unless they are open and curious, really don't want to hear about it. I've become an expert at reading the subtle cues of disconnect—the eyes that turn away, the facial expression, the subtle bodily contraction, and the way they simply change the subject. Sometimes I feel as though I am walking through minefields, scanning for danger, sensing reactivity, not knowing when I am going to be turned off or rejected. It has been a tender thread through my life.

Furthermore, the dream felt as though it might carry the weight of previous lifetimes. While some might roll their eyes with disbelief, this is not an outrageous idea. Many highly realized beings, as well as ordinary people, not only remember previous lives but have proof in hard facts that validate the truth of their claims.

I've met several women who feel, as I do, that we were banished, murdered, or burned at the stake for our healing gifts. Overly dramatic, you are thinking. No, I remember watching a film about the Salem witch trials and finding myself reaching for a pillow to hold over my belly to protect myself against the rising feelings of terror, a bodily memory as real as if I were re-experiencing the horror, the same horror perhaps as realizing in the dream that our secret gathering in the basement had been discovered, the terror so powerful it catapulted me out of my body and shook my belief systems about levels of reality, showing me that consciousness can exist separate from the body.

Might my dream experience with a non-ordinary state of consciousness have been related to what Elena had been experiencing with her dramatic awakening? Surely yes because both her experiences and mine raise the issue of consciousness. Consciousness—the awareness of this moment and all that is present—is the foundational experience of our being. In non-ordinary manifestations, consciousness is free of time and space.

Elena's experiences with non-ordinary consciousness continued. The story of her dramatic awakening was by no means over. Her continued state was about to have a subtle but powerful influence on what happened next within our family.

A MEMORABLE GATHERING

In response to Elena's insistence about the timing, nine members of our extended family gathered at the nursing home the following weekend. Except for my father, who lived an hour away, the rest of us had to travel by plane, train, or car to get there, a challenge at such short notice and given the distances. Yet there we were, milling around the foyer getting ready to go into my mother's room.

Older family: Laura, Hob, me and Ethan

My father had assumed the role of welcoming host. Three of his four adult children were there with their two spouses, along with his grandnephew and grandniece, and Elena, the newest family member by virtue of her recent marriage to my nephew.

I may have been the most anxious one at that moment. With that flash decision, I had decided to trust Elena's channeling of my mother and taken the leap to call all these family members. After all I'd witnessed during her spiritual crisis, how would she be today when with our family? Most of them were unfamiliar with anything spiritual, much less in such dramatic form. I was aware of holding my breath as we started down the hallway and one by one entered Evvie's room.

It was early afternoon, and the room was flooded with the sunlight of a beautiful September day. Like all such rooms in nursing homes, there were a few familiar objects from our family home, and the walls displayed a favorite painting and lots of collections of family photographs. Someone had sent her a bouquet of fall flowers—red, yellow, and orange—that sat on the bureau bringing a splash of color and natural beauty into the room.

I had called the nursing home that morning and asked the attending nurse to bring the phone to my mother so I could explain that the family was coming to see her that afternoon. Of course, there was no response. She had lost the ability to speak. The only sound she could make was that heart-wrenching wail—a cry of desperation. I reassured her that we would manage the meeting and be respectful of whatever state she was experiencing at the time. Not only was I exceptionally close to my mother but I also knew the importance of keeping everything simple around someone with dementia, reassuring them about anything that might stir their anxiety.

As we walked into the room, we found Evvie sitting up in bed, her back propped against a special pillow provided to support her body. She was wearing her pink, lightly woven bed jacket. Her shoulder-length hair was silvery white, and I was struck by the brilliant blue of her eyes. Even though she had the masked face characteristic of someone with Alzheimer's, she seemed more alert than usual. Clearly nine family members walking into her room together had gotten her attention.

Elena was standing behind several family members, but I noticed that Evvie's gaze immediately went to her. In fact, her eyes were fixed on Elena, not on Ammie or any of us—her children and grandchildren—but on Elena. Everyone greeted Evvie, some kissing her cheek, others touching her hands that lay extended over the bed covers. We began to settle in no special order into the chairs around her bed, Ammie about three seats away from her. At that point, Elena spoke up gently but firmly.

"Ammie, I think Evvie would like you to sit closer, up close, next to her."

I immediately recognized what was happening. Elena was starting to speak for Evvie again, just as she had spoken through her photograph in that hallway at home. My anxiety continued, my mental commentary much like before. *Would Elena's inexplicable movements disrupt our gathering? Would she totally blow our family away with her wild behaviors? Have I made a terrible mistake in trusting her channeling?*

Gradually my concerns subsided. Clearly, Elena was in a different state, still in touch with Evvie but now relaxed, calm, and totally appropriate to the situation.

After a bit of shuffling in our seating arrangement, we lapsed into easy conversation, reminiscing, telling family jokes, and singing. Through all this, Evvie continued to look back at Elena. I kept speculating about what was happening. *What is their connection? Why is Evvie making such eye contact with Elena? Ammie and her family are all here, yet she keeps focusing on Elena. What is it between them?*

Then Elena spoke up again, addressing Ammie.

"Ammie, there are some things Evvie wants you to know. Even though she can't speak, she wants to thank you for everything—for all your visits, for your care, for your love. Most importantly, she wants you to know that she loves you as deeply as she always has."

Ammie's face softened with the fullness of tears. He leaned forward, put his hands on Evvie's shoulders, and gently kissed her—a tender moment between two people who had shared life for almost sixty years, now separated by the ravages of dementia. Evvie had had an exceptionally hard experience with Alzheimer's, including a prolonged psychosis, but this moment in which all of us were present felt like the ultimate healing of all that pain.

I couldn't help but wonder who was orchestrating this meeting. Was it Elena, or was it my mother?

After our gathering, we returned to our childhood home where Ammie still lived. We gathered the garden chairs in a circle under the huge linden tree outside the house and had a spontaneous celebration of our time together with Evvie.

At one point, Ammie silently got up and left, returning a few moments later with a huge white dahlia. He went over to Elena, bowed slightly, handed her the dahlia, and said, "Thank you for what you did this afternoon."

Now it was my turn to feel teary. I had a rush of love and gratitude. Somehow this extraordinary gathering had happened without any of Elena's wildness of the previous two weeks. She had been the one who insisted we should come together—and soon, in two weeks, not three. She had spoken for Evvie with words that had deeply touched Ammie and all of us.

The following week, Elena's extraordinary state began to fade and disappeared. Elena had been right about the timing. Had we waited, the meeting would not have been the same. Evvie couldn't have spoken through Elena.

Soon after, Evvie lapsed into the coma that eventually led to her death. Everything about this phase of Elena's spiritual awakening had been remarkable, starting with her exceptionally powerful kundalini awakening at the ashram three weeks before. The crowning moment was when she had stopped to look at the photograph of Ammie with that little photo of Evvie in the background. At that moment she had first started channeling my mother and set in motion the whole series of events that followed.

THE EDGES OF EXCITEMENT

Steamy with humidity, the air heavy and hot, the Bombay airport teems with activity even at 3:00 in the morning. I have been flying through the night, a long, tedious trip to visit the ashram and Purnima for the Christmas holidays. It's now over three months since all the extraordinary events around my mother and Elena. This is my fourth trip to India, the country that I have deeply, inexplicably loved since I was a child.

Even in my exhausted, travel-weary state, I notice that I'm drifting from one reality to another like a boat that has come loose from its moorings. I have to will myself to stay present as I proceed through the formalities of customs and the aggressive surge of porters and drivers, calling insistently, invading personal space, vying for business.

I finally connect with a driver who will drive me for two hours into the Indian countryside. I settle into the usual, somewhat tattered taxi. We head into the darkness, driving through sprawling colonies of patchwork huts. Even in the dark, the scene is alive with the early morning activity of women tending fires, men squatting by the roadside, children running amidst foraging chickens and mangy dogs.

India never seems to sleep. No matter what time of night, people are up and about their business as if it were the middle of the day. As the two hours pass, we finally turn off the trunk road that runs north from Bombay and head west into deeper country. The latter part of the trip starts to feel like a pilgrimage, and my anticipation rises as we approach the ashram.

By now, a misty light glows on the eastern horizon, and as we round the last corner where the road forks to Vajeshwari, site of an ancient devi temple, I begin to see the embankment and huge fence that surrounds the hundreds of acres of the ashram compound.

This early morning arrival has become a familiar ritual—the greetings, the hustle of luggage, the welcoming sight of ashram buildings, the sound of the early morning chant. I am home. At the same time, in my exhausted state, everything seems other-worldly and heightened—the smells, the incomparable smells of India, the burning dung, the spicy fragrances of cooking, of flowers, gasoline fumes, dust, and the smell of the earth. Nearby are the sounds of sparrows, bright and insistent. In the distance I hear the call of the ravens, India's crows, large brown and black birds that erupt with their unique call, coarse and imperious, even noisier than American crows.

And always the sound of the chant, rising and falling, coming from the courtyard that is the heart of the ashram. Before dawn every morning, this succession of chants marks the beginning of another day. Most of the devotees have been up a long time. Suddenly I see Purnima hurrying up the walkway toward me.

"Hi! Hi, Mom! Welcome! How are you doing? Did the trip go okay? Oh! I'm so glad to see you! How are you? There's so much to catch up on!"

A torrent of words, enthusiasm, and love rushes toward me.

"Oh, Purnima, I'm so happy to see you! You look great! How are you? How's it going? Oh, I can't believe I'm really here, that you're here!"

We hug and exclaim, barely listening for replies to hurried questions, the excited purrings of mother and daughter meeting after three months. She looks radiant. She's now twenty-one, strikingly beautiful with her dark eyebrows, blue eyes, and strong presence. She's wearing her favorite blue punjabi with a small floral design, a simple comfortable way to dress, not the more formal punjabis that some of the ashram women wear. Even at this early hour, I notice that she has taken time to apply a bindi to her forehead.

Laura in her 20s

As we walk, arms around each other, toward the breakfast area, I try to stay open to the rush of impressions and memories—the beauty of the grounds, the lines of palm trees leading to the Durga temple off to my right where Gurumayi had invited Purnima to participate in a special ceremony in remembrance of my mother, Evvie, her grandmother who had recently died. I noticed the path lined with statues of the siddhas rising toward the expansive garden ahead of me, the groups of devotees headed for breakfast, all this while especially aware of my daughter walking at my side. Probably sensing my weary, overloaded state, she carries the conversation with pleasantries.

We settled down at a table out under the trees, purposely having chosen a place far from the breakfast crowd so that we wouldn't be interrupted.

"So where do we begin? Tell me all that's going on," I urge her.

"Well, so much has happened since my last letter, and it's all really huge for me. Believe it or not, I'm now George Afif's assistant, you know, Gurumayi's right-hand man, but for me, it turns out to be a lot of *sevas* (service to help with the work of the ashram) rolled into one. As far as I can see, he's practically running the ashram, involved in so many things you'd never believe. And I can't believe it, that this is where I am, working for him."

While she's been explaining her new role, my mind has wandered to another time when I first saw this man George. He was overseeing a sprawling construction project. In the midst of the dust and mist of the early morning light, he was a striking figure, tall, dark-haired, and impeccably groomed with a strong, lithe physique. He was dressed all in white while the other workers, mostly Indian women, adavasis or country folk, from the surrounding valley wore their tattered, soiled, cotton saris tucked up around their thighs to free their legs for the heavy work. George was pacing around the site, shouting orders in Hindi or Marathi, the local dialect, but not lending a hand to work alongside the heavy laborers. He only moved around the construction site like a great, watchful cat seeming to exert an invisible hold over the whole chaotic scene.

I learned later that he was originally from Lebanon. He met Baba, and after Baba's death, when Gurumayi had become the successor, he had moved rapidly up the ranks of the ashram hierarchy. I detected a tone of awe, even fear, when people spoke of him. He seemed to be ubiquitous, the director of many activities, the alpha male of the ashram, Gurumayi's right-hand man and bodyguard. Whether you happened to meet her in the farthest reaches of the ashram grounds or amidst crowds of people pressing to be close to her, he cleared the way and protected her. When she walked slowly into the huge meditation hall, he followed her at a discreet distance, his gaze dropping slightly, presumably out of deference and respect.

I used to wonder why sometimes I saw him as strikingly attractive while at other times he struck me as sinister. Why these polarities? I sensed that he had powers of some kind. Surely he was a shapeshifter—the only way I could account for my polarized perceptions of him.

Undoubtedly there's an explanation of why certain scenes from our past remain indelibly imprinted like the incisions carved into metal to create etchings. We don't realize how vivid and enduring the image is until circumstances reactivate it, as for me in this moment as I sit listening to Purnima. Perhaps the psyche recognizes at some unfathomable level that this incident or person will reemerge in time. At this time, I still had heard nothing about George's dark past. Or had I heard something and forgotten?

Purnima's voice pulls me back from my reverie.

"It's an unbelievable experience working for George. He never seems to sleep—well, maybe three or four hours. So there's to be this major production of the Ramayana for the Christmas intensive, a full-scale performance with a cast of almost a hundred that will be performed on Tapovan, the hill behind the ashram. Preparations are in full swing—huge sets, complicated props, an array of tents for all the activities, makeup, costumes, lights, sound systems, designers, carpenters, electricians, musicians—it goes on and on, everyone drawn from the masses of people who've come for the holidays. It's wild! It's unbelievable to be his assistant in all this, and it sure calls on all my training in theater and an awful lot more than that. I'll tell you about that later. It's just all off the scale."

She sounds incredulous at her own words. Clearly, she's excited and challenged. I recognize the headiness of her state, the impression that everything has speeded up and intensified as if all experience is magnified, seen through a magical lens.

My attention is drifting again. Purnima's state has evoked vivid memories for me. This headiness is familiar in the ashram when a big project involves working nonstop, sleeping very little. I've experienced it many times. The environment is intended to push people beyond their limits. When great numbers of people, inspired by a shared vision, work diligently for long hours, all in the name of guru seva, they create a cauldron of intensity. Invariably it leads to spiritual highs.

Hob, a seasoned Buddhist practitioner and psychotherapist, used to detect this state when I returned from the ashram. I thought I was in an expanded, yogic state, but he detected that it was inflated, overexcited, and out of balance. I had become too enmeshed in the dynamic of ashram life, a subtlety that escaped even my psychological training. Propelled by his concerns about my involvement in Siddha Yoga, he had an unerring ability to shatter my insulated reality. His words would come with a definitive thrust, often painful. I deeply resented his barbed reactions because I couldn't yet see how I was caught in the illusion of having attained some elevated yogic state.

Once again, Purnima's words draw me back into the moment, sitting under the shade trees, eating breakfast together.

"There's a whole other piece that's happened since my last letter," she begins. "A few weeks ago, Gurumayi told me I had another seva, that I was to become head of Prasad, the social service arm of the ashram. That really blew me away. Why me? There are several people in that department who have worked professionally as rural development specialists. They really know what they're doing. This is their field, like one guy who's a former Oxfam expert and others who are really experts in the stuff that Prasad does. There are about sixteen people on the staff, and I'm even expected to run the staff meetings. There's lots of other stuff that I don't know anything about at all. It all blows me away."

She pauses as we both watch the raven that has landed on the far edge of the table, hoping to pirate some discarded treasures from our breakfast. At that moment, the incongruous sound of a portable phone breaks into our conversation. For the first time, I notice that a bright red handset lies next to Purnima's shoulder bag on the table.

She takes the call and decisively passes along a series of directions to the caller. From the fragments of conversation, I realize that one of the swamis has called, and she is handing out the order. How incongruous. Ordinarily, it would be the other way around.

"A portable phone? Here in rural India?" I inquire, as she puts the phone down. During my last visit, I had to travel two hours into Bombay to make an urgent call, and now the ashram—Purnima herself—has a portable phone!

"Oh, it's George's phone, but he gives it to me when there's a lot going on. We're working with the swamis on the production. I know, all this is weird for me too," she continues, "but I end up passing along George's orders to the swamis and other key people.

"But back to the subject of Prasad. You know how it is at the ashram. Sometimes people get certain sevas, and we don't understand why. That's sure true for me with Prasad. Sometimes I have no idea what I'm supposed to be doing, but part of it is that George follows everything very closely."

I'm astonished at everything she's been telling me and ask, "So how are you managing to do all of this? It's unbelievable."

"Well, it's really tricky sometimes," she explains. "George oversees just about everything I do, and I have to report to Gurumayi a lot about what's going on at Prasad. There's some other stuff—it's all pretty complicated—which I'll tell you later when you're settled in. But come on, let's go and take your stuff to your room. You're staying in the main building in a room with one of the swamis."

This bit of news takes me by surprise. Swamis are usually in rooms by themselves, and the main building is primarily for long-term staff members, not transient visitors like me. Clearly, because Purnima is working for George and is head of Prasad, I'm being put in a special room. I feel grateful to be in a room with only two other people, a privilege in a crowded ashram. During my last visit, I lived in a dormitory with thirty other women.

As we walk toward my room, I find myself mulling over the implications of all she's been telling me. She's thriving in this community where one advances by being a hard worker, by being devoted to the guru, and by being discreet. Discretion is the operative work for sensitive jobs that you quietly do without talking about what you're doing. It contributes to the mystique that surreptitiously appears in groups where hierarchy prevails, more so when a guru is part of the picture.

In the last three months, I realize, Purnima has moved into the "inner circle," those people who are closest around the guru. I remember in the early days around Baba certain people received VIP treatment—the well-known, the rich, the powerful, leaders in their field, politicians, actors, actresses, people with connections and money. They had special seating, choice rooms, private darshans with the guru.

The system felt dissonant to me then. It still does. Discrimination is wrong anywhere but even more inappropriate at an ashram where seekers come from all kinds of backgrounds and should be treated equally. My social conscience is marching along in high gear. In spite of it, however, I notice that I'm really happy to be in this spacious room with only two other people.

Before I start unpacking, I stand by the window looking out over the village of Ganeshpuri toward distant Mount Montagni, a favorite landmark in my memories of this beautiful place. Like the weaving of an elaborate design, I notice the intricacies of my feelings, heightened surely by the combination of travel-weariness and excitement. From all that Purnima has told me, I feel a mixture of joy and pride, tinged with uneasiness. She's ebullient, radiant, and totally immersed in the heady roles she's playing. But something about it feels off and troubles me. Why has she been made head of Prasad? She's inexperienced and barely twenty-one. Why all the responsibilities for the Ramayana production? And why, above all, the dominance of George in all of this?

I notice that twice she's made veiled references to something more that she wants to tell me. She wants to wait until I'm settled in, but I'm aware of a vaguely unsettled feeling about all she's told me. I've always been fairly successful at balancing a mixture of feelings about this tradition that I've been part of for a number of years, profoundly grateful for the beauty and power of the practices but uneasy about the inevitable politics of a large spiritual organization. I smile as I remember my father once correcting me when I used that term. He'd never been involved with a spiritual tradition or darkened the door of a church, and yet he had the wisdom to tell me, "There's no such thing as a 'spiritual organization.'" I would soon learn about that in a dramatic form.

EATING HONEY OFF THE KNIFE

I immediately become immersed in the intensity of ashram life. The days are more pressured than ever because of the huge production of the Ramayana. Purnima continues to be unbelievably busy. She works well into the night, starts before dawn, and can only meet me for a cup of tea or a quick lunch. We've managed to meet today for lunch, and once again, she decisively leads me away from the dining area to a distant table out under the trees. Though very subtle, I sense an urgency to how she is moving. Before she even starts eating, she picks up from our previous conversation.

"So what am I going to do, Mom? When I told you about working for George, there wasn't anything at first, just some vibes from him. But now he's turning up the heat. I think I can handle this, but sometimes I'm not so sure. He has this really bedazzling energy. I can hold my own by teasing and challenging him on the little things, the safe things. But I'm not so sure about where this is heading. What do you think I should do? I feel so trapped."

I'm stunned, aware that I'm feeling suddenly hot, ambushed by this piece of information. What indeed! I murmur some automatic reply. I have no idea how to respond. He's her supervisor. He is twenty years her senior. He's a powerful man, running this ashram. I'm getting lost in a cross rip of feelings.

She continues. "I didn't mention that he's asked me to meet him after the evening chant, somewhere where we end up being alone. He's my supervisor, so it's really tricky, really confusing."

"Could you ask Gurumayi about it?" I respond hesitantly.

"No, no way! I've had the feeling that she's been angry with me lately, and I can't figure out why. I don't know what's going on, what I might be doing that makes her so cool and distant."

The red phone rings. She glances at me with a knowing expression. "I'll be right there. It'll take five minutes." With apologies, she gathers her things and walks briskly toward the main building.

As I watch her walk away, I have a sudden flash of memory. I've heard it several times—about George's powerful role and that he's not only Gurumayi's bodyguard but perhaps also her consort. Is it true? That would put Purnima in an impossible triangle. The prospect is appalling. I can hardly bear the dissonance of my thoughts and the cascade of powerful feelings—disbelief, shock, anxiety.

In the last few days before my return home, Purnima and I had been meeting more often. The Ramayana production was over. Now our conversations were almost all about the George situation. She explained how she'd been moved into a room with Gurumayi's first secretary and asked to report to her several times a day about her activities. Who was behind that, and what was their motive? My first reaction was that perhaps Gurumayi was trying to protect Purnima by pulling her closer. No, Purnima said, she was told not to tell anyone about what she was being asked to do, told to be discreet, even told to lie.

I felt lost in the confusion of the situation. I had no idea how to help my own daughter. To think that I was her mother and that I had no idea what to do. Even with my psychological training and ashram experience, I was deeply uncomfortable about my feelings of helplessness. I sensed flickers of dissonance. I loved this place and the practices so deeply, yet Purnima had been sharing extremely troubling information. I felt paralyzed by twisted threads of feelings—my pride in her position, my happiness for her, and the respect and affection that so many people had for her. But then there were all the dark innuendos, twisted relationships, and Gurumayi's harsh responses to her requests for guidance.

Then there was my uneasiness about the gifts and advances of George. I was all too aware of my disconnected feelings. I felt as though I'd been swept into a maelstrom of forces I couldn't decipher. I vaguely sensed an insidious combination of factors. There was this sprawling, international community held with power, intensity, and a hierarchy that involved secrets. Then there was the power of the spiritual practices and the great beauty of the ashram and its extensive gardens. A kind of brilliance permeated everything about it.

Perhaps I had been blinded by all of it. I left India feeling uncertain and troubled. What was really going on behind the scenes in this ashram where everything appeared to be so extraordinarily beautiful, inspiring, and serene?

Throughout the spring, Purnima and I stayed in touch through correspondence and several clandestine calls that she made on George's portable phone. "Call me at the office," I'd said to her, both of us recognizing the wisdom of keeping this tangled story from Hob who had always had his concerns about Siddha Yoga.

Purnima's life gradually unraveled into confusion, fear, and pain. Everywhere she turned, it seemed she ran head-on into power struggles, manipulation, and secrets. In her one letter, she wrote, "My sadhana [spiritual life] is very difficult right now. I am *really* being tested. I suppose in the Siddha Yoga lingo it's called "burning." It's hard, and every day I think about leaving. I'll write and explain soon."

As she was to explain in another letter, the dominant theme of those months was triangles. Purnima found herself caught between George and Hemananda, the swami with whom she shared a room and to whom she was supposed to be reporting several times daily. They both milked her for information, swore her to silence, and ordered her to cover up and lie. Then she was caught between Gurumayi and George, reporting to both yet being given conflicting messages. She felt whipsawed between her guru and her supervisor.

Meanwhile, I struggled and anguished from afar, still trapped by my feelings of helplessness. Given Purnima's distress and confusion, I was astonished that Gurumayi seemed to be doing nothing to help her. If anything, Gurumayi was a major part of the problem. In this devotional tradition, the guru is referred to as "the grace-bestowing power."

Why was Gurumayi doing nothing to support Purnima? Surely in the Byzantine scene around her, she must know something about what was going on. Why didn't she intervene?

Another letter came from Purnima. "Boy, have I been in the fire. Gurumayi loves me and wants to make sure I *get* it and learn from my mistakes. So all of Hemananda's checking is really for my own good. I've gotten to thinking about issues such as when is it okay to be critical, and when do you be quiet and let life unfold as it's meant to? Honesty—how do I know if I am honest or if something is just a delusion of my mind? Seeing God in other people—not as easy as I thought.

"If I think something is good and Gurumayi thinks it's bad, do I remain true to myself or change my mind simply because it's not what Gurumayi thinks? If I have too much doubt, it will become a monster and throw me off the path. How do I keep a healthy, trusting perspective and also keep my eyes open?

"If it's true that God is the most important thing in my life, why are all of these doubts even manifesting? Why can't I trust him completely? It is a much harder life here, and for a long time I believed that it was worth it because this is where I experience *true* happiness and bliss. During this hard time, it is difficult to maintain that awareness. Home is seeming very golden and free now. If anyone handed me a ticket, I'd pack right away. By the time you receive this, it will no doubt have changed as everything does. That's just about my one true hope these days."

Even though Purnima wrote those words, at the time I surely must have tempered their force, squeezed them through the sieve of my Siddha Yoga assumptions. The fact was she wanted desperately to leave the ashram, but she couldn't. As a senior staff person, the protocol would have been to ask Gurumayi, but in view of how coldly Gurumayi had been treating her, she couldn't imagine asking. Little did I know then that this kind of situation is a typical way in which cults keep their followers psychologically trapped. She was too embroiled in an impossibly complex situation. She would just grind through the remaining months.

On a beautiful summer afternoon, Purnima arrived home from her year in India. In our family, homecomings are marked by high spirits and animated storytelling. Something was different this time. Purnima looked exhausted and pale, a shadow of her former self, nothing like the ebullient beauty who had greeted me in Ganeshpuri months before. Instead of her outgoing, effervescent self, she was subdued. Her eyes seemed veiled as if she were in hiding, like a bird with a broken wing holding still to protect the hidden wound, waiting for it to heal.

She seemed muted, as if she were living at a great distance from herself and the world around her. Why was she so hesitant to talk about Ganeshpuri? For me, it was too painful to allow fully into awareness. It cast shadows too dark for me to bear. I finally got part of the picture. She simply didn't want to talk about it at all. I was heartbroken by the depth of her emotional numbness. She was cut off from her feelings, caught in a vice of isolation.

When I dared to touch the tender place beneath the surface of our relationship, I could feel the presence of a growing darkness, elusive and oppressive. As her mother, still devoted to the path we had once so joyfully shared, I couldn't bear to feel her struggling. I felt shut out, but I could see that she needed these walls of privacy and protection. I, too, retreated behind my own walls of pain. Our relationship felt dislocated, our bonding around Siddha Yoga now ragged and torn. A perilous abyss had opened between us.

In spite of her devastation, something pulled her back. She wanted to visit the ashram in the Catskills where Gurumayi had returned for the summer. She wrote to Gurumayi about her intention to visit and her anxieties about the prospect of having to deal with George. She asked Gurumayi for guidance. The reply came. All it said was, "We've moved on from all that. It's time for you to let it go."

Purnima was stunned. What an appalling response to someone who had been traumatized. Yet still she moved ahead with her plans to go. I was amazed at her courage. Was it her slender hope that going back might bring some reconciliation?

A few days after Purnima's return from the ashram, I came home to find a hastily scribbled note lying on the kitchen counter.

"Mom, I've gone to the emergency room at Mount Auburn. Please come quickly."

I found her in a hallway in the hospital, lying on a gurney waiting for the doctor to return. Ashen, barely able to speak, she was curled up in a fetal position, lying terribly still.

Mom, it's kidney stones. The doctor says they're really big—really bad case."

She stops suddenly, vanishing into the pain. It seems forever before she speaks again, weakly, in a whisper.

"This is the karma of the year in India . . . in my body . . . my rage . . . grief . . . all the pain—the worst pain. Will you call Hemananda and have her ask Gurumayi for blessings?"

I'm taken aback at her request. She'd been pulling away, but now, in her terrible pain, she was reaching back, desperate for some thread of connection and hope. She sinks into another cycle of piercing pain. Silently, I sit beside her, stroking her forehead. I'm scarcely able to think clearly. I'm overwhelmed seeing her in such pain, again unable to help except for the gentle stroking of my hand against her sweating forehead.

I couldn't think about the larger issues. I could only comfort my daughter in her pain and stay with her during the next two weeks, which involved hospitalizations, procedures, and finally lithotripsy to break up the kidney stones. The doctor told us that she had the worst case of kidney stones he'd ever seen in a person so young.

By the following winter, the full force of her pain shifted the balance. Purnima wrote a letter to all her Siddha Yoga friends. She told them not only her personal experiences but what she had observed in the organization. She wrote about the dark side of the hierarchy, how she had been abused by the guru's right-hand man and then blamed for being responsible. She wrote about the convoluted meanings of the word *discretion*, a synonym for cover-up, deception, and lies, and about how irreparably wounded she'd been by the whole Siddha Yoga experience.

"I'm bleeding inside with emotional pain and spiritual doubt," she wrote. "I have given ten years of my life to this faith, and when I most needed help, I was scolded and turned away like a misbehaving child. I have been deeply scarred by that period of my life. NO THANK YOU!"

She signed the letter "Laura" and asked everyone to stop calling her Purnima.

I continued to ruminate about issues raised by my first conversation with Purnima when I'd arrived in India for Christmas. After more than ten years in this tradition, I was very familiar with the inspiring, challenging, sometimes overwhelming intensity of this yogic form of life dedicated to spiritual practices intended to burn away the stubborn vestiges of the ego in order to realize one's innate divinity, one's true nature or essence self. Now Laura's situation confronted me with a litany of troubling stories, all in searing opposition to what a yogic path is supposed to be about. Both of us were lost in a very dark place.

LOST IN THE LABYRINTH

As I accompanied Laura through two harrowing weeks of her health crisis, I was trying desperately to balance the incongruities of our situation. Here was my daughter—physically broken and spiritually devastated—trying to find her way in unfamiliar territory. Here was I, holding on to all the gifts of the path while wrestling with the enormity of what she'd been telling me.

Both spiritual practices and psychological training are rooted in cultivating attention, clear seeing, and openness to the truth of the moment. When I dared to look directly into the situation between Laura and me, I was besieged by uncertainty. I was aware that my usual clarity and decisiveness felt elusive. I had images of a web or labyrinth comprised of all the dark threads of the tradition's history, Laura's troubling stories, and Gurumayi's inexplicable responses to her pleas for help.

I wondered if perhaps I was caught in this web, a web spun out of the innumerable gifts of the tradition, spun out of my natural idealism and my places of unconsciousness. I had a deeply ingrained tendency to look for the best in people and situations. I had grown up in a family with secrets, the most charged being my mother's several breakdowns and her delicate emotional states, which explained my father's fierce protection of her. In our family, when we expressed any powerful emotions such as anger, fear, or grief, we were banished to our rooms. The family norm was to remain upbeat, positive, and optimistic, regardless of how you might be feeling.

Family patterns spilled over into how I reacted to Laura's situation. I was struggling mightily with the stories she had told me over the phone and in her letters, but I had a way of disconnecting emotionally, even as she, too, was desperately juggling her interpretations of what was going on. Undoubtedly, she had learned some of these coping mechanisms from me as she dealt with the darkness, confusion, and complexities of the guru scene.

I tried to reconcile her stories with my experiences, but I wasn't sure that I was seeing clearly. When I thought about her former position at the ashram as George's assistant, head of Prasad, and carrying an unbelievable amount of responsibility, I couldn't help but feel proud as her mother and happy for her flourishing. During my time there, people kept telling me what an extraordinary job she was doing, how much they loved and admired her.

During our fervent conversations just before I left the ashram, I sensed that somehow I was being blindsided by the brilliance and spiritual power of the whole scene, blinded by the light like a deer paralyzed by the headlights of an oncoming car. I had already lived through enough of the dark chapters of Siddha Yoga's history. I was vaguely aware that at some level I had detached and dissociated from the dissonant information. I'm not sure I realized, however, just how deeply enmeshed and attached I had become. My devotion to the teachings, practices, and community had numbed me even to the reality of my own daughter's suffering.

Like Laura reaching out to Gurumayi in the depths of her pain from the kidney stones, I, too, found myself writing to Gurumayi about my distress over Purnima's struggles. Gurumayi replied with two sentences—"All I can say is that Purnima likes to have drama. She has really succeeded in creating one and dragging you into it."

I was incredulous at her response, but I didn't let myself feel the full impact of its implications. After the enormity of what Laura had been through, Laura was being blamed! I couldn't bear to let Gurumayi's words in, much less identify the cause of my sickening feelings—stirrings of distress and doubt—as if some part of me was turning away from the full force of a truth I couldn't bear to see.

I was lost, entrapped by my powers of denial. Once again I ignored my body's knowing. After all these years, I became adept at compartmentalizing the dissonances. I dismissed my discomfort with yogic explanations: *It's just my attachment to wanting things to be different. Perhaps there are karmic patterns here that are beyond my understanding. Perhaps this is just a passing phase in Laura's and my sadhana.*

Soon after Laura's letter to her Siddha Yoga friends explaining why she had left, she came to a dramatic turning point. She attended a lecture on mind control and cult behavior. She explained to me afterwards what a liberating experience it had been. The speaker described in great detail the dynamics of what happens in cults—the markers, components, and dynamics of cult behavior. Shockingly, he was describing in broad terms exactly what she had experienced in India. The parallels were so similar. She felt as if he knew exactly what she had been through. She had witnessed and experienced all the identifying patterns firsthand. The inner circle was undeniably a cult and the entire organization as well. For the first time, here was the explanation for the depth of her trauma. Like having a mysterious illness diagnosed, she felt enormously relieved to hear an expert talk about cults and the damage they perpetrate on their members.

As she read about cults and attended other lectures, she began to see more clearly the forces in which she had been entangled—forces too convoluted, obscure, and painful for her to understand at the time. She had had no objective context that year, only the official picture of the ashram scene. Imagine the dissonance, the ashram supposedly a place of benevolence, kindness, and blessings but which she had experienced as a hell.

Laura announced to me that she planned to meet with the cult expert a few times for counseling. She felt that he was the first person who could help her to sort through the enormity of her experience.

"But Mom, this means that I'll have to be distant from you for a while. I really need to learn more about this whole subject of mind control and cults. Don't worry. It's only for a while."

How ironic, I thought. For years I'd tracked the cult issue very carefully, or so I thought. I had raised the issue voluntarily while giving orientations for new people when they arrived at the ashram. Naturally, the environment with all its cultural anomalies often triggered that concern for newcomers. I rationalized Laura's experience by attributing it to the culture of the inner circle, not about what the rest of us experience.

Hadn't I already wrestled many times with the shadows in Siddha Yoga's history? Of course there are difficulties in any community. That's life, just the way it is. But how much darkness is tolerable? The gifts of the path, I reassured myself, still outweighed the transgressions. Yet my own daughter had been abused and irreparably wounded by those very transgressions. How could I still hold the pain of this dichotomy? Was I somehow manipulating her revelations to immunize myself against the even darker truths that were about to emerge?

I watch as a large, variegated, brown spider weaves its web beneath the eaves at the corner of the house. I'm sitting on the loveseat by the full-length windows in the family room. I've stopped reading to watch. Slowly, intricately, the spider weaves. The pattern emerges, spun out of careful movements, each leg reaching out, spinning, turning, connecting until the creation hangs there, trembling in the light breeze, resilient in its magnificent geometry.

I watch the spider, musing at how we weave our own intricate webs—what we call reality. How tenuous our creations, these inner worlds we spin!

An image spontaneously emerges, my own subtle weaving of memories, dreams, rituals, practices, inspirations—all the intricate threads of my spiritual journey. I see the image of a translucent, iridescent realm like a magnificent bubble, beautiful and inspiring. This realm is woven of all that I've experienced on this path over the many years. The weaving of images unfolds . . .

. . . the first time I saw a photograph of Baba with his penetrating gaze, famous for awakening people through that photograph alone.

. . . the memorable dream in which he appeared, creating some mysterious bond though I hadn't even met him.

. . . the incomparably beautiful chanting of the Rudram, an

ancient chant that touched some deep chord of familiarity and evoked tears of joy.

. . . the wonder of rising long before dawn to do the practices—yoga, meditation, and chanting—all opening to the divine mystery.

. . . the pilgrimage to Nasik and the profound experience while meditating at the Trimbekeshwar Temple.

. . . Gurumayi arranging a *shanti puja* (peace ritual) at the Durga temple to commemorate my mother's death and to bring peace to her soul.

. . . the memories of India where a sense of the sacred is palpable at the temples, places of pilgrimage, in the land itself.

. . . the memory of Purnima's return from her first trip to India—radiant, self-assured, healed by her months of living in the ashram environment and attending the international school there.

These numinous threads are the inspired weavings of my Siddha Yoga reality. They are resilient, like beaten gold. They can't be tarnished by passing darkness. I know that the dark threads are there as well. I've listened to the allegations, made inquiries, written letters, and talked with swamis. I've done my best to address the darkness that tugs and tears at the integrity of the luminous sphere. Still, the center holds—that deep, mysterious core of sacred experiences with which I've been gifted. I reassure myself that every community has its share of troubles. That's the human condition. How could it be otherwise?

But the urgent question is, how much am I able to hold? What is my bottom line? So far I've managed to hold the growing tension between the light and the dark, the positive and the negative. The difference now is that Laura's story has moved into the center of my reality. And it isn't numinous. It blazes with pain.

The distance between Laura and me is growing. She seems cool and contained, our conversations perfunctory, freighted with forbidden subjects. I can't bear the barrenness. Something is terribly wrong, but I can't process anything with her. I feel as though she is keeping me at a distance with a psychic wall of judgment and pain.

Despite her occasional reassurances that the distance between us is temporary, everything screams for attention. I must remain silent. Whenever I pay attention, I notice a sinking, sickening pain deep in my body—unexpressed anguish silently screaming. Our once precious relationship seems mutilated. I feel as if I am suspended in the interminable, oppressive stillness before a great storm.

Finally, Laura announces that she wants me and her brother, Ethan, to meet with her for a daylong session with her counselor, the expert in cults. We need to know the whole story, she explains, and she wants the presence of someone who is a professional in the field. She'd rather not have Hob there, she says, because he already has plenty of critical feelings about Siddha Yoga.

The morning of the meeting, to marshal all my inner forces, I made a list of wise sayings culled from various spiritual sources. I tucked the list in a pocket, vowing to stay steady during whatever was going to happen. Laura's counselor, Steven Hassan, arrived with another man named John, a former senior staff member whose name I vaguely remembered. Laura explained that John had been recruited by Hassan to attend the meeting since he had extensive experience of the inner workings of the ashram community.

We gathered in the family room where only a few days before I had been watching the spider weave its intricate, magnificent web. I returned to my favorite place on the loveseat by the tall windows while the others, including Ethan, drew up chairs in a semicircle in front of me. In a fleeting image, I felt as if I were in front of a firing squad. I drew a shawl around my shoulders, more for a sense of protection than for its warmth. In my hyperobservant state, I noticed that John murmured to Steven that wearing shawls was a familiar ritual within ashram culture. Many people meditated with shawls because the body's temperature tends to drop during meditation.

Laura began the meeting by thanking us for coming and explained that our time was primarily for sharing information that she wanted us to know. Stories and facts began to pour forth. Laura elaborated on her experiences in India and how her life had spiraled down into chaos, confusion, and pain.

"I had just turned twenty-one," she explained, "and I got caught in the cross-rips, power struggles, and deceptions of the inner circle, a powerful group of people with George and Gurumayi at the top."

She continued. How could she have known the stories about George, that he had a criminal record and had been convicted of statutory rape in the state of California only six years before? Gurumayi had apparently publicly forgiven him and invited him back to continue at her side, even as he continued his abusive behaviors, especially the sexual abuse of a number of young women.

Speaking rapidly, her voice taut with pain, Laura blurted out, "People want to know the details, but I won't talk about that. He asked me to meet him after hours, invited me to his room, took me to places where we would be alone. He was grooming me, showering me with gifts, compliments—all the usual ploys of a sexual predator. All of it is violation, all of it part of his conspiratorial web—the sexual stuff plus all those other ashram conspiracies going on. Horrible! All of it horrible!"

She described her confusion with the intrigue and secrecy that dominated the inner circle and her difficult relationship with Hemananda into whose room she'd been moved. She told how she felt caught between Hemananda and George, how she was asked to "report" on people, a common practice, a way for the guru and the inner circle people to know what was going on. Hemananda frequently reminded her to be discreet. Gurumayi was equally involved in the convoluted system, adding a final shocking directive when she said to Laura, "Never talk to anyone about any of this, and be sure never to tell your mother."

The stories tumbled out, how she felt like a pawn, used and manipulated, trapped in a vortex of secrets and lies. Gradually she became isolated, cut off from her friends and other ashramites. She was warned about honoring secrets and the rule of silence. The silence stifled honesty and communication and covered over a multitude of unsavory, illicit activities.

Then there was another triangle, she said, the worst of all. She was caught between Gurumayi and George. What was Gurumayi's relationship with George anyway? Despite the mystique about the guru tradition and supposed celibacy, several people assumed that Gurumayi and George were partners. If so, Laura's position was a nightmare. Perhaps that explained Gurumayi's treatment of Laura throughout the spring. She had been enigmatic, cold, hostile, even cruel, treating Laura as if everything was her fault. Laura was desperately asking for help, some shred of guidance. What she got was hostility and verbal abuse. In yogic traditions, this pattern is justified as "ego busting," the rationalization for showing disciples where they are overly attached, driven by ego.

As I listen to the streams of stories about hidden activities, I am stunned by each new revelation. Ethan is stunned too. At one point, he blurts out, "Isn't there anything you can believe in?"

His voice is constricted, taut with pain, on the edge of tears. I would find out later what he was going through, but now, tangled in my own suffering, I barely notice his outcry. Numbly, I observe how wildly I'm swinging between my own experiences and the newly revealed facts. The organization always had its official explanations for the more serious episodes, but for the most part, being such a large, widespread community, most people never heard about any of this. Today, the facts appear in a new and ominous light. For me in the past, even though the balance between polarities had wobbled precariously, my commitment to the practices and teaching had been so unshakable that I could reestablish the balance.

But now? What possible explanations could justify any of what I was hearing? Suddenly the official explanations collapse into whitewashing and lies. Faced with the shocking array of new facts, this so-called Siddha Yoga reality begins to crack. Have I lived in a partial reality, blinded by my trust and beliefs?

Now I'm in a battle of opposites—good and evil, truth and lies. My outrage grows. I know the dharma rises and falls according to inexorable laws. How could all these people have gotten away with this? How could all these deceptions have been so skillfully executed? How could there be so much good yet so many lives broken? I'm paralyzed by the dissonances. The truth roars in my ears. All I can hear now are the abuses, cover-ups, denials, lies, and violence.

I'm ricocheting between realities, torn apart by brutal facts, waves of disillusionment. I can no longer hold the polarities. Suddenly in one cataclysmic moment, the whole reality shatters, collapsing in on itself. That luminescent, opalescent realm I once visualized totally shatters. I plummet into a maelstrom of feelings—horror, rage, despair, grief, total desolation. I'm totally broken, racked with sobs, then vaguely aware that Laura has come over and is holding me. She, too, is crying, mother and daughter now fully sharing in the brokenheartedness of spiritual disillusionment.

JOURNEY INTO DARKNESS

While Steven and John had discreetly left the room, they would return later for processing and integration of the day. Meanwhile, Laura and I shared bits and pieces of what we'd been through, hardly aware of the great deal of healing that lay ahead. I'd never experienced the kind of pain that was coursing through my body, fire and numbness fighting with each other. I was barely able to talk, my mind assaulted by all the distressing stories I'd just heard. I felt as though something had ignited a depth charge in the deepest recesses of my mind/heart, blowing apart any vestiges of the depth and beauty of this path I'd been on for so many years.

I told Laura that what I most needed was to go for a walk by myself. Numb and proceeding with robotic movements, I put on my coat and walked out our door into the cold, March afternoon. I had no destination. I just started walking in a painful daze down our street.

I was gone less than five minutes when I approached a familiar, neighborhood intersection with a traffic light. At first glance, I couldn't figure out what was happening up ahead of me except that clearly somebody was in serious trouble. A woman was collapsed on the sidewalk. She was holding her head and sobbing loudly, her cries almost hysterical.

As I approached, I suddenly realized she was an Indian woman dressed in a sari, now wrapped awkwardly around her collapsed body. To see an Indian woman was a very unusual sight in our part of town. I could hardly believe what I was seeing.

I hurried up to her, knelt down, and asked gently if I could help. With wild eyes, she looked up at me, blood oozing from a wound on her forehead, flowing down her face, and covering her hands. Struggling to speak between sobs, she explained that she had dropped something from her purse and had leaned down to pick it up. When she stood up, she'd hit her head on a sharp, metal protrusion on the lamppost. Her forehead had a deep wound.

"How can I help?" I asked again. "Do you live near here?"

"In the Fernald apartments," she replied, "about a block away."

"Here, let me help you get home. I'll walk with you."

I wasn't carrying anything to staunch a wound but offered her the scarf around my neck. She couldn't accept. "Thank you anyway," she said and crumpled up the corner of her sari that she held to her head.

She protested my offer to walk with her, but when she held onto my arms as I lifted her up, she realized she was too dizzy and unsteady on her feet to walk alone. After pausing for a few moments to let the dizziness pass, she accepted my arm, and we started toward her home.

Two women, slowly walking along—an Indian woman in her sari, physically wounded in a bizarre accident, and me, spiritually wounded from a heartbreaking meeting. The symbolism of our encounter was almost impossible to believe.

In the days and weeks that followed this devastating experience of being counseled away from the cult of Siddha Yoga, I began the slow, arduous process of healing from spiritual disillusionment. It turned out that I had the company of thousands, and not just from Siddha Yoga because the experience of teachers going astray is pervasive through many spiritual traditions, from the Catholic church to the Mormons, to mention only two.

In 1994, an exposé was published in *The New Yorker*. The Siddha Yoga organization had gone to unbelievable lengths to try to suppress this extremely detailed account of Siddha Yoga's history.[5] They went into the editorial offices of the magazine in New York City and tried to dissuade the editors from publishing the exposé, and they apparently

5 For a comprehensive history of Siddha Yoga, see "O Guru, Guru, Guru," by Lis Harris, *The New Yorker*, November 14, 1994.

bought up all the issues of the magazine in Sullivan County, the location of the ashram, in a desperate effort to stop the spread of this alarming story to the region around the ashram.

The efforts to cover up and deny the truth of the allegations are typical of cult behavior. More immediately demanding, however, was the experience of those of us devastated by disillusionment. There were many meetings of former devotees in the greater Boston area to share stories and find support. The journalist who wrote *The New Yorker* article, who had interviewed Laura, said that in her long journalistic career, she had never encountered such a ferment of distress, disillusionment, and anger—so many thousands of people betrayed by what they had mostly deeply loved.

One might ask about the difference between this kind of pain and the pain from other crises in life like the end of a marriage or job, or the death of a loved one. Whether recognized or not, we all have a sacred place within that connects us with a greater reality, the sense of something eternal and infinite. We might call it the mystery, spirit, soul, the light within, God, Goddess, or other ways to describe the ineffable. Both deep and vast, that sacred space within is beyond the personal, beckoning us toward liberation and ultimate freedom. To have that violated through some form of disillusionment or betrayal feels like a particularly devastating, soul-level form of pain.

To deal with these challenges, three of us—fellow practitioners Priscilla, Donna, and I—decided we wanted to delve more deeply into our experience and find ways to deal with the pain. We began to meet before work in Priscilla's office at 6:30 a.m. every Tuesday morning. Our dedication was impressive. In the winter, we were often meeting before dawn. I remember one heroic day when we forged our way through snow and ice, determined to meet despite the dangerous weather.

Priscilla always assembled a beautiful altar as an expression of devotion to the sacred. We wrapped ourselves in blankets against the cold, sipped hot tea, and always started with a short chant and meditation as we then moved into an ongoing, deep analysis of all that had happened. As psychotherapists, we had a lot of training in that field, but now we were in unfamiliar territory. We tirelessly explored all the thought-provoking issues of a tradition gone awry. How does one come to terms with the betrayal of the sacred feminine by a guru who was a woman? How does one withdraw the projections inevitably at play in a guru tradition? How does one stand fully in one's spiritual sovereignty? Endless questions, urgent probing, we sometimes commented at our own astonishment at the complexities and depth of our exploration.

Besides recognizing the harsh reality of having been in a cult, how does one hold the truth of one's inner experiences, the beauty and depth of the practices, and the seeming solidity of the community of practitioners? The common expression then was how "not to throw out the baby with the bathwater." Many people, devastated by learning the harsh realities of Siddha Yoga, threw out everything, not only their affiliation with the cult but also all the practices that had been part of it.

I remembered Ram Dass's words from many years ago when he had emphasized the importance of keeping the sacredness of the teachings separate from the teacher. All too often, teachers turned out to violate their trust by abusing power, sex, or money. The pressing question was how to hold the paradox of the light with the darkness that coexisted with it. Each of us felt the same sense of urgency—a desperate wish to salvage what was precious and inviolable about our experience, having all had a dedicated practice that was the organizing principle and inspiration in our lives. Fortunately for the three of us, our grounding in the practices was so strong that jettisoning the relationship to the guru and the organization did not affect our commitment to meditation, chanting, dharma study, and the rest.

We affectionately named our little gatherings after the first initials in our names—Priscilla, Olivia, and Donna—and became the POD group. We continued to meet for well over a year until this group merged with another, which I'll describe later and which, amazingly, still exists over twenty-five years later. Such was our commitment to healing from spiritual disillusionment and to continuing the inner journey in the company of fellow seekers.

Besides the explorations of the POD group, I needed to pursue other forms of healing. Many people who go into therapy—even therapists themselves—don't realize the importance of body work that will allow the client to move beyond simply talking about their problems, which limits the process in a mental-emotional mode. No amount of talking, even with a lot of emotional expression, will touch the deeper levels where pain is held in the body. All our life experiences, including the most seemingly insignificant, are encoded at a cellular level in the body. The power of this work was a surprise even to me when I found a very skilled therapist in what was called body-oriented psychotherapy.

Lying on a massage table covered only with a sheet, this therapist invited associations with different parts of the body, using touch to amplify what needed to be expressed along with whatever sounds were inevitably part of the process. Like striking a match to gasoline, my response was rage—blind rage. Nothing compares to a mother's rage over her child's violation. Nothing was held back in body or voice — violent, full-throttled expression of all that was held in my body, guided by a gifted body-oriented therapist who held the enormity of the pain.

This deep level of body work turned out to be a pivotal part of my recovery, as was another form of healing. Also in the year after leaving Siddha Yoga, I went regularly to an artist's garage studio where four of us pursued the artist's way in whatever form called to us. I had worked in a lot of different media over the years, usually during vacations or by taking courses. Now I decided to try a new medium. I shared with Barbara, our teacher, that I was passionate about figuring out any and all ways to help me recover from a devastating betrayal. I chose to work in acrylics, and she encouraged me to work expansively on big canvases.

After about two months of painting up a storm of abstract expressionist images, Barbara invited me to put them up on the walls all around the studio. As I tacked up one after another, I could hardly believe the dramatic display of colors in broad, powerful strokes, all fueled by unbridled emotion.

After I'd finished putting them up, she invited me to stand back and see the results of my creative expression. As I stood there looking at all these vivid, powerful symbolic paintings, a rush of feeling flooded my body, and I broke down. Almost without realizing it, in one large painting after another I had portrayed the immense pain that I was holding in my body. Though I hardly needed it, my three artist friends validated the power of the paintings. They pointed out how the early paintings mostly felt dark and tortured, whereas gradually warm colors began to appear, oranges and yellows, as light gradually emerged out of the darkness. Painting had been another invaluable element in the healing process.

Meanwhile, Laura and Ethan were involved with their own efforts to heal from the enormity of their experiences. Laura explained how helpful it had been to be in school and then college throughout the Siddha Yoga years. Her life always had this other context—a learning community, friends, and activities, all very compelling. After she left Siddha Yoga, she focused on educating herself about the cult phenomenon and welcomed her return to the life of a college student. Later she would have two careers, first in the field of health and healing and then as a school teacher.

Laura and I were fortunate that we never chose to move to the ashram as many people did. Granted, Laura took a gap year in India before her junior year in college. I made many visits to the ashram in the Catskills and India, but I always had a career, my marriage, family, and many activities unrelated to ashram life.

Ethan

After Ethan's anguished cry in the midst of my exit counseling, he explained to us what lay behind his painful realization in that moment. He, too, was in a cult, a group that had evolved around the teachings of Gurdjieff. The group was held in secret under the authoritarian hand of a man named Robert. Members weren't supposed to share last names or contact information and not tell anyone—even their partners—about the teachings and their activities. Yet Ethan's participation in the Gurdjieff group had launched an exceptionally creative phase in his life—singing, art, drama, and other creative arts—a time of expansion and flourishing. As he disentangled himself from the hold of the group, one of his responses struck us as a brilliant reframing. He and his fiancée, Elise, had just acquired two little kittens. He named one of them Robert. What a satisfying way to demystify the power of a cult leader!

Olivia and Laura

Now imagine Hob's situation. All three of his family members were in the process of healing from disillusionment, each in our own way. There was no question that we—all four of us—were a family of spiritual seekers. Three of us had stumbled unwittingly into the all-too-common phenomenon of cults. Hob, too, must have been dealing with shock and disbelief at what was happening to each of us. I don't remember him saying anything judgmental or critical, a significant change from his earlier comments. In truth, his judgments had been how he expressed his concern. He once confessed to me that he had been afraid of losing me, that I might become a swami and choose ashram life over my marriage and family. I never remotely considered such a choice, but it shows the tender issues that can lie beneath the surface of relationships. During this phase, I only remember Hob's steady presence and characteristically wry humor about life. He was an anchor and loving presence for all three of us.

I wondered if a surprising event two years earlier had contributed to how Hob was able to respond to our family crisis. He had done several retreats with Thich Nhat Hanh, informally called Thay, as indeed had I, for I continued to do occasional retreats in other traditions even with my Siddha Yoga affiliation. Totally unexpectedly, Thay had invited Hob to ordain as a Dharmacharya, or senior teacher, a singular honor. Not only was Hob surprised, he wasn't even asked to consider it. He was simply told to be in France about four weeks later for the ceremony of ordination. Through this ceremony, he was initiated into an ancient Vietnamese lineage and received two new names in Vietnamese: the first translated as "True Vehicle" (conveyor of the dharma), the second as "Boundless Heart."

Both names were inspiring to me. Spiritual names are given as a form of aspiration. They seemed to honor Hob's gifts as a teacher and also perhaps the healing needed for his peek-a-boo heart, which was how a former colleague had aptly described his tenderness toward expressions of love. Boundless Heart—given what we were going through at that time, all four of us needed to take refuge in that name.

Finally, after my various efforts to find healing, I had a striking dream about Gurumayi. The dream contradicted everything about her and her appearance. After all, she carried the bestowed power of having been chosen as Muktananda's successor and initiated into that role in an elaborate ceremony that involved a number of Brahmin priests. For years, she had presided over ashrams around the world, all part of a vast international community of many thousands of devotees. A beautiful Indian woman then in her forties, she always wore the orange of a renunciant, invariably an elegant silk sari-like garment that set off her slim figure. Given her training from the time she was a young girl, then for many years as Baba's translator, and finally as the guru herself, she was not only physically beautiful but a compelling presence.

The dream contradicted all of that. In the dream, she appeared wearing an enormous necklace, by far the most dominant feature, eclipsing the usual beauty of her clothes. Hanging around her neck down almost to her waist, the necklace was a collection of dark, ominous objects—small skulls, shards of dark broken glass, bones, jagged rocks—a frightful assortment emanating darkness and danger, an ominous blending of the darkness of Kali with the horror of a Medusa.

It was only a dream fragment, but its power symbolized the initiation I had been going through for the last two years—an initiation into the darkness. That initiation had been as valuable as the original initiation many years before. I could never have anticipated that my determination to heal from this version of trauma would reveal new depths of experience through shared inquiry with friends, through art, through bodywork, and through facing into the darkest corners of my psyche. From a path that had emphasized the transcendent, this was a journey into full humanity, accepting the paradoxes, the play of opposites, the joys and sorrows, the light and darkness.

Disillusionment had not destroyed my commitment to the path of practice. That now included once again the search for a teacher, one that had started twenty years earlier with the landmark book *The Way of the White Clouds.* Newfound wisdom had come from the lessons about the perilous territory around spiritual teachers. I had done the inner work with fierce dedication. I waited until the time felt right, and then I picked up the thread of seeking the teacher I had tried to meet twice before. I was ready to move into a new chapter.

THE MEETING

After a fifteen-year interlude while involved with Siddha Yoga and after almost two years of arduous inner work to heal from spiritual disillusionment, I made a third effort to contact Domo Geshe Rinpoche. I wrote to him explaining in one page what had happened, how I'd been practicing in a devotional tradition from India, had discovered that it was a cult with a dark shadow, and that I'd left Siddha Yoga but had continued my practices. Because I recognized the role of a teacher in one's practice, I was hoping that this time I might meet with him.

By then, having suffered through the knocks and blows along the spiritual path, I sent off the letter with an open, unattached attitude. This time, I received an affirmative answer to my request to meet him. I found a B&B in the Beaverkill Valley in the heart of the Catskill Mountains where his place was located and a month later set out on the six-hour drive.

I found myself thinking back to Lama Govinda's *The Way of the White Clouds*, which included the account of how Domo Geshe's reincarnation had been found. Everyone in the Tibetan tradition knows about the process of identifying the reincarnations of high lamas and the accompanying assumption that they would be taken into monastic training at a very young age.

Stories like these challenge our Western mindset where so many people are skeptical about the reality of reincarnation. They assume that such stories must be apocryphal. But they aren't; they are supported by facts. Although many records about his life were lost with the Chinese invasion of Tibet, he was known for his ability to remain neutral and help arbitrate in some of the most politically divisive Tibetan crises such as the conflict between the regent and the ex-regent. He was widely known with countless followers, famous also for the *rilbus* he compiled for healing and protection. Even Chinese soldiers came to him seeking protection. Too highly visible as a spiritual leader and seen by the Chinese as part of the resistance, in March 1959, shortly after the war broke out, Rinpoche was taken prisoner by the Chinese.

Theoretically he should have escaped imprisonment because he had been born in Sikkim and was not a Tibetan national. But he was too visible for the Chinese to ignore. For two years, he was subjected to the most appalling conditions, forced to clean out pigsties and sewers and driven to carry heavy slabs of concrete because he was the youngest prisoner. But one of them fell on him, seriously injuring his back, an injury that plagued him for the rest of his life. Meanwhile, because of his eminent status, the Chinese attempted everything to brainwash him into submission. But when that failed, for several months they put him in solitary confinement in total darkness in a tiny cell where he could not even lie down.

Rinpoche survived these unimaginable conditions. Finally, as a result of continued political pressure on the Chinese, he was released from prison, but his health had been seriously impaired, which would have an ongoing impact later in his life. At the risk of his life, he spent his remaining days in Lhasa collecting sacred texts, priceless manuscripts, and holy objects to be shipped out of the country for safe keeping. Ultimately, the Chinese expelled him from the country, and in 1961, he left for India with nothing but the robes he was wearing and a wooden bowl.

At one level, I could hardly understand what quiet force was propelling me to follow through on this impulse, which had been set in motion almost twenty years earlier when I read about the previous Domo Geshe Rinpoche in Lama Govinda's book and then my friend Margot met him in a department store, of all places. That's when I became determined to find a highly attained teacher, hopefully in circumstances where I might have a more direct student-teacher relationship than had been possible in a large, international community with a world-famous guru. I had made two previous attempts to meet Domo Geshe, neither of which had worked out.

Meanwhile, the whole Siddha Yoga chapter passed by in fifteen years—seventeen if I counted the dream in which Muktananda first appeared. Despite the unacknowledged darkness and the shocking experience of my daughter Laura, those years had introduced me to the gifts of devotional practice, the beauty of everything surrounding the tradition, its ancient roots in Indian culture, the beautiful chanting, the powerful and the spiritual intensity of a guru-oriented community. Again and again the question would arise—how do we negotiate the extremes of so much light and so much darkness? Surely this is one of life's greatest challenges, one that many of us meet at one time or another, whatever form it takes.

As I approached this meeting with Domo Geshe, I was only two years away from having left Siddha Yoga. I'd been plunged into the darkness and pain of spiritual disillusionment and was still close to the challenging process of trying to heal from it. What in the world was I doing once again moving toward another spiritual teacher? I couldn't explain it, even to myself. Others might harbor their judgments on how this was one more unconscious effort to find some form of security in an uncertain world or that it was some unresolved issue around spiritual leaders in positions of power. As a psychologist in a healing process, I had thought deeply about all the facets of this issue—the guru-disciple relationship fraught with complexities, the tension between so much light and so much darkness, the imponderables of the spiritual journey itself—and I'd done my best to confront them head on. Yet here I was, once again wanting to meet this teacher.

The circumstances, however, could hardly have been more different. There was no huge, international scene around Domo Geshe. He didn't offer public teachings. I'd heard that in his line of reincarnations they alternated between being exceptionally public and extremely hidden. Domo Geshe was more like the latter; he lived in a remote mountain valley providing guidance for his monasteries far away in India and Tibet. He didn't give talks or write books. In America, very few people had heard of him.

What then was calling me? I couldn't answer but simply held steady with this deep intention, wherever it came from. The facile explanation might be that I had some karmic connection to Domo Geshe. Karma is a highly mysterious subject, inexplicable to the rational, very literal Western mind that wants to figure things out by what can be seen, measured, and proved. Some of life's mysteries simply can't be figured out. As Westerners, we are deeply conditioned to rely on the intellect, yet much of this wondrous world is far beyond anything the intellect can begin to comprehend.

These were some of my ponderings as I came to the end of the long drive and eventually found the two white posts that marked the entrance to the Dungkar Gompa Society's property. That's when I remembered something else I'd heard. While still in Sikkim after his release from the Chinese prison, Domo Geshe had apparently had a vision of the land where he'd be living once he moved to America. He had described the lions on the gateposts, peacocks at another gate, a "vase" image (*bumpa*), a river, a lake, and an "earth lotus" (a reference to the undulating hills like the petals of a lotus encircling the valley), and "a sky lotus" (perhaps referring to the openness to the sky of the great meadow or the lake).[6]

Whatever one's beliefs about visions, all of these signs were there, as I would soon see for myself. I was greeted at the door by Ann who, along with Danielle, manages Rinpoche's place. The large white, rather formal, French style house seemed somewhat incongruous in the Catskill Mountains of rural New York, but it was a welcoming place. She led me through a big, open living room, now the shrine room with an altar at one end and chairs along the sides, then up two steps into a smaller dining and sitting room combined. The dining room table was at the end of the room where a large picture window looked out over a small pond to the big meadow bordered by the Beaverkill River. The other end of the room had a couch, a couple of chairs, a fireplace, and a swinging door leading into the pantry and kitchen beyond.

Ann invited me to sit at the dining room table while she disappeared through the swinging door to get tea. I took in the details of the simply furnished and welcoming room—the thangkas hanging on the warm yellow-orange walls, a bookcase filled with books about Tibet. I wasn't nervous but certainly on extra alert as one is when entering any house for the first time, especially given all that had led to this moment. If anything, because of all that history, I felt as though I was also in a kind of dream

6 Ursula Bernis. *His Holiness Domo Geshe Rinpoche: A Biographical Sketch*, 51.

state, hardly believing I'd come all this way to meet this stranger known only to me through a book and a friend's stories. Like being suspended between all I'd left behind—fifteen years in Siddha Yoga—and whatever lay ahead, a complete unknown, I sat alone, surveying the room and the view out the window. The place felt remarkably peaceful.

Ann brought in the tea tray with cups, a pot, and some cookies as we made easy conversation, presumably waiting for Rinpoche's arrival. Finally the pantry door swung open, and Rinpoche walked in. Slender and slight of stature, he wore the brown robes of a Tibetan monk. I sensed traces of physical frailty, undoubtedly from his treatment in prison, but totally overriding that was his authority and inner strength somehow combined with a felt tenderness and deep calm. His expression was serious yet kind. He walked to the far end of the table, clearly his seat, with his left side to the wide window and Ann at his side. I was sitting on his right at the end of the table. I had no idea what the protocols might be in a situation like this, but it seemed respectful to wait until he spoke first.

Domo Geshe Rinpoche

Looking at me briefly with the same serious expression, he turned to Ann and spoke in a soft voice. I had heard that he was very soft-spoken, and indeed I could only pick up a few words of his English. It became apparent that she was like an interpreter, not from Tibetan to English but making clear whatever he'd said in English. There was a brief exchange of pleasantries, welcoming me, hoping I'd had an easy trip, and then a pause.

I began to speak, repeating very succinctly what had been in my letter; that I'd tried to meet him twice before in the late '70s, that now (1996) I was grateful for the opportunity to meet, that I had had years of Vipassana practice followed by fifteen years in Siddha Yoga, and that I was healing from the realization of its hidden darkness. I may have said all that in about three sentences, startling myself that I could condense all that intense life experience in so few words.

There was another pause, and then he started speaking, not in response to anything I'd said, even though I felt as though I had just handed him twenty-five years of my life in a dispassionate synopsis. As he spoke, because of his soft voice I knew I was missing the flow of whatever he was saying. I tried to catch up because to my amazement, he was now talking about the Silk Road, about exchanges of wisdom between East and West, about a part of the world I knew practically nothing about. I was trying to stay clear about what was happening, but he'd gone at right angles to what I'd said. There was no acknowledgement that he'd heard me, no effort to connect my synopsis with what he was now talking about. I had heard that teachers could be inscrutable in their actions, an invitation to projection and confusion for the student, but I certainly didn't know what to make of what was happening. I was aware of being intensely aware of the subtleties of relationship with someone newly met, especially a spiritual teacher about whom I'd read and heard so much. I was most aware of his gentle presence, deep interiority, and compassion.

Because I had dropped into some kind of timeless state, after about twenty-five minutes or half an hour I sensed that the meeting was coming to an end. Rinpoche glanced toward me, and to my own surprise, I heard myself say, "May I come back sometime?"

Without a pause, he replied, "Come back in the spring when the leaves are starting to come out."

He rose quietly, asked Ann to give me a box of Tibetan incense, and left the room back through the swinging pantry door.

I was left with Ann who, with great patience, answered my questions. I was assuming, of course, that he meant solitary retreat because except for occasional private programs, there were no teachings, no initiations, no public programs. Where would I stay? I would stay in Bata, the small cottage between the farmhouse and the barn, or later on maybe in one of the three little cottages up through the woods by the lake. Would I get to see Rinpoche? Yes, probably at the beginning and end of my retreat.

After thanking Ann and leaving, I could hardly make out what had happened in this long-awaited meeting. We certainly hadn't had any ordinary kind of conversation. I barely felt acknowledged except by his gentle, kindly looks. As someone both impressionable and quick to trust, I had to be careful of any stories I might start to tell myself about the meeting—for example, that maybe a whole lot was going on at a deeper, beyond-the-mind level; that his inner state, presumably unfathomable to me, might account for my trusting him and our unusual encounter, even though on an outward level not much seemed to have happened. What a conundrum!

The answers to my questioning would start to unfold over time. Whenever I talked about him, my eyes filled with tears. I returned for that first retreat the following spring and felt incomparably cared for. At our initial meeting, I asked him for teachings, for I had been told that in this close teacher-student relationship, you only got teachings when you asked. He told me to do shorter practice—a complete turnaround from the long sittings to deepen concentration and develop samadhi in the Vipassana tradition or the extensive liturgical, chanting practices of Siddha Yoga.

Memorably, he once came with Ann to Bata, the little retreat cottage where I often stayed. He had come to offer me the savory rice soup that he had made, mysteriously delicious like no soup I'd ever tasted. But then much to my surprise, he stayed. He sat down at the little kitchen table, and with Ann translating his idiomatic English, he told me one unbelievable story after another about life in Tibet. For instance, he talked about trance running and about the famous yeti, the legendary creature said to inhabit the most distant reaches of Himalaya. He spoke about miraculous happenings and other mind-bending stories.

I was very touched by the time he took to introduce me to these esoteric aspects of Tibetan culture and, in retrospect, felt sure that the ultimate purpose of these stories was to reveal the many other levels of reality that my conditioned, Western mind could never decipher. His stories weren't about what I did or didn't believe; they were an invitation to open up to subtle realities far beyond my ordinary experience. I would look back at this meeting as a treasured event in my relationship with him. He had introduced me to the realm of non-ordinary states of consciousness, something I would explore later in surprising ways. Furthermore, the Tibetan tradition involves many complex visualization practices that are an invitation to subtle dimensions of reality. I was again struck that whenever I thought back to our meeting, I became teary with gratitude.

I continued to be profoundly touched by Domo Geshe's extraordinarily kind and tender presence. His movements, speech, everything about him exuded kindness. His deep, calm presence was a teaching in itself. Even the deer that lived in the fields and forests around the main house trusted this simple, gentle monk. Once, standing by the living room window, I could hardly believe what I saw. A wild deer—unafraid and totally trusting—was eating from his hand.

Then one day down by the river, I saw a deer at the edge of the meadow near a stand of bushes. Without even thinking, I slowly reached down and picked a fistful of grasses and started to walk, slow step by slow step toward the deer. She was watching me, unmoving, ears totally alert. I kept eye contact, hardly breathing. Like a very slow dance, the distance between us closed. Still she didn't move. As I slowly extended my offering of grass, she stretched her tawny neck until I felt the soft skin of her muzzle and then the gentle movement of her lips as she ate out of my hand.

I had no illusions that this precious encounter had happened because the deer around the property had come to trust Rinpoche's gentle nature. Still, I was filled with wonder, astonishment, and gratitude for these remarkable moments with the doe—a rare gift.

Rinpoche was to give me my first simplified version of a Tara sadhana, Tara being the beloved goddess in the Tibetan tradition, a manifestation of the sacred feminine like Kuan Yin or Mother Mary. Further along in visualization practices, I realized how they were intended to open us into subtler realms of reality, thereby loosening our attachment to the apparent solidity of the phenomenal world and especially to the persistent hold of the ego.

As I continued to do solitary retreats and meet with Rinpoche at the beginning and end of each retreat, he kept encouraging me to do shorter practice periods of meditation and to include the chanting and artwork that I so loved. I saw how he was working on my tendency to be over-zealous toward practice and to assume that sitting meditation was the high road to wherever I thought I was going. Obviously, the fullest understanding of meditation is to cultivate total absorption and full awareness to all our activities while acknowledging that working with the mind/heart through sitting meditation is an incomparably powerful practice.

Who was Domo Geshe? This gentle, soft-spoken Tibetan had not a shred of personality noise. Most striking was his kindly, quiet, and wise presence that commanded immense respect. This was no ordinary guru scene. There weren't other students around or a single picture or any sign that anything remarkable was going on here, yet I continued to be moved by my brief meetings with him. I couldn't help but feel that some kind of transmission was going on at a level beyond my mind.

The news came suddenly. Domo Geshe had passed away on September 10, 2001—the day before the September 11th catastrophe when the hijacked planes created chaos and destruction in three places across the country. Again, here were the extremes, polarities that tear at our vision of reality, in this case the passing of this compassionate Tibetan who had had untold impact throughout his life juxtaposed against the violence and destruction of the hijacked planes.

Looking back, I realized that I'd met Domo Geshe in 1996, the year my husband, Hob, had been tentatively diagnosed with Alzheimer's, leading to his death in November 2001, ten weeks after Domo Geshe died. I appreciated what a blessing it had been to have Rinpoche's presence in my life during those six challenging years and, of course beyond to this day. The image keeps arising and can still bring tears to my eyes. Like a great bird's wing extended over me, his kindly, gentle presence had accompanied me through the most difficult time in my life.

SELF-ORDINATION AND THE DANCE OF FREEDOM

In that liminal state at the edge of waking, I heard a voice repeating, *We're a small group of six, and our lives depend on it.* The dream repeated the statement again. *We're a small group of six, and our lives depend on it.* Though still more asleep than awake, I picked up the refrain, repeating it, determined not to forget it. The words in the dream carried urgency and import. I *must* remember them!

The Self-Ordination Circle in the late 1990s

I knew the dream was about our Self-Ordination Circle. At that time, the group was composed of six women, but why the dream's urgent statement that our lives depend on it? Still barely awake, I found myself drifting back to a memorable time when the circle had its beginnings. It was a raw, January day in 1997. Several good friends were gathering with about twenty others for daylong teachings with Tsultrim Allione, a teacher in the Tibetan Buddhist tradition. Her book *Wisdom Rising: Journey into the Mandala of the Empowered Feminine* had had widespread impact, and she planned to teach on this subject.

As I climbed the steps to the front door of the rambling, brown-shingled house for the meeting, I felt a flash of anticipation and anxiety. I was about to turn sixty. Even with all that I had to be grateful for, I had been feeling unsettled—a gentle nudging toward something new in life, but I had no idea what that might be. It was like an echo of the Spirit Bird dream, a liminal time with intimations for change but no clear direction. *Maybe today's meeting will help shed some light on what's going on*, I thought to myself. *That's my hope and intention for today.*

As we gathered in the spacious front hall before the teachings began, the conversation turned to the astrological indications of the day.

"It's the full moon of January," someone commented, "and looking at the astrological implications of today, there's an unusual harmonic convergence, meaning that several planets are in an auspicious configuration. That amplifies subtle energies, and even if we don't feel them, this is a particularly powerful day for us to be meeting."

At the time, I'd been reading an arresting book, *Anatomy of the Spirit* by Caroline Myss, an exploration of the subtle body and the opening of the chakras or energy centers in the body through yoga and spiritual practice. When the six of us gathered during the lunch break, I began to share thoughts about the book.

"I don't know if you all can relate to this, but I was really interested when I read her assertion that when the throat chakra opens—that's the communication center—the pertinent words are a form of calling, 'I'm ready. Show me my task.'"

I was really struck by this statement because the book goes on to explain that the throat chakra is connected to the subject of ordination. It's different from traditional ordination bestowed by some priest.

"Thank heavens!" one friend broke in. "We've all had enough of patriarchy and priests. Where are the priestesses?"

There was a ripple of laughter, and I elaborated further about the book. "This different form of initiation comes from one's community, from the collective. They see and affirm your gifts as a spiritual teacher. It is a calling to honor and fulfill one's unique task in life. It's neither hierarchical nor patriarchal but rather initiated through the vision of one's community. That feels really different to me."

By this time, it was clear that the topic had ignited a lot of interest among the six of us. Three of us had been invited to traditional ordination. We had all declined for different reasons. I'd declined because I was still healing from spiritual disillusionment. The others didn't feel called to traditional ministry, and one of them spoke of her discomfort with the paternalistic language of her tradition and especially the prospect of ordination coming through a priest.

As the conversation continued, I shared more about the significance of the throat chakra. The five of us were huddled close to listen, for clearly this topic had captivated all of us.

"According to ancient wisdom," I continued, "women's enlightenment is also connected to the opening of this center. Women are called to speak their truth in new and powerful ways, free from the constraints of patriarchy. And listen to this. A friend of mine was meditating on one of the Black Madonnas in a French church when she heard the words, 'When we are ready, we give birth to the clarity of the Word—the Truth.'"

There were murmurs of appreciation around our little circle. What an inspiring vision had come into our midst.

"All of these revelations are really striking," I said. "Something about the symbolic meanings, the connection between the throat chakra and ordination, as well as women's enlightenment touches me so strongly. I think we should find some way to continue exploring this together."

Propelled by the energy of that conversation, we brought together two small groups and began to meet monthly, calling ourselves the Self-Ordination Circle. Primarily, the origin of the name related to a non-traditional form of ordination. For us, it also assumed another dimension. We shared the vision of continuously evolving into an expanded sense of Self, a readiness to move toward the next challenge or calling in one's life. This theme was always central to our group's vision of ordination.

We were intrigued by how the S-O group, as we fondly called it, unfolded. We rotated meetings among us. The host for the meeting created an altar. The altars were always unique, a way to acknowledge that we were creating sacred time and sacred space. We started with chanting "Devi devi," a melodic Sanskrit chant to the sacred feminine, followed by fifteen to twenty minutes of meditation.

The heart of our meetings involved a check-in from each person—ten to twenty minutes of uninterrupted, reflective sharing. This invitation was like dropping a plumb line into one's life to assess its depths and crosscurrents in the present moment. Through this process, we might identify an area in life where we were called to take the next step, to speak our truth, to stand forth in some new way.

An important part of the sharing process was to give thoughtful feedback. We might point out an unconscious pattern, clarify a complex issue, or support each other in moving forward in an empowered way. Sometimes the issue was dramatic—perhaps it was time to leave a job or relationship—and sometimes it was subtle, like raising a sensitive issue in a relationship, stepping out professionally, or risking some new behavior. As a specific example, one of our members had asked her revered mentor to write the introduction to her book. The mentor wrote virtually nothing about the author but focused instead on her role in originating the project. For our member, it was a Self-ordination issue to confront her mentor with and explain why she couldn't use the introduction, a challenging situation that took diplomacy and courage.

As a group, we'd sense when it was time for an ordination ritual, for ritual exists to honor significant passages in life. When we sensed that one of us was ready to move to a new level of Self-ordination, she would stand in the center of the circle, the others gathered around her. Wearing something special to honor the occasion, the group stood as witnesses to her next step, their hands on her shoulders in a form of blessing. We listened in silence as she declared her statement of intention, clarification, or affirmation to move forward in her life in a courageous, empowered way.

Over the years, our gatherings continued to be a treasured time. Sometimes we arranged to have overnight, extended meetings where we had ample time for open-ended conversation, sharing latest discoveries, and abundant fun—walks, a restaurant, a movie.

Besides the organizing principle of Self-ordination, we were deeply bonded by being dedicated dharma practitioners. Dharma issues were often a subject for thought-provoking discussions. Furthermore, all of us were drawn to the exploration of new forms of consciousness—a range of modalities that included channeling, psychics, spiritual healing, NDEs (near-death experiences), UFOs, crop circles, and the quantum reality of contemporary physics. In one of our favorite activities, we regularly turned to the wisdom of the Tarot. We would each shuffle the deck to connect with the energy of the cards and then draw a card. Reflecting on the image, we would use that as a springboard for receptive writing, followed by shared readings.

In meetings laced with laughter, we shared books and resources, listened to each other's latest discovery, and once even spent a weekend at a rustic getaway by a lake in northern Vermont. We swam, walked, sky-gazed, and simply enjoyed the luxury of leisure. In a memorable moment, someone discovered a small cement monument only a few yards from our cabins. Set in the middle of a wide spread of mown grass, the little monument—incredibly!—marked the border between the United States and Canada. No fence. No official building. No border patrol. Only an open, unprotected border. The six of us lined up, one behind the other with a foot in each country, and immortalized the moment with a photograph.

To provide a striking example of an ordination issue, during one of my check-ins, I expressed some sensitivity about my Ames ancestry. Priscilla, one of our members, immediately picked up on the feeling-tone of my sharing. She was a therapist and gifted astrologer, intuitive and wise. She had interpreted my chart several times, which meant that she was familiar with the psychological and spiritual patterns that influenced my life. Now she spoke up.

"I think you have some unresolved legacy issues with your Ames heritage and that there's more here than you're aware of. I have a suggestion. It would be a first for us, but why not?"

Priscilla emphasized the last few words, almost like a challenge. "Why don't we spend a day at your grandparents' house in North Easton. The day will be for you to tell us all your stories, your memories, and whatever issues come up for you, and let's see how they relate to our S-O group and our issues with patriarchy and spiritual authority."

As I listened to Priscilla, I was incredulous at her proposal. A whole day! Yet I knew how perceptive she was. Listening to my body, I recognized a heightened sense of excitement that often arose when the subject of my Ames ancestors came up. The excitement was out of balance, amplified by tender feelings like how to reconcile my pride in their accomplishments with my fear that my privileged background would separate me from others. I had lived with this tension since my teenage years.

Priscilla's suggestion launched a momentous day. A few months later, the six of us drove the hour from Cambridge to North Easton. Because I was a family member, I got permission for us to spend the day in the house, which remained closed to the public except for one day a week when the mansion was open for tours. We spent the first part of the morning on a leisurely tour of the mansion as I provided a running commentary—rooms filled with GrandB's paintings, mostly portraits; glass-fronted cabinets displaying stuffed birds or artifacts from around the world; the historic room filled with Civil War memorabilia; letters from Presidents; Benjamin Butler's Civil War army uniform with medals; an antique American flag; GrandB's third-floor art studio with its easels, color charts, and works in progress; the butterfly cabinet with drawers displaying exotic species collected from around the world; the dining room with its large model of a clipper ship hanging over the mahogany table; the cavernous front hall over which presided, on a pedestal, the marble bust of "old Oliver," GrandO's father who had been the Governor of Massachusetts.

We ended up in the library, the six of us gathered in a circle in front of the fireplace at the far end of the vast room. Following our custom, we created a simple altar on a small table with flowers from my garden and a few treasured objects brought by each friend. We launched the meeting with chanting Sanskrit mantras, the ceremonial way we started all our gatherings.

It was incredible to me that, thanks to Priscilla's initiative, I'd brought my five close friends to witness a part of my story about which I'd been ambivalent for so long. The stories poured forth, a torrent of family information that I'd hidden in the back recesses of memory, protected from others. My friends urged me onward, calling for more, holding everything with their curiosity and caring. Blown open—the tendency to censor. Blown apart—the shards of embarrassment. Blown away—the habit of hiding. I felt as though a brisk wind of freedom was blowing through me, releasing subtle burdens and old patterns. All the storytelling led to the two crowning events of the day.

Throughout our meeting time, I had been wearing an ordination stole in soft earth colors, woven by the indigenous people of Central America. As if called to a moment of truth, I got up and stood in front of the fireplace, facing into the cavernous library. My five friends had fallen silent and were watching, witnesses to whatever would happen next. I raised both arms wide and high in a gesture of openness and triumph, and started to speak to my ancestors. I invited their presences to join us. In a stentorian voice, I told them who I was, the discoveries I'd made, the

Addressing my ancestors

distances I'd traveled. I told them about the inner journey and the ground upon which I stood before them. I thanked them for their gifts and honored their lives. I affirmed my choices and my spiritual journey. By the end of my oration, I had spoken the truth of my life to those hallowed, book-lined walls and to whatever presences might have been present. I had declared my freedom to them —and from them.

That truth-telling gesture might have brought closure to the day, but another spontaneous event unfolded. We started to chant Kali Durge, a favorite rollicking chant from Siddha Yoga, the meditative path that several of us shared. Kali, the dark goddess and an archetype in the Hindu pantheon, is depicted as black, wearing a necklace of skulls to symbolize her fearlessness. Her fierce expression and dancing body portray her power as the goddess of both creation and destruction. The chant—melodic and spirited—began to fill the vast library with the echoes of our lusty voices.

Dance of freedom on GrandO's desk

Almost without thinking, I took off my shoes and socks and jumped barefoot onto my grandfather's desk—now bare of papers and books—and began to dance. The others gathered in a circle around the desk and began dancing around it, clapping with exuberance while I danced wild and free on top of the massive, formal desk, the chant rising and accelerating with our shared exultation. Another triumphant and celebratory moment. Another expression of unbounded freedom.

Something profound about my relationship to legacy had been transformed that day. I had experienced the freedom to choose what to honor and what to relinquish. Above all, the need to remain hidden had been transformed. I had spoken, declared, and danced my way into a new freedom that both embraced my past and liberated me from it.

The day at my grandparents' place was a compelling example of our small group's commitment to the principle of Self-ordination. For me, the way opened to further dharma teaching with a new focus on issues of aging and eventually to writing my second book, *Aging with Wisdom*. Given the group's dynamic energy, we have continued to evolve, responding to our aging and ongoing commitment to spiritual practice.

Most inspiring, the S-O group has provided an inner compass for us individually and collectively. As a small but powerful collective, we've collaborated in this journey of consciousness, always exploring, always evolving. As one member once said, "Self-Ordination is a recognition of one's own inner spiritual authority and taking action on that basis." Or as another put it, "We need no religious denomination to grant us the authority to perform rites and ceremonies. Challenging issues arise in our lives that need special attention and empowerment to resolve."

For more than twenty-five years, the group has been our centering point amid turbulent times. This surely explained the urgency of the words in my dream, *We're a small group of six, and our lives depend on it.* From an excerpt in a book to our initial gathering through many years of exploration, the Self-Ordination group has been a source of inspiration for us all. We always sensed that we were part of what is called the Great Turning or the Shift, the transformation of consciousness needed to create a more sustainable world. We lived with questions of how to relate to the urgency of the times and whether to move into social justice or political action. Our vision has been influenced by the revelations of quantum physics wherein everything in the universe is intricately interconnected down to the level of individual thought. We trust that the impact of our inner work, our intentions, and actions have radiated to touch the lives of others, even into the quantum where assuredly our small group has offered light to our darkened world.

THE GIFTS OF ADVERSITY

The origins of our Self-Ordination group had evolved from my Clearness Committee, a practice from the Quaker tradition, I had convened when my husband Hob's life began unraveling from the ravages of Alzheimer's. We were facing one of life's greatest challenges, and as his primary caregiver, I needed support. Especially in the last three years of his illness I was focused on just surviving the ruthless succession of losses and crises. Often the challenges were overwhelming, even with the help of our psychological and meditative training. In those days, it seemed inconceivable to me that there could be any gifts hidden in the darkness.

But there were. As I came to see it, two influences were at play for us. The first was Hob's background in literature, his gift for memorization, and his love of words. He was forever playing with images, quotations, and humor—one of the ways he dealt with the enormity of Alzheimer's. The second was because he was by nature a reflective person. His many decades of dedicated meditation practice and teaching contributed to his wisdom about the nature of the mind/heart. These may have been exceptional gifts particular to him, but there were many instances where his comments, quotations, or observations felt like gifts to all of us. Let me share a few of the memorable ones.

From the beginning, I had asked Hob to let me know what he was experiencing as much as he could. Considering that both of us were dedicated students of understanding the mind through meditation, this wasn't a surprising request. Some people with dementia, however, either can't speak about their experience or choose not to. Hob, on the other hand, was glad to provide what we humorously called "his reports from the interior."

For example, at some point in the middle stages of his illness, he came up with a vivid image to describe his inability to express something.

As he declared one evening, "The words get stuck. I've got this galloping brain drain. I know what to say, but the word horde is locked up. It's like a corral filled with horses all pushing against each other to get out, but they can't find the gate. Now that's a great image!"

Then he broke into laughter, delighted by his whimsical way of describing what was, in fact, frustrating and painful.

Thanks to my Clearness Committee gathering that morphed into our Self-Ordination Circle, I had done my best to prepare for what lay ahead after Hob had received the tentative diagnosis. But no one is ever ready for the overwhelm of this illness. It's a slow-motion robbery job that gradually steals away the words, the memories, and finally the last vestiges of personality. Still something remains—some deep essence that can be touched and awakened through touch, song, poetry, and, above all, love.

Now, more than twenty years since Hob's death, I'm more aware than ever that we live in a timeless universe. Although we spend a lot of time being governed, even tyrannized, by linear time, I marvel at how much I experience the timeless nature of life, especially now that I'm in the Elder years. Loved ones like Hob, my parents, grandparents, and other dear ones feel more present to me than I remember in my younger years. Has a mysterious process started to soften the boundaries between linear time—*chronos*—and eternal time—*kairos*? Might this be a gentle preparation for what lies in the beyond—the other side of our leaving physical form?

My view across time has slowly worked its alchemical wonders on the most challenging chapter of my life, accompanying Hob on this journey with dementia. Everyone knows how utterly devastating it is. How, then, is it possible for me to talk about the gifts of adversity? How did this harrowing of our lives also become a valuable part of my spiritual journey? How can I find anything redeemable in such a heartbreaking experience?

Like flares of light in the darkness, certain bits of wisdom still inspire me across the years. Naturally, the workings of time provide perspective. I wrote my first book, *Ten Thousand Joys & Ten Thousand Sorrows: A*

Couple's Journey Through Alzheimer's, as part of my own healing, but even more because I knew that what we experienced would be helpful for others. It was an urgent calling, plain and simple. Now, years after the book's publication and all the countless talks, articles, and interviews that followed, the process of transformation has worked its way even deeper. Once again, I'm compelled to share my perspectives, now updated—what I call wisdom treasures from a journey to hell and back.

There was our background in psychology and meditation, and there was Hob's playfulness and sense of humor. Frustration, grief, and fear also lurked in the hidden recesses in both our hearts—of that I'm sure. There was no way to minimize the harrowing process of this illness. At the beginning, there was also incredulity and anxiety about the unknowns that lay ahead. Yet that was what brought the first wisdom treasure. Soon after the diagnosis, we had a conversation about wanting to live with the challenges as consciously and lovingly as possible. "Consciously and lovingly" became our shared vision, floating somewhere in the background but always an aspiration.

Buddhist philosophy teaches about the importance of the "view," and having the "right view" is one of the steps on the Eightfold Path described in the fourth Noble Truth. Because Hob and I were both immersed in Buddhist practice, we came up with this simple but compelling "view" without even realizing that we were calling upon a key teaching. We simply framed it in our own words.

Ever since I heard Ram Dass use the phrase "conscious aging" way back in the mid-1970s, I had embraced the invitation inherent in the phrase, sometimes as if my life depended on it. What does it mean? Probably something different for each of us. Surely it's a wake-up call to the preciousness of life—each day, each moment, that preciousness amplified as we age. With aging, new and sometimes overwhelming challenges arise. Don't avoid, don't deny, don't run. Look directly at what's unfolding, no matter how hard, even the diagnosis of a life-threatening illness, maybe *especially* the hardest news. Once more, these words are also for myself, exhorting me to remember! As we learn from meditation practice, open to whatever arises, and greet it with curiosity and acceptance. Hold it with the kindness and compassion of your open heart. It's far from easy but an invitation nonetheless and intricately woven into our situation.

As I reflect upon it, the phrase "conscious aging" has key components, each one an essential part of spiritual practice whatever your tradition—acceptance of change, openness to the unknown, living with awareness, acceptance of our mortality, and finally, awakening to our deepest nature through meditation or any contemplative practice that works with the mind/heart. What a compelling list—a recipe for waking up! All those elements were at play in our exhortation to greet whatever was coming "consciously and lovingly."

In the early months, I went to see a longtime spiritual friend, or *kalyana mitra*, the Sanskrit name for one who values and supports your inner life. I had met Tulku Thondup many years before. He was the first person I sought out in my search for a highly attained teacher. A tulku is someone who has been identified as an emanation or reincarnation of a previous Buddhist master. Tulku Thondup, born in Tibet, had been identified at age five, received traditional monastic training, and eventually moved to the United States, having taught and authored countless books ever since.

When I first met with him, I wasn't ready to adopt the complexities of the Tibetan tradition. Nevertheless, a mysterious seed of connection was planted then. Although I didn't turn to him formally as a teacher, occasionally I found myself seeking him out when faced with a perplexing life issue. This time it was the prospect of living with Alzheimer's. Those occasional visits were made easy because he lived only a few blocks away, and he always generously agreed to see me even though I wasn't formally his student.

As I found my way to his small apartment on a back street in Cambridge, I formulated my essential question—how might Buddhist perspectives help us to negotiate Hob's illness? What was the highest understanding we could bring to these challenges? While we sipped green tea and started with the initial pleasantries of any visit, after about fifteen minutes, he slipped into a kind of meditative monologue. From my previous visits, I knew this pattern well. He looked slightly away from me and seemed to move into another gear where a stream of observations seemed to arise from a source deep within his gentle presence.

"You and Hob have common karma," he began. "Any situation can be a source of growth. This is difficult, but it is a teaching, a training, a blessing. And so you should try to use it as much as you can. Feel gratitude for all the blessings of your lives. Feel them. Then this whole situation becomes a healing process."

There was something deeply comforting about his compassionate presence and evocative words, but at the same time, I was experiencing prickles of resistance, shadows of doubt. Could I follow such an exalted view? "A blessing?" How could he say that? It struck me as utterly impossible at that moment. I was to ponder these words many times. A teaching, a training, a blessing—I recognized that this invitation was at the heart of transforming life's biggest challenges into unforeseen opportunities, a principle in Buddhist philosophy that I'd read about. Nevertheless, it was still daunting to me.

Tulku Thondup went on to explain how to transform the most ordinary activities of caregiving into the perspective of meditative practice.

"Taking care of him will become a meditation for you, a practice. If you need to help him, you will be practicing the six *paramitas* (the six perfections: patience, generosity, discipline, diligence, contemplation, and wisdom). This is the most important practice. Even giving him a spoonful of food could include all these perfections."

He elaborated on the various perfections and how they related to caregiving, how generosity can be a form of dedication and a service to others.

"Do whatever you do joyfully because discipline—the true meaning of the word—is characterized by doing something with joy. Even the little things, see them as an opportunity, a blessing, a meditation, a spiritual practice. Then, even if it's difficult, it will be good. If you use hardships in a proper way, they can even bring inner peace."

The visit to Tulku Thondup was a landmark event for me in the course of Hob's illness. He had said that accompanying Hob could be a teaching, a training, even a blessing. His invitation to accept this radical view provided a compelling challenge. I would return to it, repeat the words to myself, and swing wildly between questioning and embracing his statement. Of course, I often forgot, but with his teachings, some mysterious process began to work deep within, a kind of slow alchemy that kept refining his invitations, nudging me back to the wisdom of his words. He had truly offered me an inspirational framework, a reframing of a heartbreaking situation. His teachings helped to fuel my motivation. He gave me aspirations in which to take refuge; that is, when I remembered!

The inexorable, mysterious process of Hob's dementia unfolded over more or less six years. The first three years after his tentative diagnosis, he continued to drive, teach, and enjoy much of his life as it had been. The last three years got progressively more challenging. We used to joke about the phenomenon of the "well buckets" in our relationship. When one well bucket went down, the other bucket went up, and vice versa. We couldn't help but rise to a difficult situation if the other's well bucket had plummeted.

When he sank into despair, depression, or fear, I could feel all my psychic powers mobilize to help him toward some more encouraging refuge. Depending on circumstances, of course, I might turn to singing, a story, a walk, a reminder about something we shared, a new activity, or simply distract him as one would with a child. Over and over again, I felt this fierce determination to keep making his life as bearable—even enjoyable — as I possibly could. I felt as fierce as a mother tigress protecting her young. Primal fierceness—it was another form of superpower like the determination and resilience that got me down Mount Abraham that night in the midst of the storm.

Besides Tulku Thondup's inspiration, I had received another wisdom gift many years earlier. I was only in my early forties at the time. Hob and I were part of a small weekly meditation group that rotated between our houses. There were seven of us, all seekers of one kind or another, all following a meditation practice, eager to practice together and to discuss whatever arose. Mary was one of our members. She was a gifted artist who had created a striking series of paintings that explored the dance of life and death—animals, bones, flowers, and mystical forms —evocative images that settled into one's psyche, startling one into unexplored attitudes toward death.

Mary was living with cancer. She was a lovely looking woman with a warm, open expression, her white hair drawn back in a bun with its errant whisps that somehow accentuated her very blue eyes. She was an inspiring Elder for me, a strong, quiet presence, thoughtful and wise. At one meeting, she held one of those long-gone, blue airmail letters and explained that her European friend had written a helpful letter about dealing with illness and physical limitations. In particular, Mary wanted to share a quotation from the letter. It was a reflection from Father Teilhard de Chardin, theologian and mystic.

She started reading aloud. "In my younger years, I thanked God for my expanding, growing life; but now in my later years, when I find my physical powers growing less, I thank God also for what I call the grace of diminishment."

Though still far from that stage of life myself, the phrase "the grace of diminishment" hit me with the force of truth—a thoroughly surprising idea. How could diminishment involve grace? Who wants devastating losses? Where was the grace in that?

I knew that I needed to reflect on the meaning of the phrase. I copied the words from Mary's letter. When I went home that day, I started a file labeled "Aging and Wisdom." In retrospect, the name was prophetic. Some years later as I moved into the Elder years myself, not least because I'd accompanied Hob through Alzheimer's, I ended up writing my second book, *Aging with Wisdom*, giving talks on the subject, and offering courses on aging, awareness, and awakening.

Still another invaluable teaching came in an unexpected way. Hob and I were at a New Year's retreat, the last one he was able to attend given the advancing symptoms of dementia. We were in our separate rooms, spending the days alternating between sitting and walking meditation and listening to dharma talks, an immersive experience in meditation practice. Although the retreat center had discouraged reading to minimize distractions from deepening meditation, I had brought a collection of poetry by Rumi, the fourteenth century Sufi mystic and poet.

On the morning of New Year's Day, to greet the turning of the year, I decided to open the book at random, look halfway down the right-hand page to see what message might appear in honor of this special day. Fairly often I would play with this practice. I would open a book, decide ahead of time where to look on the page, and wait to see what message was awaiting me. This time, before my eyes was a powerful, utterly appropriate teaching for exactly where Hob and I were. In my wildest dreams, I could never have come up with such a surprising statement. Drawing on an image from alchemy—the transformation of copper to gold—the poetic fragment ended with an astonishing conclusion.

> Always check your inner state
> with the lord of your heart.
> Copper doesn't know it's copper
> until it's changed to gold.
> Your loving doesn't know its majesty,
> until it knows its helplessness.

The message leapt off the page. Rumi was linking the acceptance of helplessness with the majesty of loving. This is such a surprising, counterintuitive statement. Most of us avoid feelings of helplessness at all cost. After all, we live in a culture that extols independence and fortitude. Here the poet proposes that we discover the majesty of our loving in the very depths of what is most difficult for us to accept.

That moment on New Year's morning was the beginning of an extended contemplation of these words. The poetic fragment struck me as a gift from the universe, an answer to my longing for an inspirational message. We were both dealing with helplessness—Hob's helplessness with the loss of language and his life as he'd known it, my feelings of helplessness as I witnessed his diminishment and pondered how best to help him in increasingly difficult circumstances such as the most recent development of his symptoms—episodes of passing out. The message provided inspiration. It proclaimed that all was well at the ultimate level because in the end, love triumphs over everything, including feelings of helplessness. Copper to gold—the most difficult realities transformed into the gold of loving.

When Hob started to pass out, something that happened several times both at home and in public places, we were suddenly in very different territory. It often involved EMTs and my fierce efforts to keep him out the hospital, which are hell realms for anyone with dementia. The day after such an event, he always kept me close to what he had experienced. Like the sun breaking through the clouds of confusion that naturally accompanied these serious emergencies, his words would be back—always a miracle. Alluding to his near-death experience, he went on to describe how he experienced it.

"Now that I've died once, I can use that as a guide. This passing out, it's simple. There's nothing scary here. Not a big deal. In fact, it's just fine. If dying is this easy, no problem. . . . You've got to get in the habit of letting go. You can't live without doing a lot of dying along the way."

Having just come back from a harrowing experience, he was still able to move beyond the enormity of nearly dying. There was a long pause, and then he added, "And I'll go ahead and explore the next chapter for you."

Those touching words dropped into my heart. How remarkable that he could come up with such a statement when he was still recovering from the confusion of the previous day. It was enough to be retrieving the tenuous threads of his own consciousness, much less express his compassionate wish for me.

About the same time as these dramatic episodes, probably in the late middle stages of his illness, Hob startled me once again. He was in a quiet, thoughtful mood when he suddenly said, "This Alzheimer's . . . it's a different truth. It's not to be worried about."

What did he mean? How could he say that? For me, it was like a Zen koan, a paradoxical riddle given to the practitioner to challenge conceptual thinking and provoke flashes of insight. I suspected he was alluding to the two truths of relative and ultimate reality that I described earlier in connection with the allegory of Plato's cave and its impact on me. On the level of relative reality, having Alzheimer's was a nightmare to be coped with as well as we could. On the ultimate level—that which is beyond conceptual mind—Hob's consciousness was as open and free and unencumbered by illness as it had ever been. Free to play, free to make a statement like that, even though he had been losing words and experiencing aphasia. In other words, at that ultimate level of reality, all was well.

We never know where we are in the arc of a life, our own or another's, especially when the end might be near. Hob had declared several times that he wouldn't live into the late stages of his illness. He'd seen what my mother went through when she had Alzheimer's, and he was determined not to end his days as she had. Who knows where the mystery of intention may relate to the timing of one's death, but one day, seemingly out of nowhere, Hob said haltingly, "I hear a voice saying, '*Leave him to heaven.*'" Long pause. Then he continued. "I really have to keep track of myself . . . of who I really am. But as soon as I wake up from this dream, I'll be in heaven."

There was another long pause. I could see the strain of concentration in his expression, his eyes very focused. I sensed that he still had more he wanted to say. But now the words were ever more elusive, difficult to find. After a long silence, he spoke again. This time it was a poetic fragment, something he must have memorized many years before.

"I warmed both hands against the fire of life,
It sinks, and I am ready to depart."

I'd never heard him recite these words before. This was an example of grace. He could convey the depths of where he was with a poetic couplet. How incredible! I always tried to write down his words, especially the poetry, because I knew they were his gifts, not only as a way to communicate something no longer possible for him with ordinary words but because I needed to ponder their meaning.

These words were a clear message. A couple of weeks later, Hob had a stroke, and seven weeks after that, he died peacefully at home in a hospital bed in our living room next to the altar I'd set up right beside him. After six years with all the ups and downs of illness, a journey marked by the inevitable sorrows and occasional joys, I felt sure that he had died on his own timetable.

I've always felt that the last chapter of life is the most heroic. That's far from our culture's view of the Elder years, but when you consider that often the greatest challenges come toward the end of life when one's energy and capacities are diminished, it's inspiring to see how Elders often deal with those challenges. Heroic for sure! As for us, I came to see that our journey with Alzheimer's had been a form of initiation. There were many phases of that initiation. I've described several of the most memorable ones—our determination to live with the illness as consciously and lovingly as possible; Tulku Thondup's radical perspectives on how the illness could be a source of growth—a teaching, training, and blessing; the wisdom treasures of Teilhard de Chardin and Rumi; and finally Hob's reports from the interior. Like flashes of lightning on a summer night, the landscape suddenly illuminated. Hob's recall of poetic fragments always struck me as gifts, flashes of light that softened the darkness of his illness.

I'm inclined to think that the pains of loss through illness are similar to the pains of childbirth. In a similar way, the memory of pain softens over time so that one can retrieve some of the gifts hidden in the experience—not an infant to hold in one's arms but a recognition about loving that was precious in its own way. The gifts were there, along with the insights and, yes, the blessings. With the perspective of time, I can look back and see how we had been held in the fires of transformation. As a wise one once said, "What is to give light must endure burning." We had been burned and burnished until the gold of love shone unobstructed between us. Ultimately, that was the blessing and the gift of the journey.

GOODBYE, BRIGHT ANGEL

In one of those in between, daydreaming moments, a memory started to unfold unexpectedly, compelling and still moving after so many years, from that time when I was only twenty-two.

How could I forget that day when we had to say goodbye? We didn't know if we'd ever see each other again, and what had passed between us could never become anything permanent, much as each of us longed for exactly that.

We had only those last four days together—sublime days spent in the great spaciousness of the Southwest. On a hot, brilliant blue day from the North rim of the Grand Canyon, we descended a long, treacherous trail composed of dizzying switchbacks. Besides the awe-inspiring, ever-changing play of light and color on the walls of the canyon, I remember those resting places where the mules, having been trained to stop at the outermost edge of the trail, left us sitting suspended virtually over the abyss. The sheer wonder of the canyon triumphed over all fears of falling, perhaps even dying in those great chasms.

Late that afternoon, we arrived at the bottom of the canyon, crossed the great Colorado River on a wooden bridge, and entered Bright Angel Canyon, a tributary to the Colorado. As the vertiginous walls of the canyon slowly stole away the daylight, we wandered up the gentler banks of Bright Angel Creek and gathered the rose-colored stones, unique to this dramatic landscape.

Later, when night had fallen and the full moon had risen above the dark canyon walls, we walked slowly back to the bridge and stood there for a long time, arms around each other. We were silent, looking and listening as the great river thundered beneath the bridge. Neither of us mentioned it. It was too poignant, for this was our last night together, to be spent in this place of mystery and consummate beauty.

It seemed that between us, we, too, were dwelling in that same mystery and beauty. So close had we become, how could we not be together? Over the years that followed, with luminous clarity, I would remember how I felt that evening — loved, loving, totally complete. Our two lives had crossed, met, and awakened something utterly new for each of us. Nothing was missing. If some supernal being had come along at that moment, tapped me on the shoulder, and announced that it was my time to die, I would willingly have gone.

Inexorably, the day of departure came. I would be flying west; he would be driving east. I ricocheted between memories of the previous night and the reality of today. We said goodbye. The plane took off and veered westward. Stunned, I sat racked with sobs, having plummeted from fullness, like that moon, to emptiness. Would there ever be another meeting, such love, such wholeness? From the joy of Bright Angel Canyon to total desolation in a matter of minutes.

Keith Taylor at Grand Canyon (1959)

Forty-five years later, Keith and I—for it was we who had shared the Grand Canyon experience—were sitting across a table from each other in a sunlit Thai restaurant in London. We began to weave the stories of two lives—a tender, tentative, exploratory journey of reconnecting. We had stayed in touch intermittently across all those years, even met occasionally when one of us was in the same city on the same continent. What was this slender thread that still connected us? It was stronger for me now that I was on my own since Hob's death, but still impossible because he was married.

Over those many years, I had ventured into realms totally foreign to him—the new therapies, encounter groups, psychedelics—and above all, a dedicated spiritual practice that was the organizing principle of my life. I had done innumerable retreats in two traditions, including six trips to an ashram in India. I inhabited an utterly different world from his traditional English life with his work in industry, international consulting, and commitment to the military, seared into his being from being drafted at nineteen and sent into active duty in the Korean War.

During those moments of reconnection, I was struggling quietly with something I couldn't understand, maybe just the longing for relationship—any relationship. Mainly because I had to be clear with myself and with him, I made a pronouncement. I declared quietly, "I think that we'll always be loves, but never lovers."

"I don't know," he answered after a long pause. His answer came from a distant place within and left me puzzling. Then with eyes shining with tears, he reached beneath the table and pulled something out of a crumpled brown paper bag. He kept it hidden in his hand.

"This is for you," he said. "I want you to keep it." He opened his palm. There was a rose-colored stone mounted on a black plastic stand into which was inscribed, "Taken from Bright Angel Canyon, October 10th, 1959."

Our lives moved on. Keith's second marriage dissolved, and once again he contacted me. He explained that he was coming to the United

States in connection with his military interests. Could he visit? I said yes, but ever since the meeting in London, although I occasionally thought about him, I had settled on the incompatibility of our two lives.

As I drove to Logan airport to meet his plane, I was feeling both anticipation at seeing such a memorable person from my past and apprehension about being together for several days. What would it be like? What expectations did he have? What were my expectations? I had no idea. I was just aware of feeling vaguely unsettled and curious.

As I stood in the airport, waiting by the exit doors from immigration, I remembered the moment almost fifty years earlier when Keith had walked through the door of the English Speaking Union in San Francisco. I had just started my first job there after college. He was tall, handsome, and well-dressed, with the erect bearing of someone who'd had military training. His jet black hair was neatly combed back. He had blue eyes and an open, welcoming expression like someone always eager for life's next adventure. He looked like a British gentleman right out of central casting, including the captivating accent.

The man who walked through the exit door in the Boston airport now had white hair and a slightly heavier physique from his earlier days as a rugby player. We hugged in greeting like old friends. I had suggested we spend our three days together at our family place in Vermont. It was early September, a beautiful time of year. As I drove us northward and in addition to all the catching up since my London visit, I introduced him to a tape of Taizé chants, beautiful choral music from the ecumenical community in southern France. As we had fifty years before, driving through the Southwest on our way to the Grand Canyon, once again we were singing together, both of us being lovers of music. Keith had a beautiful singing voice. He told me that he had sung with the Westminster Abbey Special Choir for fourteen years, performing all the choral masterpieces of sacred music.

The days were leisurely, filled with stories, mountain hikes, listening to music, and drinking wine over timeless dinners. What was it that had originally drawn us so powerfully together? I remember feeling flashes of tenderness like embers still glowing from an earlier fire. How could some of those feelings be stirring in me once again even as I continued to be incredulous at my attraction to this traditional Englishman, as different from Hob as he could possibly be.

Hob was always a maverick, separating himself from his traditional background, drawn to a diversity of friends, leading international work-camps, and very active in the anti-war movement. His independence from social norms even increased in his later years. He had embraced the downward path with his work shirts and old khakis, almost never wearing a suit and tie, both to be comfortably informal and as a subtle statement of his identification with the working class.

The three days in Vermont with Keith were a tender reweaving of the threads from our original time together in San Francisco, the four days traveling through the Southwest, including the Grand Canyon, and subsequent short visits over the intervening years when our paths crossed in one another's country. The original pull into relationship reawakened, not as dramatically as before for me but slowly and surely the same tender and powerful thread of connection that had overturned our lives back in 1959. I continued to harbor a secret place within where I wondered at the mystery of our shared karma, the unlikeliness of now being together, the echoes of my relationship with Hob. With Keith, our relationship felt like an old and deep love, beyond this life, always mysterious yet deeply welcomed.

After Hob's death, Keith and I continued to visit back and forth. He accepted that I was thoroughly embedded in my life. I was teaching, writing a book, participating in two small groups, and had a wide circle of friends, as well as being close to my two families. He, on the other hand, had retired from his consulting business. When he suggested that he might move so we could live together, I felt a cross-rip of feelings. How ironic! I had experienced the same hesitancy before Hob and I had married. I wondered playfully to myself if I'd been a nun in some previous life! Although it had been five years since Hob's death, I still felt the magnetism of our lives together—above all, the spiritual journey that we had shared, all our explorations, the adventures with psychedelics that appear in the next chapter, and at the center of it all, our precious connection.

Even though I still had luminous memories of my last four days together with Keith, especially of Bright Angel Canyon, I had traveled immeasurable distances since that time. I continued to be sabotaged by the superficial appearances of this traditional Englishman. But deeper feelings prevailed, and something in me leapt over my ambivalence. Even though the focus of our lives had been so different—his more outwardly engaged, mine more inward, delving into the mysteries—nevertheless, the deeper bond prevailed, intensified by the attraction that originally drew us together. We shared long conversations in which he proved to be insatiably curious about my life and all my explorations. We also shared a love of music and singing. I was now in my seventieth year. He was seventy-five. I could only attribute this renewed relationship to the play of karma, those mysterious callings that the mind can't possibly explain. The heart always prevails.

Keith in Iona, Scotland (2010)

The day came when Keith arrived to live with me. The next day, we sat in the dining room of my Cambridge house waiting for the moving van to arrive. A huge truck eased its way into our little side street, slowly rounded our dead end circle, and stopped in front of the house. Three men began unloading Keith's belongings, forty-three boxes filling the dining room and spilling into the hallway. I was feeling waves of panic. *What have I done? Am I ready for this?* I'd grown so accustomed to being on my own, forging my new life without Hob. I was thriving. Surely I loved Keith, but this felt like a British invasion. Keith held my hand as both of us beheld this pile of boxes. I started to weep, and when I looked up at him, he, too, was weeping.

What were our different experiences in those moments? For him it was a huge life change and leap of faith. He had pulled up stakes and left his home, crossing the ocean to a new continent, separating from his three adult children, six grandchildren, and circle of friends. For me, it would be necessary to make accommodations—letting go of the solitude I'd come to cherish, figuring out how he would fit into the life I had created for myself, and resolving the incongruities between the very different worlds the two of us had inhabited.

We slipped easily into living together. Mysteriously, even though we lived life at different levels—his more on the surface, mine seeking within—our deep bond prevailed. He was an adventurer at heart, though of a very different kind than Hob. With his work and nomadic spirit, he had already traveled to thirty-seven countries across five continents. He created the Soldiers Fund, a charity to help British veterans, and then went on to author four books.

Hob and I had been seriously immersed in the Vietnam anti-war movement, ready to go to jail were it not for our two young children. I hadn't realized the depth of my aversion to anything military. Now, because of Keith, I was meeting military personnel, listening to Korean War stories, hearing about reenactments, and learning about military connections involved with his veterans' charity. I once opened the front door to a man in full uniform with an impressive gold braid across his chest—the British Military Attaché from Washington, DC. A soldier on my front steps! Soon after, I found myself entertaining an eminent British general who was also Gold Stick to the Queen, the highest honorary position as a symbolic bodyguard to the Queen, riding on horseback behind her carriage on ceremonial occasions.

Keith's traditional background and military connections seriously challenged me. All my opinions, prejudices, preconceptions, and aversions were right in my face. Praise be for Buddhist practice with its brilliant practices for dealing with these self-created tangles! I stretched. I let go. I opened to new and unexpected situations. I also sometimes burned and contracted with disbelief, aware of the superficial influences that assaulted me.

Because of the bond between us, unlikely as it seemed to me, there was always the deeper truth. Keith's open and generous heart drew me into his circle of loving. But the poignant thread in our relationship was to continue. Because of my vision issues, I knew I had to move into an Elder community. I was also ready to downsize, burdened by managing the house and its garden.

There was, however, a complication. Keith had no US health insurance, and there was no way to move into any Elder community without it. Once again we were faced with separation. His attention was also pulled back to the United Kingdom because of his daughter Gayle's inoperable brain tumor and eventual death, an unbearably painful time. After fifteen very fulfilled and happy years of living together, once again we began to live separately. The situation was easier for me as I now lived in community, sometimes participating in activities, but mostly savoring my solitude. I continued to teach and write but was able to fulfill my contemplative nature more easily when on my own.

Keith and I found ourselves visiting back and forth once again. Given our ages, we had no way of knowing how long that might continue. Nevertheless, I continued to marvel at the mysterious force that had brought us together over sixty years earlier, the spark that had ignited an enduring love with so much in common and so much to share.

Although our relationship seemed destined to have its unexpected interruptions, what endured was the bond that, for me at least, triumphed over the complexities and brought the gift of loving connection.

Keith and Olivia in the UK

EXPLORATIONS IN CONSCIOUSNESS

Now in my last chapter of life, new voices were calling. What issues needed attention? What were the priorities? Having taught extensively in the field of aging, which includes death and dying, what about my own mortality? As an abbreviated version of the Five Remembrances from Buddhism reminds us, death is inevitable, the time of death is uncertain. What is the most important thing?

These questions evoke the subject of consciousness, that subtlest realm in which we dwell without giving it a thought. What happens to consciousness at death? The mind stops when we try to think about these unknowns. I thought back to the 1970s, when Hob and I, like many others, began to venture into the exploration of consciousness through the sacred medicines—psilocybin, MDMA, and LSD in particular.

One unforgettable day, Hob came home from a meeting and began telling me about a psychiatrist and shaman named Salvador Roquet. A highly qualified MD, Roquet had been trained by the famous Mexican shaman Maria Sabina who had been visited by many Americans in the 1960s when the psychedelic movement emerged, often inciting a lot of controversy.

"Apparently, Roquet offers weekend retreats," Hob said. "It's a two-day intensive experience where he promises you will experience both your madness and your death."

"Well, that doesn't exactly sound like a day at the beach," I replied, thoroughly daunted by such a prospect.

"I know, it sounds pretty challenging, but I've never had a near-death experience, and I'm curious about it," Hob said. "It sounds like an important part of one's training not just professionally but personally as well. I'm thinking about doing it. And believe it or not, his next weekend retreat will be in Lincoln, just over the mountains from us in Vermont."

"Unbelievable!" I exclaimed. "What is it about Lincoln? That's where I finally met Lama Gursam!" I couldn't believe that tiny village over the Lincoln Gap from our valley was coming up again. When Hob asked if I wanted to join him on the retreat, I said I'd think about it.

Because of my mother's several breakdowns, I had always been afraid that I might suffer a psychotic break. To face that fear, I decided to go with Hob. Was I afraid? I certainly was, but once again Hob, the fearless adventurer of the spirit, was opening the way.

Several weeks later, we walked into a somewhat rundown Vermont farmhouse in the woods on the west side of Mount Abraham, the mountain where I'd spent my nighttime vigil. Salvador was probably in his early sixties with white hair and dark eyes framed by black-rimmed glasses. He had a strong presence and a quiet authority that suggested an iron will combined with kindness and compassion. His reputation preceded him. As a medical doctor, psychedelic therapist, and shaman, he had worked with the most distressed patients—drug addicts, recidivist criminals, the severely depressed, and cancer patients fearing death. His protocol was dramatic, criticized by some of his associates in the field for being too aggressive.

He interviewed each of us, a clinical intake of sorts, and gave a lecture on the history of shamanic traditions, sacred rituals, the borders between worlds, the vast realities that lie beyond the limits of ordinary mind, as well as the deep healing that can happen not just personally but for others whose lives we touch. Then it was time for the journey to begin.

Twelve of us are on mattresses on the floor. We have six guides, including Salvador and his teenage son, an apprentice in this shamanic tradition. Many of us are therapists, engaging in further training. Salvador has explained that the preliminary phase of the journey involves sensory overload, the purpose being to gradually break down our hold on ordinary reality. The shamanic drumming begins, increasing in tempo and intensity. There are three large screens at the front of the room with fast-moving images projected onto all three simultaneously. The images are alternately beautiful images of nature, people, flowers, and then violent and horrific with death camps, war scenes, natural disasters flashing by while abrasive music thunders through the room. I feel as though I'm being assaulted from every direction between the cascading images, loud drumming, and the floor vibrating beneath me.

Ordinary consciousness can't sustain itself in the face of such an assault. My heart is pounding. I want to flee, but it's too late. I've made a choice. Something deep within keeps calling, keeping me there on the floor with my fellow travelers. There's already a strong bond between us. We're given blindfolds to intensify the intrapsychic experience, along with ingesting the sacred medicines. I'm taking LSD for the first time, frightening to me because it's a chemical, not a plant.

I'm aware that my sense of identity is being shaken, overwhelmed, and shattered by the sensory overload. I've taken the tab of LSD and vaguely wonder how long until it takes over. I feel myself trying to hold onto my sanity, some thread of who I am, then slipping, dissolving, until it's just pure experience with no "I" to identify with any of it. A lot of rhythmic, beating sound. I am dying, being shot over and over again . . . in Nazi war camps . . . standing against a glaring white wall, being mown down by a stream of bullet-sound. . . . I'm everyone who has ever died in battle or been shot in the street or died in the jungle . . . dying over and over again.

I become a lion, roaring, rearing up, trying to take down one of the guides, clawing at his leg like some possessed madwoman as he gently disengages my grip and lays me back down. Now I'm an African dancing around the ceremonial fire with my black brothers and sisters, wildly ecstatic . . . then images of death, plane wrecks, piles of bones, all in whirling vortexes of sound and color. . . . Somewhere in this chaos, there is the faintest awareness of wanting to find God.

Then the ketamine kicks in, a dissociative drug that in higher doses causes out-of-body experiences. Suddenly I'm being propelled like a rocket from a launching pad, tearing upward into the cosmos. Fear, terror, a cataclysmic death . . . only a fragment of consciousness remains, catapulting through space at a million miles an hour.

As I feel my consciousness breaking apart, I make one final effort and shout into the room, "Oh God, I'm going! Take care of Ethan and Laura!" I'm streaming upward through the tunnel . . . then the breakthrough . . . all the movement ceases. Into Light, clear Light, radiant Light, Light is everywhere, luminous, brilliant gold, peaceful, blissful, timeless, all One. Sublime peace.

Timeless. For how long? No one, nothing to know. Eventually the sound of sacred music. Bach . . . the B Minor Mass . . . consciousness beginning to reassemble, alternating between pure Light and rainbow light . . . alternating between the One and the multiplicity, the one Light and the seven colors . . . Fauré's Requiem . . . knowing it, a miniscule effort to hum along with it . . . consciousness slowly returning . . . like an old friend except there's a profound difference. To the core of my being I've experienced other realities beyond time and space, beyond body and mind, beyond words to describe it. There have been many deaths, the death of the little self, but what remains is a deep trust in the meaning of existence, an immense affirmation of this life and a life beyond. I've been woven into a vast web of loving interconnection with everyone and everything. The heart is broken open, overwhelmed with love. Death, God, and Love, all interwoven, become the essence of this initiation.

The impact of the experience continued for weeks and months afterward. I spent a lot of time integrating it, not only the day of integration that followed the all-night journey with my fellow travelers but when I got home through writing, painting, and quiet reflection. The fear of death softened while the link between love and death was forged more strongly. What ultimately shone through the psychedelic experience was the deepening in love, the love that transcends even death.

The journey deepened my inner life, leading to states of absorption in meditation beyond the awareness of "I" as I pondered the promise of going beyond suffering, the Buddha's third noble truth. I also felt a pervading sense of interconnectedness with all life, all beings, and eventually I decided to become a hospice volunteer and be present at the death and dying of those in hospice care, including family and friends.

Shortly after this life-changing experience, I came to the realization that I didn't need to do any further journeys into non-ordinary states of consciousness. Something momentous had been completed. All the exploration just stopped. I had not the slightest inclination to continue.

Forty-five years went by. Then surprisingly in my mid-eighties, something shifted. What was it that impelled me to explore once again? It was certainly the reality of being closer to death. My death was no longer an abstraction or a distant memory of a powerful psychedelic journey. I was also living with challenges to my vision and the possibility of going blind. What might be the role of consciousness with visual loss? As the essence of all experience, profound changes in consciousness would surely be involved with the loss of sight.

After all those years, I decided to continue my exploration with the sacred plants. The protocol was far more gentle—a pre-session meeting with the guide, eight hours for the session itself, and a follow-up session. I had worked with Peter many years earlier when I needed some short-term therapy. He was a skilled therapist, teacher, and healer with almost twenty years as a shaman, a guide for exploring non-ordinary states of consciousness. I deeply trusted him.

As I walk into the session room, I'm stopped by the beauty and sacredness of the space. The light is gentle. On one wall, three Tibetan tangkas hang above a low altar adorned with sacred objects from different cultures. On the opposite wall are three exquisite works by indigenous artists, one an intricate weaving of an elaborate mandala. At the far end of the room stands a life-sized Buddha. The room feels wondrously peaceful.

This journey is being held in sacred ceremony. I share my invocation with Peter, then his invocation, and finally my intentions for the journey—to surrender to the wisdom of the plants (the understanding of indigenous cultures), dedicate my healing to the healing of my family and ancestors, ride the waves of consciousness with openness and curiosity, and be open to an experience of death.

As consciousness shifts and dissolves, I speak to Peter several times in the early hours. Three separate times I speak to him.

"I want to be so far out there, there's no one left to be talking."

"Take me beyond any remaining sense of "I."

"There's still further to go."

Now beyond ordinary mind, from deep within, I am asking for a very powerful experience. He asks whether I (whatever remains of me) want the LSD. Now it follows the psilocybin. He sits quietly, taking notes.

The journey unfolds, primarily about the karma of this life—memories streaming through consciousness . . . wanting to die as an abandoned infant . . . mother's breakdowns . . . father's admirable life . . . the hard work of labor, especially giving birth to Ethan . . . the Siddha Yoga betrayal . . . the darkness of spiritual disillusionment . . . my daughter, Laura, sacrificed on the wheel of suffering . . . who cares about siddhis (powers) when you hurt people like that . . . I just want to help others get out of their prisons—that wheel we're all stuck on . . . men who came onto me . . . men who oppress women . . . oh god, the rage at men who oppress women everywhere.

So many karmic threads spinning, untangling, pulling consciousness here and there across a lifetime, a life also woven with so much good fortune, plenty of suffering, so many blessings. Through all of this unfolding karmic display, there is awareness, though at one point totally dissolved for over an hour and half—a gentle death. Gone, gone beyond. I am totally absorbed, with no fear. A priceless gift of consciousness.

Months later, another journey, entirely different. Again I return to Peter's sacred space. I've clarified my intentions to open to the play of consciousness, once more to dedicate the session to healing— mine, family, ancestors, other loved ones, and for all who suffer.

Again, the ease of surrendering to the shifting inner worlds that start to unfold. Already thoughts are more attenuated, less dominating, more like clouds floating across the screen of awareness, not as solid as in ordinary reality. All attention shifts as waves of energy start coursing through my body. They begin at my feet and shudder upward in smooth, undulating patterns, seeming to reach beyond the crown of my head. A lot of sounds, long "ahs," even shouts because the energy is so strong, but always ending with dissolution into laughter. Over and over again, for hours—through this utterly timeless realm—an endless stream of ecstatic, orgasmic waves of pure energy—sounds erupting, then dissolving into laughter, bathed in sheer joy, released into freedom—released and free over and over again.

"Peter, come along for the ride. This is really wonderful. This is ecstasy."

Karmic threads are weaving in and out of all this bodily movement. Concerns for Keith, talking to him, hoping he's okay. "If you're dying, I pray for your liberation. Don't hold onto me because death is perfectly safe." Memories interweaving—my UK friend living in Council housing, two other dear ones, sons of immigrants born into poverty. The injustices of the world. Why my world, why their world? Different journeys for every one of us. Remembering the men I've loved. Knowing and trusting that huge angel that a clairvoyant once saw behind me. Protection. Such good fortune, such blessings.

Just two days after the journey, I attended a week-long retreat, the end of the five-year training in Dzogchen, a Tibetan Buddhist practice. The first morning of teachings focused on how these practices were purifying the subtle body. In a moment of insight, I suddenly flashed back to my recent journey and realized the essence of what it had been about. All the hours of physical movement naturally involved both the physical body and the subtle body. I saw the connection between an outrageous statement I'd made to Peter— not once but twice— connecting sexual ecstasy and childbirth. I now realized that all those hours of release and delight were a dramatic purification. Through that wondrous process, the waves of energy were giving birth to the freedom of my soul—the recurring theme of this life—the longing for freedom, for ultimate liberation.

The journeys into non-ordinary states of consciousness are memorable landmarks. They involve many striking insights—the feelings of interconnection with all beings, not only our loved ones but our connection with all beings, and especially vividly to the sufferings of the world. The plants, with their mysterious wisdom, dissolve all feelings of separation and show us other worlds. They open us to realities we could never imagine. Each time, I feel the call to be of service, to bring the gifts of the journey to others through kindness and compassion, teaching and writing, and presence to the suffering of others.

There is an inner shift from the tenacious hold of the ego to letting go into pure consciousness, riding the waves of change, no matter how dramatic, trusting that we are held by something beyond ourselves. With the dissolution of the ego's grasping on to reality, the fear of death is softened. Each journey has broken open the heart into the love that permeates all of creation, paradoxically including even the darkness and suffering. We have the insight that these explorations are not for ourselves alone. We vividly experience that we're inextricably interwoven with everyone and with all of life, a wondrous revelation.

VISION QUEST

Some years ago, I found myself at the beginning of yet another kind of journey. I received a medical prognosis that I would probably lose my vision. What I only learned over time was that the loss of vision would lead me to experience totally new realms of consciousness. I began to perceive an intimate connection between my journeys into non-ordinary states of consciousness and the prospect of losing sight.

In my mid-forties at my first visit to get reading glasses, the ophthalmologist who examined my eyes got very quiet. Then almost incredulously, he announced that there was considerable loss to the optic nerve in the right eye. Hadn't I noticed changes in my vision? No, I hadn't. The brain is so brilliant, it kept compensating. Besides, if you'd asked me then, I would have said blindness would be dark, whereas I experienced subtle points of light, sometimes with iridescent halos, a sign of glaucoma. I had never known about that symptom. I learned that I had been born with Chandler's Syndrome, a birth defect in the lens of the eye that created the pressure that destroys the optic nerve.

As I struggled to accept the challenges of this diagnosis, I remembered once again—for I'd never forgotten—that my mother had told me what had happened when she'd been institutionalized after my birth. At the time, our family dog was a German Shepherd named Zilla. Apparently Zilla began to stay very close to this newborn family member, sleeping by my bassinet, accompanying me when I was carried outside—overall taking a proprietary role in becoming my constant companion. I was a failing-to-thrive baby, and animals are well known to sense and respond to human suffering.

In retrospect, Zilla's loyalty strikes me as especially poignant. She had gone through the training to serve as a seeing eye dog, but she couldn't be entrusted to a blind person because her trainers couldn't break her passion for chasing birds. I had to smile over that. Birds are often regarded as symbols of freedom—a lifelong theme for me—and here was Zilla, a failed seeing eye dog because she chased after birds.

After various surgeries and all possible treatments, I became blind in my right eye and was diagnosed with macular degeneration in my left eye. What an unimaginable prognosis. Our senses are such an intimate part of ourselves that we scarcely think about them until one of them is threatened, especially sight or hearing. When one loses sight gradually, as I had with the right eye, the adjustment is gradual and almost unnoticeable. Most of the time I forgot about my blindness until I bumped into someone in a crowd or collided with something on my right.

The prospect of going blind was totally inconceivable, the most dreaded of possibilities. Living in darkness was unimaginable. I experienced a towering wall of disbelief as everything within me cried out, "No!" All my life, I'd reveled in the glories of sight, especially with countless hours and days of pure seeing, rendering landscapes, flowers, and symbolic forms into watercolor, ink, pastels, and oils. I'd enjoyed the feast of sight, in love with nature, in love with the world. How could I lose the wonder of all that?

In minimal ways, I started to open to the world of the blind. Close friends began to send me materials on blindness, a moving poem or a book filled with interviews with the blind. I was inspired by their courage, how they adapted, the inner worlds they discovered, and, unbelievably, several who said if offered their sight back, they wouldn't accept it. I played with putting myself into their situations. I was determined to face this challenge with their courage and full awareness toward an inevitable process.

Then the startling changes began to happen. First, small holes appeared in my vision, threatening to interfere with ease of reading, and then came the so-called floaters, a small collection of very faint spots that moved around with my focus and started to interfere with my visual clarity, not yet affecting my overall visual field but interfering with finer activities such as my artwork, threading a needle, reading piano music, or reading small print.

A tectonic shift in consciousness was happening. I was more aware of how subtle changes in my vision were impacting life. I felt as though I was living with a new companion, a presence that had crashed into my life, unbidden, to keep reminding me about loss and impermanence. This becomes the reality for every Elder when a companion appears—whether a disease like cancer, Parkinson's, or dementia—that will accompany us out of this life.

Whenever faced with a challenging life issue, I invariably search for inspiring perspectives on how to handle it. The opportunity arose when I was attending a meditation retreat with Anam Thubten, my primary teacher in the Dzogchen tradition. I knew he had both spoken and written about his dread of blindness. He had developed this fear as a boy because of a blind relative who was such a sad person. Surely losing one's sight, he had said, must be the most fearful loss one could suffer.

He was always very accessible to his students, so when the morning break came on the second day of the retreat and he remained sitting quietly in his chair, I immediately went up and kneeled down in front of him so we could be at eye level. Since my first impulse is to make physical contact, without even thinking, I reached for his hand and began speaking.

"I would like to ask a question about losing my vision because I'm already blind in my right eye, and the vision is slowing going in my left. I want to approach these losses as consciously as possible and hold them with the inspiration of the dharma, but what might you say?"

He paused for a moment. I sensed the depth of his response, for he turned slightly away for a moment as if absorbing my words and then turned back, looking directly into my eyes with great compassion. He started to talk about Helen Keller.

"She is one of my heroines, an inspiration to me and to all of humanity. I wrote about her in my book *A Sacred Compass*. She once said, "The most beautiful things in the world cannot be seen or even touched. They must be felt with the heart."

He got quiet for a moment and then continued. "There was also a famous lama in Tibet who went blind, but he had attained the highest state. People were very drawn to him because he shone with a kind of radiance.

So whatever happens to us, we need to find transcendence in the situation. We need to find inner freedom and the highest understanding."

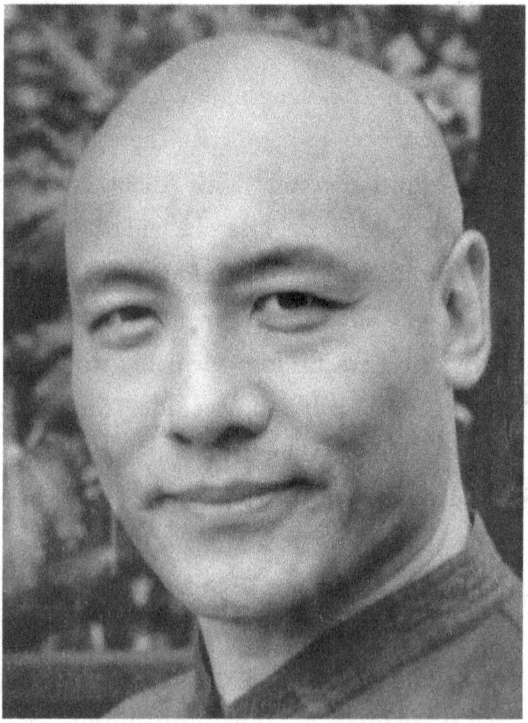

Anam Thubten Rinpoche

Because he spoke quietly, especially in a situation where others were talking while awaiting their turn, I was unable to hear everything he was saying due to impaired hearing. Frustrating as it was, I realized that ultimately it didn't matter; his presence and our profound connection were the gift. In the moments when I was unable to hear, I only remember that certain words flashed forth like beacons—*ultimate attainment*, *transcendence*, *enlightened vision*, and the thought-provoking statement, "Growth in consciousness is blinded by sight." I've pondered those words, which suggest that the expansion of consciousness is unaffected by loss of vision.

When I sensed our exchange was complete, I added, "I want to accept this situation, live with it consciously, and trust that ultimately whatever happens to us needs to be held in love."

Although inexplicable, I felt that Rinpoche had become an ally in my situation. His words—even those I had barely heard—were a balm, a covenant between us, or so I framed it. I further realized that his embracing, compassionate presence was even more important than whatever he said.

About the same time as my conversation with Anam Thubten, I was introduced once again to the realm of invisible mysteries. For years I'd had a good friend who was a health professional and healer. She introduced me to a relatively new field, a form called environmental healing. It involved an expanded world view, both scientific and spiritual, that explores the energy of the body's organs to help restore their energetic balance. Through a form of meditation, one creates a wave field, or environment, that helps to entrain the original energetic balance within a particular organ. By creating two-dimensional forms that reflect the organ's energy field, one can use these patterns as a focus for meditation, or by drawing them to invite an energetic resonance that helps to promote balance.

For my vision, the dominant image that resonated with my eye was a spiral. I immediately resonated with it. I've always loved spirals. I doodled them endlessly as a girl, drawing them over and over again in the margins of my school notebooks. Later I would learn that spirals were classically regarded as a symbol for the soul since they depicted the unfolding process that occurs over a lifetime.

The spiral pattern became my constant companion. I copied it onto a notecard and placed it beneath my computer for frequent glimpsing. Every day I drew the pattern many times—a kind of meditative focusing exercise that captivated me, back to childhood doodling but with a higher purpose! Although I had no illusions about the reality of the body's inevitable diminishment, I felt that I was invoking healing energies. It became another facet of spiritual practice, along with several other modalities that my friend introduced.

From my training in Mind/Body medicine, I had read many studies that proved the power of mind over body with inspiring outcomes from many forms of healing. With my friend's guidance, I felt as though we were co-creating a positive energy field for my vision. That in itself was an inspiration and a comfort.

After some months, I wrote to her, "Whatever is happening is mysterious and very welcome. There are subtle changes in my vision, but what's most striking is the ease of heart I'm experiencing—a significant inner shift—with less anxiety and disbelief along with greater acceptance. I've also noticed that vision is affected by states of mind. If I dwell on the losses, they seem amplified, whereas if I appreciate what I still have, my visual field becomes clearer, more complete. The combination of ease and serenity somehow diminishes the changes and enhances the vision. A warm thank you for how you have helped."

Although it's natural to hope for physical improvements, any healing at the emotional, mental, or spiritual level is ultimately the gift—something I clearly had experienced.

Always on a quest for inspiration, I also reached out to Tulku Thondup, the first person I had contacted in my search for an enlightened teacher. As I mentioned in an earlier chapter, over the course of more than fifty years, he had become a *kalyana mitra*, the Sanskrit term for a spiritual friend. I explained that I wanted to talk about how to hold the prospect of blindness with acceptance and the wisdom of the dharma.

Tulku Thondup Rinpoche

One brisk spring afternoon, I walked across the little park that abutted Tulku Thondup's Cambridge apartment building. I was always filled with anticipation when I was about to meet with him because these meetings were like no other. This one seemed particularly poignant because the previous winter he'd been hospitalized in the intensive care unit and nearly died from Covid-19.

Tulku-la, as he was sometimes called, met me at the door. In his eighties, he'd had a long convalescence from the severity of his illness. I could see that he was thinner and frail, but his warm, welcoming smile quickly eclipsed those first impressions. We walked through his living room, not like any other for it was almost entirely devoted to an elaborate altar. It was a visual feast, characteristic of Tibetans who love bright colors, elaborate designs, and exuberant expression—Buddha statues, pictures of saints, cabinets filled with Tibetan artifacts, a set of offering bowls, several vases of flowers, and many ritual objects. High above the central part of the altar was a picture of Guru Rinpoche (Padmasambhava) who brought Buddhism to Tibet and is known as the second Buddha. I couldn't begin to take in the complexity of the altar, but I experienced a kind of force field that seemed to surround and emanate from it.

I followed him as he walked slowly into the little sitting room, an extension of the living room. The windows looked out through giant sycamore trees to the Charles River, a beautiful view from his fourth-floor apartment. I settled onto the couch as TT, as I fondly think of him, took his usual chair to my right. He now had a slight, grey beard, unusual in length and narrowing to a point like an ancient sage. I'm struck again by his wide-set eyes, always emanating warmth, equanimity, and quiet joy.

After catching up since my last visit, I posed my question about how to greet my visual challenges with the inspiration of the dharma. He looked slightly away from me, paused for a long moment, and said, "I don't know what I'm going to say in answer to your question. I'm just going to say whatever comes into my mind."

With those words, he eased into his familiar way of responding to whatever concern I've introduced. I sensed that he was shifting to an interior realm, accessing the depth of his experience, his wisdom, and compassion. He no longer maintained eye contact, yet I could still feel the strong connection between us. He kept glancing toward the living room altar to his right, pausing between phrases, using the fragments of speech characteristic of his meditative monologue.

"Whatever comes, try to imagine Guru Rinpoche, the buddhas and bodhisattvas—or whatever form appeals to you—and feel their unconditional kindness and compassion. It is important to have some sort of inspiring image, statue, or painting. They all have wisdom power and are helping us with this power, freeing us from suffering and problems. "

Is he referring now to a problem like losing my vision and that cause of suffering? I fleetingly wonder.

"They are looking at me . . . looking at us . . . and we're unifying with them as they unify with us. Feel their presence. Enjoy it. The mind is being transformed into the Buddha's mind, the mind of pure perception and lovingkindness. I see them and pray, *Om Mani Padme Hung*" (the most well-known Tibetan mantra).

TT looked steadily toward the altar, humming the mantra quietly, his voice filled with devotion. He continued, "This is the world of devotion; you have been transformed into them. Your mind and the Buddha's mind become united. No subject, no object. Unified, one. With amazing openness and devotion, close your eyes, and even if you don't see—not seeing, but feeling—you can feel their lovingkindness and feelings of joy. If you see them with devotion, your mind will be transformed, illuminated."

I'm absolutely still, reaching for his words (he speaks beautiful English but with a Tibetan accent). The words carry me effortlessly into a deep calm. I sense that this is an initiation—an introduction to realms almost beyond my comprehension but stirring my heart, which feels very open and full.

Now TT was almost constantly turned toward the altar as if his words were creating a bridge to ease my awareness into the world he inhabits.

"Be totally open. Do not try to grasp, but allow the images to open your mind. That is the role of devotion. Include every being with your devotion . . . open our minds and hearts . . . feel their presence, their boundless nature, their blessings. . . . That's all we need. . . . That answers all our questions."

I sense that he's come full circle, back to my original question. I'm suspended in some altered state, open, receptive, quiet mind, energized body. I hear the traditional dedication.

"Dedicate the merit of these practices to all beings. May they be enlightened. My meditations may be simple, but that kind of devotion opens us up. That's what we try to do. We try to let go, enjoy this waking up . . . this devotion . . . these blessings."

As our meeting came to an end, the focus shifted from TT's teaching to casual conversation. At that moment, his wife, Lydia (monks are allowed to marry in his lineage), who had been sitting with us, volunteered something unexpected.

"Like you, Tulku-la also has macular degeneration. With supplements and specialists, we are also doing everything we can to preserve his sight."

How ironic! I'd come to TT in hopes of getting some inspiring perspectives on my vision issue, and here he was dealing with the same challenges. Our meeting left me with much to ponder. He had started by saying that he didn't know how he was going to answer and that he was going to say whatever came into his mind. What followed was a meditative prayer on devotion, an outpouring of his love and connection with Guru Rinpoche, the buddhas, and bodhisattvas—the inspirational beings of his tradition.

After almost twenty-five years of practicing Tibetan Buddhism, I had embraced the essence of these teachings, though sometimes I had to let go of the cultural complexities. TT's extended soliloquy on devotion was his answer. It felt like an unusual form of initiation. He had been shining the light of his understanding on a difficult prospect, one that we shared. The words had poured forth from his heart, conveying the depth of that love. He had addressed my question indirectly, but I treasured the answer. The wise response was to greet whatever lay ahead with love and devotion.

GIFTS OF AWARENESS

There is a classic saying from Lao Tzu, the Chinese philosopher. "Those who know don't talk. Those who talk don't know." Not surprisingly, a similar truth was stated by the Western philosopher Ludwig Wittenstein when he wrote, "Whereof one cannot speak, thereof one must be silent." At the risk of talking about what is elusive and ineffable, I look back at some of the landmarks along the way—not the outer events of life as much as the inner ones—and marvel at the evolution. This is not a linear process. The following vignettes, mere bits and pieces, describe something about the mysterious path along which I have been led and where it has brought me. Because these vignettes are beyond space and time, we need to suspend ordinary ways of seeing and let the images reveal from beyond the words. All of these vignettes are ultimately about freedom—the freedom inherent in human existence, a recurring thread in my story.

Colombo, Sri Lanka

In 1982, still basking in the inspiration from the transpersonal psychology conference, Hob and I arrived in Sri Lanka as part of a post-conference trip. Besides our guide, there were only three in our little group, our fellow traveler being a Jungian analyst. On our first evening in Colombo where we stayed at a rambling, colonial era hotel overlooking the sea, she began telling us about a Sufi master she'd been told she must meet. He lived in the outskirts of Colombo. She knew very little about him, only that his name was Guru Bawa Muhaiyaddeen. She had his contact information and had been told that he held teachings every morning at seven o'clock before the day got too hot. According to the story, he had spent many years in solitary practice in the jungles of northern Sri Lanka and had emerged as a wise and compassionate teacher.

Early the next morning, the three of us squeezed into a small taxi and headed through the chaotic city traffic toward the quieter suburbs. We arrived at a modest row of houses. We'd been told that the front door was always open, so we let ourselves in and climbed the rickety stairs to the second floor. The stairs opened into a small room and a surprising sight. A man, very slight of stature, sat cross-legged on a bed. The bed had been placed incongruously in the middle of the room. In that first flash of taking in an unfamiliar environment, I noticed that the legs of the bed stood in little cups of water to prevent any tropical wildlife from crawling up. Even though it was still early morning, it was already hot, and a ceiling fan turned slowly above the bed, stirring the air in the room.

Guru Bawa was dressed in a lightweight, white cotton garment with part of the cloth loosely covering his head. No one greeted us. The room was silent. About ten other people sat in meditation around the bed, waiting for the meeting to begin.

As I settled onto the floor, I was drawn by the serene presence of this gentle man and the stillness that filled the modest room. We'd been told that he was well into his nineties, but except for a beard, his light brown face was smooth and unlined as if never having carried the cares of the world. His eyes were closed. Silence, deep silence. Minutes passed. At last, he began speaking quietly, slowly. The morning's teaching began.

I don't remember anything he said, nor do I remember the question I asked, only that I didn't want to miss the opportunity to ask something about meditation practice. I never forgot the image that illustrated his answer.

To paraphrase his quiet words, "There is an oyster lying at the bottom of the ocean. Down in the murky darkness, the oyster lies amid mud and nature's debris. The outer surface is gray, rough, and ugly, but within the tightly closed shell, a mysterious process is occurring. A pearl is forming, a slow, hidden process. After a long time, the tough outer shell opens. The pearl breaks free. It drifts upward to the surface of the ocean toward the light . . . to gather light . . . to gather light."

The image always stayed with me, a metaphor for an alchemical process whereby the pearl of wisdom is gradually revealed through one's practice of meditation and life experience.

Cambridge, Massachusetts

I watched our teacher, a master of Chinese brush painting, as he leaned over the scroll-length rice paper and began to paint, his brush flying over the paper as if guided by an unseen force, easy and free. A landscape gradually appeared, mountains shrouded in clouds, waterfalls, trees, a gazebo, and a monk sitting in meditation. Then he picked up a calligraphy brush, moved to the top left side of the scroll, and with effortless strokes, the Chinese characters appeared, forming the poem that traditionally accompanies a painting. As he finished the scroll, he said that it was only a demonstration piece, and as the class ended, I saw that he was about to crumple it up.

"Wait!" I called out. "Please don't destroy it! I'd love to have it." To me, it was a masterpiece. To this day, that painting hangs in our front hall, a reminder of what unfolded for me from those classes in Chinese brush painting.

Our teacher introduced the preliminary practices. Nothing is preliminary, he clarified. Every brush stroke is unique unto itself and should be regarded with reverence.

"This is a meditative art because we're cultivating attention, precision, discipline, and ultimately freedom. This is an ancient art form that expresses the Tao, or the "way" of Chinese philosophy, that there is order and harmony in nature, and that divine laws regulate the patterns of life in heaven and on earth. We want our brush painting to reflect that harmony."

In that first session, before painting the entire landscape that I rescued, he introduced us to the principles of painting bamboo leaves and stalks, analogous to learning the alphabet before learning to read. He gave us samples to follow and encouraged us to practice regularly between weekly sessions.

At that time, I was in my early thirties, with Ethan and Laura still very young. I was filled with excitement and anticipation over this new art form with its philosophical view of life. Hungry for inspiration, I bought the classic text, a 650-page illustrated book called *Tao of Painting*, a translation of a seventeenth century text called *The Mustard Seed Garden Manual of Painting*.

I felt as though I'd fallen down a rabbit hole into a new world filled with inspiration and possibilities. I practiced whenever I could, even with toddler chaos unfolding around me. I loved the tools of my new practice, the black ink stick and rectangular inkstone with its shallow well for mixing the ink and water. I loved my three bamboo-handled brushes with their bristles of goat, black rabbit, and weasel hair, each lightweight and beautifully balanced, and the thin white rice paper with its subtle woven textures.

Having already studied watercolor and line drawing, I'd now fallen in love with this new medium. I was intrigued by the interplay between my brush, the ink, and the rice paper. I marveled at the subtleties of what happened, the varying intensities of the images, depending on my skill. Most delightful of all, as described by our teacher, every image reflected some aspect of nature. A single bamboo leaf resembled a crescent moon, two leaves looked like a fish's tail, three leaves needed a brushstroke like a wild goose in flight, four leaves were like the image of a wild goose alighting, five leaves were like a swallow in flight. Observations from the natural world saturated Chinese brush painting.

A few weeks after that first class, something unexpected happened. One Saturday morning, Hob had taken the kids off to a museum, and I was blissfully alone. By then, I'd been practicing a lot, painting hundreds upon hundreds of bamboo leaves, trying to copy the samples and studying the images in *Tao of Painting*. Always encouraging us, our teacher had said, "What happens with your painting depends on discipline, commitment, and reverence. Follow the forms, and you'll find your form of expression."

He'd told us to always start with the basic strokes for bamboo leaves, like practicing scales for a pianist. I started with the basic forms, by now loving the meditative process of applying ink to paper and watching what emerged. Suddenly a shift occurred, imperceptible at one level, totally apparent at another—a mysterious process unfolding within my very being. The brush, the ink, and the paper seemed to flow effortlessly together. There was no longer any sense of "I" the artist trying to create something. I felt an ultimate freedom. I was in the flow, this ancient art form manifesting in this moment and the next and the next. Artist, the act of painting, and the image came together in movements fluid and free in an experience of oneness.

Although it happened more than fifty years ago, that morning still evokes wonderment. It may appear like a tiny blip in the arc of life, but any experience of freedom is a gift, a joy. Practicing with the form had led to the formless—the heart of all meditation practices. Such experiences of breakthrough—flashes of freedom—may occur in seemingly small moments, but their impact is timeless. They are precious gifts, moments of awakening to our deepest, ultimately free nature.

The Big Island of Hawaii

We awoke that morning to unsettled weather, unusual for Hawaii where the sun shone into cloudless skies day after day. A brisk wind continued to stir the surface of the harbor when we found our guide for the day and the captain of the 35-foot boat that would take us out into the ocean with the hope of swimming in the wild with bottlenose dolphins.

My friend Natalie and I had experienced a dolphin swim another year, but today was my birthday, and this adventurous outing was her gift to me. Our guide was named Joan Ocean, surely an adopted name! She was well known for her worldwide experience swimming with both whales and dolphins about which she had written several books. We knew we were in capable hands. Both she and our captain knew the patterns of certain dolphin pods and where we might find them. I had already voiced my concerns about the unsettled weather and strong swells. We were planning to snorkel so we could dive and get closer to the dolphins, but I was concerned that the windswept sea would make that more challenging.

We headed out into the open sea and cruised slowly northward along the coast. The eight of us onboard had fallen silent, attentive only to any changes in the surface of the sea that might indicate the presence of dolphins. Then Joan spoke. "They're coming. Let's get ready." She pointed to where a few dorsal fins alternately surfaced and dove through the waves, still far from us.

I felt a rush of excitement. My heart began to pound, my breath in ragged gasps. Once before with the dolphins, I'd experienced the same waves of energy, almost overcome with the thrill of swimming with these creatures of the deep. I hurriedly pulled on my flippers and adjusted my snorkel. In a fleeting moment, I noticed how the lens of the mask was altering my vision. As I stood by the rail looking at the wind-driven waves and the oncoming pod, a wave of fear swept through, then excitement, then an unfamiliar power like being propelled by a force beyond myself.

"Stay with me," ordered Joan as she slipped deftly over the gunnel of the boat into the sea. I followed, easing myself into the water. Swimming with long thrusting breast strokes, I took a huge, deep breath, enough to stay under for as long as possible and heard it whistle loudly through my snorkel.

Then came a blur of experience. I saw Joan's lithe body, hands pressed by her sides as she dove beneath the surface, more like a fish than a human, undulating with decisive, powerful movements. Then the beautiful gray bodies came flashing by, too fast, too agile to keep up with, until one appeared in my peripheral vision. The majestic being was swimming more slowly, maybe slowing to swim alongside me. Then we were eye to eye. Gazing into that eye was like looking into the eye of the universe. For how long? Seconds? An eternity? Then more sleek, graceful bodies streamed past me. Suddenly desperate for breath, I surfaced.

The rest of that day was dreamlike—more dives, a duet of excitement and fear, the wind rising, a heavy sea finally forcing us to return to the harbor, the drive home into a fierce storm with high winds and torrential rains. There was an unprecedented storm up-island from where we'd been, with eleven inches of rain, they said. The road was littered with debris from the floods, and on the drive up the mountain we were accompanied by huge, arching rainbows, almost half an hour of rainbow light, phenomenal and wondrous.

Beyond any rational explanation, the presence of the dolphins continued to permeate everything I experienced, especially that night when, eyes closed but not sleeping, I slipped into an unfamiliar state of consciousness. I watched, incredulous, at what started to appear in my inner vision—realms of light unfolding in wave upon wave of luminous lines, pulsating, expanding, evolving into an endless series of exquisite geometric forms. It was an inner kingdom of light with designs never seen, never imagined, and realms like new worlds being born, second by second. I was transported into another dimension of reality, overtaken by visions as the ethereal patterns of light endlessly evolved, changed, and disappeared into infinity.

The experience lasted for several hours, utterly unique, beyond time. Might the visions have been some form of communication from that magnificent creature with whom I had shared those timeless moments? Much has been researched and written about communication with dolphins. There are countless stories of miraculous encounters, of healings, of dolphins saving people from drowning; of their intelligence, their sounds, their communications; how dolphins may be assisting human evolution, serving as gateways to other dimensions of reality; theories about interspecies transmissions. Was that moment of contact between us a transmission? I don't need an answer. I only know that the visions that night were sublime, mysterious, and beckoning, and that ever since the encounter, I've felt an indelible bond with dolphins. I've tried to capture the experience in words, and with acrylics I painted a series of paintings of how it felt to swim with them. I was left with a deep love for them and with gratitude for these luminous visions of other realities—incomparable gifts of consciousness.

Gifts of Awareness

The finger pointing to the moon is only an invitation to look at the moon. This classic image is merely a reminder not to mistake the finger for the moon and that ineffable experiences are beyond words. Several vignettes from daily practice are mere pointers.

Upon waking: Before any thoughts have arisen, the words arise from my Christian past: "This is the day the Lord hath made; rejoice and be glad in it."

On my deck that faces south to the weeping cherry tree and conservation land beyond, I greet the morning with movement before meditation, my hands in *namaste*, silently repeating, "With great respect and love, I bow to this body, home of the self, vehicle for awakening, abode of pure awareness."

In the meditation corner: a simple altar, a vase of flowers, photos of inspiring teachers, a few natural objects—rocks and feathers—and a candle.

The sound of my Himalayan gong made by masters who have hand-beaten seven different metals to form a melodic fifth—a low D and a high A—the overtone. The sound of the gong is associated with the heart chakra, its long, deep resonance continuing for almost a minute, the form of the sound slowly dissolving into silence. From form to formless, the play of phenomena, all held in awareness.

Daily practice on generating the mind of enlightenment: At the end of teachings with His Holiness the Dalai Lama, he gave us an ancient vow and encouraged us to repeat it daily—only three sentences, starting with the wish to free all beings while affirming refuge in the Buddha, dharma, and sangha. The second sentence states the intention to generate the mind for full awakening for the benefit of all sentient beings. Finally, one dedicates the rest of one's life to dispelling the sufferings of the world (you can find the text of his vow and his brief teaching in the Appendix).

Further refuge: "I take refuge in infinite spaciousness, primordial awareness, and boundless compassion, which is the nature of everyone's heart/mind, for the sake of all."

Remembering a beloved Elder's words: "Reflecting on space is a practice," she had said. Blanche was in her mid-nineties, blind, a woman of wisdom. "When looking at a tree, look at the spaces between the leaves." The mind continuously attaches to form, she explained, but let it ease into openness, free of commentary.

The space between thoughts: flashes of pure awareness woven through meditation and throughout the day—the play of mind and awareness.

The heart of practice: "Remembrance is Bhairava" (Remembrance is the Lord), a phrase from the Shiva Sutras etched in memory. Every moment of returning to awareness is sacred.

Throughout the day: the weaving of awareness moments, waking up fully to the experience of the present moment, responding with awareness to whatever arises whether within the mind or outside. Dharma teachings unfolding effortlessly.
Sometimes the short version of the Tara mantra (*Om Tare Tam Swaha*) arising spontaneously for heightened attention to stairs or uneven ground.

Meditative Dialogue: (A whimsical conversation between awareness and the mind)

Awareness (A): "Oh friend, come home from your wanderings. You are always on the go between past and future—looking, wanting, driven by desire. Know that this—pure awareness—is your refuge."

Mind (M): "Nothing happens there. I want to keep moving, occupied, busy, with my running commentary on life."

A: "Everything happens here. All is open, spacious, vast, loving."

M: "If I come home to awareness, what happens to desire, curiosity, movement, play?"

A: "All fragmentation, all separation is included and transforms into peace and pure being."

M: "Not very interesting. What of life's intensities—joys and sorrows, anger and fear, outrage and passion, all the vividness of life?"

A: "Everything is included. All those are honored, experienced, enhanced. All afflictions are transformed—the end of suffering. Peace of heart/mind, equanimity, loving kindness, joy, rapture. Just this."

M: "What then of 'I, me, and mine,' my organizing principle?"

A: "All is transformed into the One heart/mind—loving, compassionate, and free."

M: "Ah . . . if awareness is all-inclusive, mind's role continues, continuously transforming—a harmonious relationship between mind and awareness."

A. "Yes, you've seen the light, the light of awareness. That is all."

Om Gate Gate Para Gate Para Sam Gate Bodhi Swaha.
Gone, gone, gone beyond, gone completely beyond. So be it!"

(Excerpt from the Heart Sutra)

In the end, we discover that there are many times in life when we are left without words. There have been many memorable experiences, but increasingly I have found myself simply living with moment-to-moment awareness, the most precious gift of all.

POSTLUDE

I wonder if you have ever stopped to watch a snail. We know how slowly they go, often with stops along their leisurely way. The delightful fact is that some snails leave an opalescent trail. How extraordinary! I've studied their wakes and marveled that this modest little creature can create something of such beauty—an iridescent trail. No matter that the opalescence usually lies amid dirt and nature's dark debris. The snail with its trail is a metaphor. The beauty and the darkness are all inevitably part of life.

Whimsically, I saw a comparison between that little snail and my own journey. Whether proceeding at a very slow pace like the snail or dedicating oneself rigorously to spiritual practice, the inner process is hidden, slow, and intermittent. There may be desert periods, disconnection, or dark nights of the soul—or blessed periods with big dreams, deep meditations, and sudden insights, wondrous light and wondrous darkness. All are part of the trip. Whatever is happening, our dedication to the spiritual life leaves an opalescent wake in the soul, a hidden process that then shines forth in our lives.

I mentioned before how we all long for stories and how they reassure and inspire us. They weave connections between us. Those connections are subtle and hidden, much like the ley lines that I mentioned in the story about Findhorn where I first heard the term. Since then, it has taken root and unexpectedly woven together many threads that appear in this book. With hindsight and reflection, I see how "my" journey was orchestrated by mysterious forces far beyond my mind's ability to fathom. A dominant theme has been the weaving of my Christian upbringing with exposure to the wisdom traditions of the East, namely Buddhism—both Vipassana and Tibetan—and from India, the combination of Vedanta and Kashmir Shaivism in Siddha Yoga. As the eminent teacher Joseph Goldstein said, there is only One Dharma, the title of one of his books, as these different traditions all spring from the same source, the One beyond the many.

Each teaching or practice is like a ley line, connecting and illuminating apparent differences with the light of awareness. In my own life, without being able to articulate it at first, I longed for devotional practices, the unbounded, dynamic expression of one's love beyond anything I'd ever seen in Western spiritual traditions. From a Christian perspective, one might have judged these non-Western practices as idolatry, but at heart they were simply an expression of love. The ley lines of love transcend all differences of form, belief, and ideology over which humankind has argued and fought.

We can also reflect on the ley lines that exist within families, all those subtle connections woven of our respective karmas that form a complex interweaving of forces. How they play out becomes the wondrous story of a family—your story, your siblings, parents, and ancestors' stories, sometimes cause for rejoicing and gratitude, at other times the source of endless dysfunction and suffering.

When I look back at my dream of the Spirit Bird and all that unfolded in my relationship with my father, I marvel at all the ley lines of connection between father and daughter that unfolded from that one dream image. I also reminisce about the years that Laura and I shared a spiritual journey with its extremes of joy and pain, all that light and darkness, and the final heartbreaking realization that we'd been in a cult. The cult, however, was only the outward form that evolved around the two gurus. The essence of the teachings and practices remain as deep and inspiring as ever.

The image of ley lines extends yet farther into the ultimately expansive view that everything in the universe is interconnected—the quantum theory of contemporary physics wonderfully expressed by the term *interbeing* offered by Thich Nhat Hanh and now widely accepted. With this view, the controversies between science and spirituality are transcended in yet another example of how ley lines subtly connect seemingly disparate theories, creating power points whether on the surface of the earth, between differing philosophies, or between various aspects of our inner experience.

Although referring to the quantum in very simplified ways, it's a wondrous prospect that everything—absolutely everything in our world, including the entire cosmos—is interconnected, a subtle network of interrelationships called Indra's Net in the Mahayana tradition. The image is perceived as a vast net of relationships, ley lines if you will, that weave in endless, infinitely intricate patterns. This vast perspective also suggests that our every thought, word, and action creates the subtlest of vibrations within the net, giving profound, inspirational meaning to our lives.

I've heard several Buddhist teachers say that we can't even begin to comprehend the complexities of karma. I believe we're given the gift of incarnation to experience these mysteries within our lives and in the world around us. Life is an invitation to fulfill that gift, each in our unique way. Whatever form it takes, the heart of the journey is about opening to give and receive love. The ley lines of love transcend the challenges of life, or to put it another way, love can hold anything that life presents, including death. We discover that we are part of something far beyond our personal stories—even, as the wise ones say, that the nature of the universe is love. The presence of truth is always accompanied by paradox. The joys and sorrows, the darkness and the light, all form part of our story, woven together with love.

GLOSSARY

Acharya: an honorific title given to an advanced practitioner in the Buddhist or Hindu traditions

Adavasis: the name for the tribal people who lived in the vicinity around the Siddha Yoga ashram in India

Ahimsa: non-violence or to do no harm, a central principle in Buddhist and Hindu traditions, often taken as a vow or spiritual practice

Arati: a devotional chant often performed with the waving of lights in front of a sacred image or *murti* (statue of a saint)

Ashram: a residential, spiritual community usually formed around a guru or teacher

Avadhut: a highly attained or Self-realized person who is beyond worldly concerns

Bhakti: the path of devotion in the Hindu tradition

Bharat Mata: a name for Mother India

Bindi: from Hinduism, a mark applied between the eyebrows at the "third eye," or energy center, that symbolizes inner divinity and spiritual vision

Bodhisattva: one who is able to reach nirvana (liberation) but chooses, through their compassion, to remain to help suffering beings

Bodhisattva vow: a commitment to achieve full Buddhahood, or enlightenment, to help alleviate the suffering of all beings

Chakra: Sanskrit word meaning "wheel," referring to the major energy centers in the body, usually the major seven centers

Channeling: an ancient practice first found in the Bible and accepted in many cultures where one becomes the medium or channel for information coming from another dimension of reality

Chela: a devotee or disciple of a guru or eminent teacher

Clairvoyant: literally "clear seeing," a non-ordinary state of consciousness where one's knowing is not limited by time or space, the ability to see events beyond one's ordinary sensory ways of knowing

Cobra posture: term from hatha yoga in which the upper body arches over backward

Darshan: coming into the presence of a holy person or statue of a deity, a valued practice in the Hindu and Buddhist traditions

Dharamsala: like a hostel or place to stay overnight for travelers

Dharma: universal truths as taught by the Buddha, divine law, right way of living, the nature of reality; further meanings in other traditions like Hinduism

Dungkar Gompa: name of Domo Geshe Riinpoche's monastery, meaning the Monastery of the White Clouds

Dzogchen: or ati yoga, a tradition within Vajrayana Buddhism; practices reveal the natural state, or *rigpa*, described as pure awareness, luminous and compassionate.

Guru: a spiritual teacher, reputedly highly attained (but, I would add, still very much with fallible, human qualities)

Karma: term in Buddhism and Hinduism that refers to one's actions in life (also previous lives); in Biblical parlance, the law of cause and effect

Kriya: Sanskrit word meaning "action"; the spontaneous movements of energy in the body that unfold through the awakened energy of kundalini

Kumkum: a form of religious marking, usually applied at the third eye between the eyebrows, made from various colored powders, often red

Kundalini: energy in the subtle body that is awakened through committed practice (hatha yoga, etc.) and through initiation; symbolically perceived as snake-like coiled energy at the base of the spine

Lama: an ordained teacher, an honorific used in Tibetan Buddhism

Lingam: a phallic-like form revered as a symbol of the creative force, or specifically the creative powers of Shiva, the male principle in Hinduism

Mahasamadhi: *maha* means "great," as in the great samadhi, to describe the passing of an eminent spiritual teacher

Mahayana: one of two major Buddhist traditions practiced mainly in Tibet, China, Japan, Korea, and some southern Asian countries

Mandala: devotional images, often circular in shape, from the Buddhist tradition, often symbolizing an ideal universe

Mudras: Sanskrit term meaning "gesture"; energy flowing postures that symbolically connect individual energy with universal energy

Muktananda: known as Baba ("father" in Hindi), a swami in the Saraswati order of monks in India

Nityananda: also known as Bade Baba, Muktananda's guru

Pranam: the act of bowing out of respect toward a teacher, statue, or sacred place

Punjabi: a form of Indian dress; a tunic worn over trousers

Rilbus: handmade by high lamas with medicinal herbs and infused with healing powers through ritual and prayer

Rinpoche: a title given to a highly respected Tibetan teacher

Sadhana: spiritual training or practice, a term usually associated with Buddhist or Hindu practices

Sahasrara: the crown chakra at the top of the head symbolized as a thousand-petalled lotus

Samadhi: meaning "to bring together," as in concentration of the mind; a state of deep absorption used in reference to meditation

Sangha: spiritual community; in Buddhism, the community of monks, nuns, and fellow lay practitioners

Seva: means service or work assigned to devotees to help with the daily running of an ashram

Shakti: the female principle of divine energy

Shaktipat: spiritual initiation where the spiritual energy known as kundalini is awakened in the spiritual practitioner

Shiva: the name of a Hindu deity, symbolizing the creative spirit and other roles embodied in one unified form

Siddha: a highly realized master of meditation; traditionally eighty-four mahasiddhas (*maha* means "great") in the Tantric Tibetan tradition

Siddha Yoga: the name Baba Muktananda gave to a body of teachings that drew from Kashmir Shaivism and Vedanta

State Oracle of Lhasa: someone who enters a trance state to receive (often prophetic) information from other dimensions; usually resides in Lhasa, the capital of the autonomous region of Tibet

Stupa: a dome-shaped structure or form of Buddhist shrine

Swami: a spiritual teacher, usually a senior member of a religious order in the Hindu tradition

Tantra: tradition within Hinduism and Buddhism that involves principles of the tantras, including mantras, meditation, yoga, and ritual

Tara: an archetypal image for the sacred feminine, a form used as a focus in meditation primarily in Tibetan Buddhism; Green Tara is one of the most popular of the twenty-one forms of Tara

Tulku: an honorific (title) given, usually at a young age, to one perceived as the reincarnation of a previous, highly attained lama or teacher

Vairocana: archetypal form used in visualization practice in Tibetan Buddhism

Vedanta: one of the six schools of philosophy in the Hindu tradition; teachings on knowledge and liberation based on the Upanishads, ancient scriptures

Vipassana: also known as insight meditation, a practice from Theravada Buddhism, found in South Asia

Yogis: people who practice yoga

APPENDIX

CREDO

of Blanche Ames Ames
(Written when she was 72)

I believe in the Motherhood of God.

I believe in the blessed Trinity of Father, Mother and Child.

I believe that God is here, and we are as near him now as we ever shall be. I do not believe He started this world a-going and went away and left it.

I believe in the sacredness of the human body, this transient dwelling place of a living soul, and so I deem it the duty of every man and woman to keep his or her body beautiful through right thinking and right living.

I believe that the love of man for woman, and the love of woman for man, is holy; and that this love in all of its promptings is as much an emanation of the Divine Spirit as man's love for God, for the most daring hazards of human mind.

I believe in salvation through economic, social and spiritual freedom.

I believe John Ruskin, William Morris, Henry Thoreau, Walt Whitman, and Leo Tolstoy to be Prophets of God, and they should rank in mental reach and spiritual insight with Elijah, Moses, Ezekiel and Isaiah.

I believe we are now living in Eternity as much as we ever shall.

I believe that the best way to prepare for a Future Life is to be kind, live one day at a time, and do the work you can do the best, doing it as well as you can.

I believe there is no devil but fear.

I believe that no one can harm you but yourself.

I believe that we are all sons of God and it doth not yet appear what we shall be.

I believe in freedom—social, economic, domestic, political, mental, and spiritual.

I believe in every man minding his own business.

I believe that men are as inspired today as much as men ever were.

I believe in sunshine, fresh air, friendship, calm sleep, beautiful thoughts.

I believe in the paradox of success through failure.

I believe in the purifying process of sorrow, and I believe that death is a manifestation of Life.

I believe there is no better preparation for a life to come than this: do your work as well as you can and be kind.

I believe the Universe is planned for good.

I believe it is possible that I will make other creeds, and change this one, or add to it, from time to time, as new light may come to me.

The Ames family coat of arms

The image of a rose appears at the top of the shield with three rosettes inscribed at an angle across the center of the shield. The Latin motto on the scroll is Fama Candida Rosa Dulcior. Although the motto has been translated in several ways, the translation I prefer is:

"The pure rose is sweeter than fame."

DALAI LAMA'S PRAYER FOR GENERATING THE MIND OF ENLIGHTENMENT

(including his words of introduction and commentary)

For those who admire the spiritual ideals of the Eight Verses on Transforming the Mind, it is helpful to recite the following verses for generating the mind for enlightenment. Practicing Buddhists should recite the verses and reflect upon the meaning of the words, while trying to enhance their altruism and compassion. Those of you who are practitioners of other religious traditions can draw from your own spiritual teachings, and try to commit yourselves to cultivating altruistic thoughts in pursuit of the altruistic ideal.

With a wish to free all beings
I shall always go for refuge
to the Buddha, Dharma and Sangha
until I reach full enlightenment.
Enthused by wisdom and compassion,
today in the Buddha's presence
I generate the Mind for Full Awakening
for the benefit of all sentient beings.
As long as space endures,
as long as sentient beings remain,
until then, may I too remain
and dispel the miseries of the world.

In conclusion, those who like myself, consider themselves to be followers of Buddha, should practice as much as we can. To followers of other religious traditions, I would like to say, "Please practice your own religion seriously and sincerely." And to non-believers, I request you to try to be warm-hearted. I ask this of you because these mental attitudes actually bring us happiness. As I have mentioned before, taking care of others actually benefits you.

AN ODE TO DAHLIAS

By Olivia Ames Hoblitzelle

I've always wondered how
these radiant blossoms, orange and apricot,
tinged with gold, emerge from slender stems—
miracles of creation.

One year they grew two stories high
Wondrous creations shining pure light,
Each a thousand petalled lotus,
Crowned with sacred symmetry.

Symbols of hope—exquisite and ephemeral—
I balanced on the ladder to gather
Beauty for the house to help
Dispel the darkness of days.

Shine! they say, Shine your light
into the brokenness of the world,
trusting that which is eternal
in the lotus of your heart.

ACKNOWLEDGMENTS

My initial gratitude is for how *Ley Lines of Love* became a book. Every book is like a tapestry, a weaving of countless influences and interconnections. As I wrote, I was surprised by joy at how the next thread of the story unfolded, adding another design to the tapestry. I was intrigued at how a mysterious force seemed to be urging me along. Altogether the experience of writing *Ley Lines of Love* has been totally absorbing and filled with wonders. So much gratitude!

First of all, let me recognize the role of my family and ancestors, especially parents and grandparents, but also my beloved siblings Joanie, Ned, and—although now deceased—my oldest brother Oakes; my son Ethan and his wife Elise; my daughter Laura and her husband Randy. Thanks beyond words to Laura, whose courage propelled a life-changing series of events for me and countless others.

What a blessing to be held in circles of friendship. Deepest gratitude to Ilona O'Connor, Penny Gill, Ann Dunlop, Charles Busch, Jeff Scannell, Sam Black, Henry Schniewind, Nigelle de Visme, Joan Diver, Jackie Merrill, Anne Nash, Prajna Hallstrom, Barbara McCollough, Shannon Gilligan, Nyia Yannatos, Sam Fisk, and Linda Coe. My soul sister Judith Laskaris may have recently passed on but is still very much present.

Heartfelt thanks go to my dear friend Louise Cochran who read each chapter and gave invaluable feedback with her insights and light touch. Her support and inspiration were treasures.

A special bouquet of thanks to Keith Taylor, my partner. His abiding love is a continuous, heart-warming gift, even though circumstances only allow for intermittent visits.

In professional categories all their own, boundless gratitude to Monique Pommier and Peter Faust for their exceptional gifts.

How fortuitous that I found Jennifer Browdy, my editor. She was a joy to work with. As well as being my cheerleader, she was a wonderful combination of equanimity, skill, and vision. Insatiably curious about the story, she kept encouraging me to write more, a quiet yet powerful force behind the book. I can't imagine any writer having a more gifted ally.

Among midwives for the book, Margaret Harding holds a unique place. As my longtime assistant, she rescued me countless times, especially with the finer points of editing when she became my second pair of eyes. Quite simply, Margaret is a miracle worker, wizard, and saint.

As for my dharma teachers, a deep bow of gratitude to each of them for lighting the way through this journey. Starting with Vipassana teachers, through the devotional tradition from India, to my Tibetan Buddhist teachers, their inspiration and wisdom has blessed my life beyond measure.

May *Ley Lines of Love* offer insight and light to others living in these tumultuous times.

Olivia Ames Hoblitzelle is a writer and dharma teacher whose work is inspired by almost fifty years of practice in Buddhist meditation, psychology and the wisdom traditions. She taught in the field of mind/body medicine where she pioneered the integration of meditation, yoga, and cognitive therapy with traditional Western medicine.

Olivia is the author of the award-winning book *Ten Thousand Joys & Ten Thousand Sorrows: A Couple's Journey Through Alzheimer's*, and more recently *Aging with Wisdom: Reflections, Stories & Teachings*. Now living in an Elder community in Massachusetts near her two families, she also spends time at the family place in Vermont where, as a lover of nature, she hikes, gardens, and sky gazes.

Printed in the USA
CPSIA information can be obtained
at www.ICGtesting.com
LVHW090527271124
797762LV00026B/118
* 9 7 9 8 9 8 9 9 4 5 2 0 7 *